T5-CVQ-490

UNIX System V Libraries: Programmer's Rapid Reference

UNIX System V Libaries: Programmer's Rapid Reference

Baird Peterson, Ph.D.

VNR VAN NOSTRAND REINHOLD
New York

Library of Congress Catalog Card Number 92-8662
ISBN 0-442-00539-3

Manufactured in the United States of America

Published by Van Nostrand Reinhold
115 Fifth Avenue
New York, New York 10003

Chapman and Hall
2-6 Boundary Row
London, SE1 8HN, England

Thomas Nelson Australia
102 Dodds Street
South Melbourne 3205
Victoria, Australia

Nelson Canada
1120 Birchmount Road
Scarborough, Ontario M1K 5G4, Canada

16 15 14 13 12 11 10 9 8 7 6 5 4 3 2 1

Library of Congress Cataloging-in-Publication Data

Peterson, Baird.
UNIX System V libraries : programmer's rapid reference / Baird Peterson.
p. cm.
Includes bibliographical references and index.
ISBN 0-442-00539-3
1. Operating systems (Computers) 2. UNIX System V (Computer file) I. Title.
QA76.063P5258 1992 92-8662
005.4'3--dc20 CIP

to Maureen, Colin,
and my mother

Contents

Preface

This book was written to help two different kinds of readers: newcomers to UNIX System V and experienced UNIX System V programmers. The book has features that help newcomers find descriptions of UNIX software development routines quickly without having to know the names of the routines. Also, the descriptions of UNIX features are organized to reduce reading time, something that both kinds of readers will enjoy.

UNIX has hundreds of commands, system calls, library routines, and file formats. This book presents descriptions of library routines for UNIX System V that are of interest in general software development. The routines covered include all AT&T System V Release 4 routines for general software development.

Acknowledgments

Many people helped to create this book. I thank my literary agent, Bill Gladstone, of Waterside Productions, Inc. I also thank the people at Van Nostrand Reinhold for their fine editorial support, especially acquisition editor Dianne Littwin and managing editor Alberta Gordon. I thank my anonymous reviewers for helping to make this a better book. I thank my wife Maureen for her constant support and encouragement.

UNIX System V Libraries: Programmer's Rapid Reference

INTRODUCTION

Notation

The following kinds of notation are used in this book.

`constant width italic` type denotes variables whose names are chosen by the user.

`constant width roman` type denotes input such as function names, constants, and the names of directories.

`function` (*`name year`*[*`letter`*]|*`letter`*(s)]) refers to a book or to a section of this book where a description of the specified function, `function`, may be found. The form

`function` (*`letter`*(s))

refers to a description of a library routine in the present book. The form

`function` (*`name year`*[*`letter`*])

gives the author name, *`name`*, of a book listed in the Bibliograpy of this book; the year, *`year`*, the book was published; and the specific book (*`letter`*) published that year if the author had more than one book published in that year. For example,

`directory` (Peterson 1991)

refers to a description of the `directory` function in a book published by Peterson in 1991.

<> indicates input that is not displayed on the screen when it is typed, for

example, passwords, tabs, or RETURN. Such input appears between angle brackets. The angle brackets themselves are not input.

<^*char*> indicates control characters. The circumflex (^) denotes the control key (CTRL), and *char* denotes some key. For example, <^d> denotes the value obtained by holding the control key down and striking the *D* key. The letter *D* is not displayed, and the angle brackets themselves are not input.

[ ] indicates optional arguments. One or more of the options enclosed by the brackets (but not the brackets themselves) are input.

| separates optional arguments in cases where only one of two listed options may be chosen. For example, in the following library routine

`function` [*arg1*|*arg2*]

either *arg1* or *arg2* may be chosen, but not both.

. . . means that more than one argument like the preceding argument may be used.

How to Use This Book

If you are an experienced UNIX programmer and you already know the names of all UNIX System V library routines, see Part 2, 3, 4, 5, or 6 for the description of the library routine that you seek. These descriptions are given in alphabetical order. Their names are given in the Contents and in the Index.

If you don't know the names of all of the UNIX System V library routines used for software development, read Part 1. You should also read the `class` section that appears near the beginning of each of Parts 2, 3, 4, 5, and 6 of this book. Each `class` section classifies the library routines described in that part. See the Contents for the page numbers of these sections.

Part 1

Unix System V Release 4 Libraries

Part 1 consists of two sections:

- An introduction that explains the format of the descriptions of UNIX System V Release 4 library routines that appear in Parts 2, 3, 4, 5, and 6 of this book, and
- A section containing definitions of the terms used in this book.

intro (CSGXM)	INTRODUCTION TO UNIX LIBRARIES	intro (CSGXM)

The descriptions of the UNIX library routines given in Parts 2, 3, 4, 5, and 6 consist of up to eight separate sections: NAME, SYNOPSIS, DESCRIPTION, ARGUMENTS, NORMAL COMPLETION: VALUE RETURNED, ERROR CONDITION: VALUE RETURNED, FILES, and SEE ALSO.

Name

Each description of a library routine begins with the name of the routine, followed by a brief summary of its purpose. The letter in parentheses that follows the name of each routine indicates the library to which the routine belongs. There are several libraries. The particular library to which a function belongs is indicated by the following letters:

(C) following the name of a UNIX library routine described in Part 2 indicates that the routine, together with those described in (Peterson 1991b) and those whose names are followed by (S), belongs to the standard C library, `libc`. The C compilation system automatically links this library. The standard C library is implemented in two ways: as a shared object, `libc.so`, and as an archive, `libc.a`. The default library for linking is `libc.so`. In order to link with the archive version, the `-dn` option must be specified on the `cc` command line. See `cc` (Peterson 1991a) and the "C Compilation System" in (AT&T 1990g)].

(CS) following `class` in Part 2 indicates that the material pertains to both Standard C and Standard I/O.

(CSGXM) following `intro` and `define` in Part 1 indicates that the material pertains to all libraries described in Parts 2, 3, 4, 5, and 6.

(E) following the name of a routine described in Part 3 indicates that it belongs to the ELF access library, `libelf`. This library is not implemented as a shared library. It is not automatically linked by the C compilation system. `-lelf` must be specified on the `cc` (Peterson 1991a) command line in order to link with this library.

(G) following the name of a routine described in Part 4 indicates that it belongs to the general-purpose library, `libgen`. This library is not implemented as a shared library. It is not automatically linked by the C compilation system. `-lgen` must be specified on the `cc` command line in order to link with this library.

(M) following the name of a routine described in Part 5 indicates that it belongs to the math library, `libm`. This library is not implemented as a shared library. It is not automatically linked by the C compilation system. `-lm` must be specified on the `cc` command line in order to link with this library.

(S) following the name of a routine described in Part 2 indicates that it belongs to the standard I/O package [see `stdio` (S)].

(X) following the name of a routine decribed in Part 6 indicates that it belongs to one of several specialized libraries. The particular library to which such a routine belongs is indicated in its descriptive entry in Part 6.

Synopsis

The synopsis subsection of the description of each routine lists any header files which must be included, and it shows the routine and its arguments. Function declarations are contained in the `#include` files indicated in this section.

The `lint` (Peterson 1991a) program checker can be used to report discrepancies even if the header files are not included by an `#include` statement.

No function, external variable, or macro given in the synopsis can be redefined by the program. (Any other name can be redefined without changing the behavior of other library functions. However, such a redefinition may conflict with a definition in the included header file.)

Description

Each description of a routine contains general details about one or more functions that do not directly invoke UNIX system primitives.

Descriptions of routines (and arguments) sometimes refer to symbolic names that are implementation specific and not necessarily expected to be accessible to an application program. Some of these symbolic names describe boundary conditions or system limits. These symbolic names are enclosed in curly braces in order to distinguish them from other implementation-specific constants whose names are accessible to application programs through header files. In order to be portable, an application program should not refer to any symbol whose name is enclosed in curly braces. For example, a program should not test the length of an argument list to determine if it is longer than {ARG_MAX}.

Arguments

Where possible (and it nearly always is), all of the information about each argument of a routine is put in this subsection. The descriptions of arguments are sorted in alphabetical order of the argument names as these are given in the synopsis. Usually, when information about an argument must appear in other subsections or in the material about another argument, the argument description will point to such material.

Normal Completion: Value Returned

Routines usually return 0 if they succeed, but in some cases they return other values. Such values are described in this section.

Error Condition: Value Returned

The error handling for functions that return floating-point values depends on the compilation mode used.

If the `cc` compilation option is `-Xt` (the default), such functions return the conventional values 0, +HUGE, -HUGE, or NaN if the function is not defined for a given argument or if the value returned cannot be represented.

If the `cc` compilation option is `-Xa` or `-Xc`, such functions return +HUGE_VAL instead of +HUGE and -HUGE_VAL instead of -HUGE if the function is not defined for a given argument or if the value returned cannot be represented. HUGE_VAL and HUGE are respectively defined in `math.h` to be infinity and the largest-magnitude single-precision number.

Files

INCDIR is ordinarily `/usr/include`. The header files in *INCDIR* provide function prototypes (function declarations that include the types of arguments) for most of the functions in sections (C), (S), (G), (M), and (X) of this book. These prototypes let the compiler test for correct usage of these functions in the user's program.

LIBDIR is ordinarily /usr/ccs/lib.
LIBDIR/libc.so
LIBDIR/libc.a
LIBDIR/libgen.a
LIBDIR/libm.a
LIBDIR/libsfm.sa
/usr/lib/libc.so.1

See Also

This secion points to related material. In general, see ar (Peterson 1991a), cc (Peterson 1991a), intro (Peterson 1991b), intro (M), ld (Peterson 1991a), lint (Peterson 1991a), math (AT&T 1990m), nm (Peterson 1991a), stdio (S), and "C Compilation System" in (AT&T 1990g)

define (CSGXM) USEFUL DEFINITIONS define (CSGXM)

Name

define—definitions of terms used in descriptions of routines in libraries that are described in Parts 2, 3, 4, 5, and 6.

Description

Character is any bit pattern that can fit into a byte on the machine.

Character array is a sequence of characters.

Null character is a character whose value is 0, representd in the C language as \0.

NULL pointer is a value gotten by casting 0 into a pointer.

Null string is a character array that contains only the terminating character. C language guarantees that this value will not match any legitimate pointer. This allows functions to return a NULL pointer to indicate that an error has occurred. The NULL macro is defined in stdio.h.

Null-terminated character array is a sequence of characters, the last of which is a null character.

size_t is a data type defined in the appropriate header files.

stream is a file and its associated buffering. *stream* is declared to be a pointer of type FILE declared in stdio.h.

STREAMS is a set of kernal mechanisms that consist of utility routines, kernel facilities, and a set of data structures. These mechanisms enable the development of data communication drivers and network services.

Part 2

libc Standard C and stdio Standard I/O Library

Part 2 has two sections:

- A section (page 7) that classifies routines in the libc Standard C and Standard I/O libraries so that you can quickly find the appropriate routine for your purpose; and
- Descriptions of the libc Standard C and stdio Standard I/O library routines in alphabetical order.

Name

class—Classification of routines in the libc Standard C and stdio Standard I/O libraries.

Description

This section classifies the routines in the libc Standard C library (C) and the routines in the stdio Standard I/O library. It points to pages that describe these routines.

Characters and Strings

Conversions

See "Date and Time" below.

Date and Time

Devices, Directories, and Files

See “Resource Access Control” below.

a64l (C) STRING/LONG INTEGER CONVERSION a64l (C)

Name

a64l, l64a—convert between a base-64 ASCII string and a long integer

Synopsis

```
#include <stdlib.h>

long a64l (const *string);

char *l64a (long long);
```

Description

a64l and l64a are used to convert back and forth between long integers and base-64 ASCII character strings. Long integers can be represented by up to six ASCII characters, where each character represents a digit in base-64 notation.

The 64 different characters used to represent digits are `.` to represent 0, `/` to represent 1, `0–9` to represent digits 2–11, `A–Z` to represent 12–37, and `a–z` to represent 38–63.

Arguments

long is a long integer whose value is to be converted to a base-64 ASCII string. If *long* equals 0, `l64a` returns a pointer to a null string.

string is a pointer to a null-terminated base-64 ASCII character string representing an integer. `a641` scans the character string from left to right (the least significant digit is on the left), decoding each character as a six-bit base-64 number. If *string* points to a string that contains more than six characters, `a641` uses only the first six characters.

Normal Completion: Value Returned

`a641` returns a long integer value corresponding to the null-terminated string to which its argument points.

`l64a` returns a pointer to a base-64 ASCII character string representation of its type long integer argument. The pointer returned points to a static buffer whose contents are overwritten by each succeeding call to `l64a`.

abort (C) GENERATE AN ABORT SIGNAL abort (C)

Name

`abort`—generate a `SIGABRT` abnormal termination signal

Synopsis

```
#include <stdlib.h>

void abort (void);
```

Description

If possible, `abort` closes every open file, all directory streams, `stdio` (S) streams, and message catalog descriptors and sends the `SIGABRT` signal to the calling process.

Arguments

None

Error Condition: Value Returned

If the SIGABRT signal is not caught or ignored and the current directory can be written to, abort generates a core dump and the shell [sh (AT&T 1990q)] writes the "message abort - core dump" message.

See Also

catopen (C), stdio (S), exit (Peterson 1991b), kill (Peterson 1991b), sdb (Peterson 1991a), sh (AT&T 1990q), signal (Peterson 1991b)

abs (C) GET THE ABSOLUTE VALUE OF AN INTEGER abs (C)

Name

abs, labs—return the absolute value of an integer

Synopsis

```
#include <stdlib.h>

int abs (int value);

long labs (long longval);
```

Description

abs and labs compute the absolute values of their arguments.

Arguments

long is a type long argument whose absolute value is to be computed by labs.

value is a type int argument whose absolute value is to be computed by abs.

Normal Completion: Value Returned

abs returns the absolute value of its type int argument.
labs returns the absolute value of its type long argument.

See Also

`floor` (M)

addseverity (C) — MESSAGE-FORMATTING FACILITY — addseverity (C)

Name

`addseverity`—build a severity level list for use with `fmtmsg`

Synopsis

```
#include <fmtmsg.h>
int addseverity(int severity, const char *string);
```

Description

`addseverity` builds a list of severity levels and associated error message strings for error conditions in an application. The list is for use by the message-formatting facility, `fmtmsg`.

The `SEV_LEVEL` environment variable also can be used to define severity levels at run time [see `fmtmsg` (C)].

Arguments

`severity` is an integer value that denotes the level of seriousness of an error condition. If a particular value of *`severity`* has not been defined by a previous `addseverity` call, the new value of *`severity`* and its associated print string (see *`string`* below) are added to the list built by `addseverity`. If a particular value of *`severity`* has been defined by an `addseverity` call, the value of *`severity`* is redefined by a new print string. The `NULL` string removes a previously defined severity level. Values of *`severity`* from 0 to 4 inclusive are reserved for standard severity levels. These values cannot be modified.

`string` is a pointer to a string that describes an error condition. Identifiers corresponding to standard levels of severity are as follows:

`ERROR` is a print string produced by standard error level `MM_ERROR`. The string indicates that the application has detected an error.

`HALT` is a print string produced by standard error level `MM_HALT`. The string indicates that the application has encountered a severe fault and is therefore halting.

INFO is a print string produced by standard error level MM_INFO. The string gives information about a condition that is not an error.

WARNING is a print string produced by standard error level MM_WARNING. The string indicates that the application has encountered an extraordinary situation that may need to be watched.

If the severity level is MM_NOSEV, no message is supplied.

Normal Completion: Value Returned

If `addseverity` succeeds, it returns MM_OK.

Error Condition: Value Returned

If `addseverity` is called with a value of *`severity`* equal to a negative number or to 0, 1, 2, 3, or 4, it fails and returns −1. If `addseverity` fails, it returns MM_NOTOK.

See Also

`fmtmsg` (C), `gettxt` (C), `printf` (C), `fmtmsg` (AT&T 1990q)

atexit (C) PROGRAM TERMINATION atexit (C)

Name

`atexit`—add a program termination routine

Synopsis

```
#include <stdlib.h>

int atexit(void (*func) (void));
```

Description

`atexit` adds a specifed function, *`func`*, to a list of functions to be automatically called without arguments when a program terminates by a return from `main` or by a call to the `exit` system. As many as 32 functions can be registered to be called. These functions are called in the reverse order of their registration.

Arguments

func specifies a function, *func*, which is to be added to the list of functions to be called without arguments when a program terminates normally.

Normal Completion: Value Returned

`atexit` returns 0 if registration succeeds.

Error Condition: Value Returned

`atexit` returns nonzero if registration fails.

See Also

`exit` (Peterson 1990b)

bsearch (C) BINARY SEARCH bsearch (C)

Name

`bsearch`—do a binary search of a sorted table

Synopsis

```
#include <stdlib.h>
void *bsearch (const void *key, const void *base,
size_t nelem, size_t size, int (*compar) (const
void*, const void *));
```

Description

`bsearch` is a binary search routine based on Knuth's Algorithm B (6.2.1).

Arguments

base points to the element that is at the base of the table. The pointer should be of the type appropriate to the type of the table element.

compar points to a comparison function used to sort the table in increasing order. The comparison function must be called with two arguments that point to the two table elements being compared. The comparison function must return an integer that is negative, 0, or positive, depending on whether the first argument is less than, equal to, or greater than the second, respectively. The comparison function need not compare every byte in the table; thus arbitrary data can be in the elements in addition to the values that are compared.

key points to an instance of a datum which is to be sought in the table. The pointer should be of the type appropriate to the type of the table element.

nelem specifies the number of elements in the table. If the number of elements in the table is less than the size that is reserved for the table, *nel* should be the lower of these two numbers.

size gives the number of bytes contained in each element of the table.

Normal Completion: Value Returned

If `bsearch` succeeds in finding a specified key in the table, it returns a pointer to the key.

Error Condition: Value Returned

If `bsearch` cannot find a specified key in the table, it returns a null pointer.

See Also

`hsearch` (C), `lsearch` (C), `qsort` (C), `tsearch` (C)

catgets (C) READ FROM THE MESSAGE CATALOG catgets (C)

Name

`catgets`—read a program message from a message catalog

Synopsis

```
#include <nl_types.h>

char *catgets (nl_catd catdescr, int setnum, int msgnum, char *string);
```

Description

`catgets` tries to read a specified message, *msgnum*, in a set of messages, *setnum*, in a message catalog specified by *catdescr*.

Arguments

catdescr is a catalog descriptor returned by a previous call to `catopen` (C). The descriptor identifies a message catalog.

msgnum specifies a message, in a set, in a catalog.

setnum specifies a set of messages in a catalog.

string points to a default message string that `catgets` will return if the specified message catalog is not available.

Normal Completion: Value Returned

If `catgets` succeeds, it returns a pointer to an internal buffer area that holds a null-terminated string.

Error Condition: Value Returned

If `catgets` fails because the message catalog specified by *catdescr* is not available, it returns a pointer to *string*.

See Also

`catopen` (C)

catopen (C) — OPEN/CLOSE THE MESSAGE CATALOG — catopen (C)

Name

`catopen`, `catclose`—open or close a message catalog

Synopsis

```
#include <nl_types.h>

nl_catd catopen (char *name, int oflag);

int catclose (nl_catd, catdescr);
```

Description

`catclose` closes the message catalog specified by *catdescr*.

`catopen` opens the message catalog specified by *name* and returns a catalog descriptor.

Arguments

`catdescr` specifies the message catalog which `catclose` is to close.

`name` specifies the name of the messsage catalog descriptor which is to be opened by `catopen`. `name` specifies a pathname for the message catalog if `name` contains a "/" character. If `name` does not contain a "/" character, the default path for the message catalog [see `nl_types` (AT&T 1990o)] is specified by the environmental variable NLSPATH unless NLSPATH does not exist in the environment or unless the message catalog cannot be opened in any path given by NLSPATH. NLSPATH gives the search path of message catalogs and specifies the naming conventions associated with message catalog files. NLSPATH ordinarily has a standard, systemwide form, making the location and the naming conventions associated with message catalogs transparent to users and programs. However, the names and locations of message catalogs can vary from one system to another. In addition, individual programs can name or locate message catalogs as needed. NLSPATH gives a mechanism for managing changes in the name and location of message catalogs by inserting substitutions in the string defining NLSPATH. For example, in

NLSPATH=/nlslib/%L/%N.cat

the metacharacter % introduces a substitution field. Thus, %L in the above string substitutes the current value of the LANG environmental variable, a variable that gives the ability to specify a user's requirements for character set, local customs, and native language by using an ASCII string having the form

LANG=*language*[_*territory*[.*codeset*]]

The value of LC_MESSAGE, as returned by `setlocale` (C), is used for the LANG variable value if the value of LANG is not set. If LC_MESSAGE is NULL, the default path given by `nl_types` is used.

In the above string defining NLSPATH, %N substitutes the value of the `name` argument that is passed to `catopen`. For example, in searching the above string, `catopen` will search in /nlslib/$LANG/*name*.cat for the message catalog.

The metacharacters used in substitutions have the following effects:

%% represents a single %.
%c specifies the value of the codeset element of LANG.
%N passes the value of the `name` argument to `catopen`.
%l specifies the value of the language element of LANG.
%L gives the value of LANG.
%t specifies the value of the territory element of LANG.

`oflag` is reserved for future use. If it is set to any other value than 0, the result is not defined.

Normal Completion: Value Returned

If `catopen` succeeds, it returns a message catalog descriptor to be used by future calls to `catgets` or `catclose`.
If `catclose` succeeds, it returns 0.

Error Condition: Value Returned

If `catopen` fails, it returns (`nl_catd`) −1.
If `catclose` fails, it returns −1.

See Also

`catgets` (C), `setlocale` (C), `environ` (AT&T 1990m), `nl_types` (AT&T 1990m)

clock (C) REPORT CPU TIME clock (C)

Name

`clock`—report the amount of CPU time used

Synopsis

```
#include <time.h>

clock_t clock (void);
```

Description

`clock` returns the amount of CPU time used since the calling process first called `clock`. The CPU time reported is the sum of the user and system CPU time used by the calling process and the CPU time used by any terminated child processes for which the calling process has executed a `wait` (Peterson 1991b) system call, a `pclose` (S) function, or a `system` (S) function.

Arguments

None

Normal Completion: Value Returned

clock returns the number of microseconds used since the calling process first called clock. On AT&T 3B computers, the value returned wraps around after 2147 seconds of CPU use. Dividing the value returned by clock by the constant CLOCKS_PER_SEC (see <times.h>) gives the time in seconds.

Error Condition: Value Returned

clock returns (clock_t) −1 if the process time is unavailable or if it cannot be represented.

See Also

popen (S), system (S), times (Peterson 1991b), wait (Peterson 1991b)

conv (C) CONVERT CHARACTERS conv (C)

Name

conv: toascii, tolower, _tolower, toupper, _toupper—convert characters

Synopsis

```
#include <ctype.h>

int toascii (int c);

int tolower (int c);

int _tolower (int c);

int toupper (int c);

int _toupper (int c);
```

Description

toascii returns its own argument with all bits of the argument turned off that are not part of a standard seven-bit ASCII character. toascii is intended to support compatibility with other systems.

`tolower` is a function that converts its argument to lowercase if the argument represents an uppercase letter. Any other values of the argument (see "Arguments" below) are returned unchanged.

`_tolower` is a macro that converts its argument to lowercase if the argument represents an uppercase letter. It is faster than `tolower` but has a more restricted domain.

`toupper` is a function that converts its argument to uppercase if the argument represents a lowercase letter. Any other values of the argument (see "Arguments" below) are returned unchanged.

`_toupper` is a macro that converts its argument to uppercase if the argument represents a lowercase letter. It is faster than `toupper` but has a more restricted domain.

LC_TYPE affects `tolower`, `_tolower`, `toupper`, and `_toupper`. These functions and macros determine the case of a character according to the rules of the ASCII character set if the locale is the C locale or a locale in which shift information is undefined.

Arguments

`toascii`

`c` may be a value inside or outside the ASCII range of characters.

`toupper` *or* `tolower`

`c` may be any character in the range of the `getc` function if `c` is an argument of `toupper` or `tolower`, i.e., `c` may be the value of the macro EOF as it is defined in `stdio.h` or any value represented in an `unsigned char`. Any other values in the domains of `toupper` and `tolower` are returned unchanged.

`_toupper` *or* `_tolower`

`c` must be an uppercase letter if it is an argument of the `_tolower` macro. It must be a lowercase letter if it is an argument of the `_toupper` macro. If arguments outside the domain of a `_toupper` or `_tolower` macro are used, they produce undefined results.

Normal Completion: Value Returned

See the function and macro descriptions above.

Error Condition: Value Returned

See the `_tolower` and `_toupper` arguments above.

See Also

ctype (C), getc (S), setlocale (C), environ (AT&T 1990m)

crypt (C) PASSWORD ENCRYPTION crypt (C)

Name

crypt, encrypt, setkey—generate encryption

Synopsis

```
#include <crypt.h>

char *crypt (const char *key, const char
*saltstring);

void encrypt (char *block, int edflag);

void setkey (const char *key);
```

Description

crypt encrypts passwords. It uses a one-way encryption algorithm that has properties intended to thwart hardware implementations of a key search.

encrypt gives access to the actual hashing algorithm.

setkey, like encrypt, gives access to the actual hashing algorithm.

Arguments

The arguments of crypt, encrypt, and setkey have the following effects:

crypt

key points to the input string (a password, for example) which is to be encrypted. All but the first eight characters of the string are ignored.

saltstring is a string consisting of any two characters from the following set: [a-zA-z0-9./]. crypt uses this string to perturb the hashing algorithm in one of 4096 different ways. After perturbing the hashing algorithm, crypt uses the input string as a key to encrypt a constant string repeatedly.

encrypt

block is a character array. It contains only the characters with numerical values 0 and 1. The array is converted in place to a similar array that represents the bits of the argument after it has been hashed using the key set by setkey.

edflag specifies decryption rather than encryption. Depending on the value of the argument, the argument either is ignored or produces an error message if it is used with the international version of `crypt` that is provided with the C Development Set. See the error condition section below. If decryption is required, use the domestic version of `crypt` that is supplied with the Security Administration Utilities.

`setkey`

key is an array of 64 characters. Each character may have numerical values 0 or 1. The character string is divided into groups of eight. The lowest-order bit of each character is ignored in order to produce a 56-bit key that is set into the machine. This key is used by `encrypt` to encrypt the *block* string, using the hashing algorithm.

Normal Completion: Value Returned

`crypt` returns a pointer to static data that consist of the encrypted input string, except that the first two characters are the *saltstring* itself. These static data are overwritten by each subsequent call to `crypt`.

Error Condition: Value Returned

`errno` is set equal to ENOSYS (meaning that the operation is inapplicable) if *edflag* is assigned a nonzero value.

See Also

`crypt` (X), `getpass` (C), `login` (AT&T 1990q), `passwd` (AT&T 1990m), `passwd` (AT&T 1990q)

ctermid (S) CREATE FILENAME FOR TERMINAL ctermid (S)

Name

`ctermid`—create a filename for a terminal

Synopsis

```
#include <stdio.h>

char *ctermid (char *string);
```

Description

`ctermid` creates the pathname of the controlling terminal for the current process. It stores the pathname in a string.

Unlike `ttyname` (C), `ctermid` can be used even if the process has no file open to a terminal.

Arguments

`string` points to a character array of at least `L_ctermid` elements if *`string`* is not a NULL pointer. The pathname is put in the character array. If *`string`* is NULL, the string is stored in an internal static area that is overwritten the next time `ctermid` is called. `L_termid` is defined in `<stdio.h>`.

Normal Completion: Value Returned

`ctermid` returns a string (`/dev/tty`) that will reference a terminal if it is used as the name of a file.

If *`string`* is NULL, `ctermid` returns the address of an internal static area where the pathname is stored.

If *`string`* is not NULL, `ctermid` returns the value of *`string`*.

See Also

`ttyname` (C)

ctime (C) CONVERT DATE/TIME TO STRING ctime (C)

Name

`ctime`, `asctime`, `gmtime`, `localtime`, `tzset`—convert date and time to a string

Synopsis

```
#include <time.h>

char *asctime (const struct tm *tm);

char *ctime (const time_t clock);
```

`struct tm *gmtime (const time_t *clock);`

`struct tm *localtime (const time_t *clock);`

`extern time_t altzone;` /* `altzone` contains the difference, in seconds, between the alternate time zone and Coordinated Universal Time (UTC). Default: 0 */

`extern int daylight;` /* `daylight` is nonzero if time reflects daylight savings time. */

`extern time_t timezone;` /* `timezone` contains the difference, in seconds, between local standard time and UTC. Default: 0. Setting the time during the change from `timezone` to `altzone` gives unpredictable results. */

`extern char *tzname[2];` /* `tzname` contains time zone names. The default is `char *tzname[2] = {"GMT", " "};` */

`void tzset (void);`

Description

These functions perform time conversions. They understand how to handle the new U.S. daylight savings time that started with the first Sunday in April 1987. They also understand the peculiarities of converting U.S. times for the years 1974, 1975, and 1987.

The system administrator must change the Julian start and end days once a year.

asctime

`asctime` converts a structure of type `tm` to a 26-character string and returns a pointer to the string. The string expresses a date and time, for example

```
Sat Apr 20 00:00:00 1990\n\0
```

The fields of the string have constant width. Before `asctime` creates the string, it makes any necessary corrections for daylight savings time and time zones. The `<time.h>` header file contains declarations of the `tm` structure, as well as the functions and external variables mentioned in the synopsis. The declaration of `tm` is as follows:

```
struct tm {
    int tm_sec;  /* seconds since minute for leap seconds
                    [0, 61]                                  */
    int tm_min;  /* minutes since hour [0, 59]               */
    int tm_hour; /* hours since midnight [0, 23]             */
    int tm_mday; /* day of month [1, 31]                     */
    int tm_mon;  /* months since January [0, 11]             */
    int tm_year; /* years since 1900                         */
    int tm_wday; /* days since Sunday [0, 6]                 */
    int tm_yday; /* days since January 1 [0, 365]            */
    int tm_isdst; /* This variable is a flag for daylight savings
    time. It is 0 if daylight savings time is not in effect and less than 0
    if no information is available. In earlier implementations, this vari-
    able was nonzero if daylight savings time was in effect     */
};
```

ctime

`ctime` returns a pointer to a 26-character string described above. See `tzset` below.

gmtime

`gmtime` returns a pointer to a `tm` structure described above. It converts time directly to coordinated universal time.

localtime

`localtime` returns a pointer to a `tm` structure described above. It corrects for the main time zone and for any possible alternate time zones, such as a daylight savings time zone. See `tzset` below.

tzset

`tzset` can be called by the user or by the `asctime` function. `tzset` makes the value of the environment variable TZ override the values of the external variables listed in the synopsis above. (The functions `ctime` and `localtime` above, as well as `strftime` (C) and `mktime` (C), also may use TZ to override the default time zone.) The TZ environment variable contains time zone information. TZ is set to its default value when the user logs on by means of the `/etc/profile` file.

If the first character of TZ is a colon (`:`), the form of TZ is specific to the implementation; otherwise, TZ has the following fields:

stdtime offset [*dstime* [*offset*], [*start* [/*time*], *end* [/*time*]]]

dstime is optional. If it is present, daylight savings time applies to this locale. `dstime` may consist of three or more bytes, including any upper- or lowercase letters and any other characters except digits, a comma (`,`), a leading colon (`:`), a minus (−), or a plus (+). See `stdtime` below.

`end` may be one of the following if it is specified:

`Jn` indicates the Julian day *n* (*n* ranges from 1 to 365 inclusive). February 29 is never possible.

M*m*.*n*.*d* indicates the *d*th day of the *n*th week of the *m*th month. *d* ranges from 0 to 6 inclusive. Day zero is Sunday. *n* ranges from 1 to 5 inclusive. Week 1 is the first week that holds the *d*th day. Week 5 means "the last *d*-day contained in month *m*." *m* ranges from 1 to 12 inclusive.

n indicates the zero-based Julian day (*n* ranges from 0 to 365 inclusive). February 29 is possible, and leap years are counted.

`end/time` is optional. It tells when, in current local time, the switch from daylight savings time to standard time occurs. If `end` is not specified, an implementation-specific default is used.

`offset` is mandatory when it follows `stdtime` and optional when it follows `dstime`. It specifies the amount of time that must be added to the current local time to derive coordinated universal time. `offset` has the following fields if it is specified:

hh [`:`*mm* [`:`*ss*]]

where minutes (*mm*) and seconds (*ss*) are optional and hours (*hh*) is mandatory. *hh* may range from 0 to 24 inclusive. If *mm* and/or *ss* are present, each may range from 0 to 59 inclusive. Out-of-range values can cause unpredictable behavior. If `offset` is preceded by a minus (−), the time zone is east of the prime meridian; otherwise, it is west of the prime meridian. This may be indicated by a plus (+).

`start/time` tells when, in current local time, the change from standard time to daylight savings time occurs. The format of `start` is the same as that of `end` above.

`stdtime` is a mandatory field. It uses three or more bytes to designate standard time time zones.

`time` has the same format for its fields as `offset` does. It defaults to 02:00:00 if it is not specified. `time` cannot be preceded by a leading sign, unlike `offset`.

`tzset` scans the environment variable. It assigns each of the above fields to its respective variable. For example, the setting for New York in 1986 could be

EST5EDT4, 116/2:00, 298/2:00

or with defaults chosen

EST5EDT4

In the first example, the value of `TZ` is as follows:

- `altzone` equals 4 * 60 * 60
- `daylight` is positive
- `timezone` equals 5 * 60 * 60
- `tzname[0]` equals EST, and
- `tzname[1]` equals EDT.

The start date of the alternate time zone is 2 AM on the 117th day, and its end date is 2 AM on the 299th day. These times are relative to the alternate time zone. Zero-based Julian days are used. The time is 2 AM if the start and end dates, but not the time, are specified. If the time and the start and end dates for the alternate time zone are not specified, the time is 2 AM and the days for the United States that year are used as default values.

`tzset`, like `ctime`, `localtime`, `mktime`, and `strftime`, alters the values of the external variables `altzone`, `daylight`, `timezone`, and `tzname`. In fact, `ctime`, `localtime`, `mktime`, and `strftime` update these variables as though they had called `tzset` at the time given by the `struct tm` or `time_t` value that they are converting.

Arguments

`asctime`

tm is the `tm` structure described under `asctime` above.

`ctime`

clock has type `time_t`. It represents the time (in seconds) since 00:00:00 coordinated universal time, January 1, 1970.

`gmtime`

clock has the same meaning as in `ctime`.

`localtime`

clock has the same meaning as in `ctime`.

`tzset`

No argument

Normal Completion: Value Returned

`asctime` returns a pointer to a 26-character string.

`ctime` returns a pointer to a 26-character string. The string is overwritten by each call.

`gmtime` returns a pointer to the `tm` structure described above. Each call to `gmtime` overwrites static data.

`localtime` returns a pointer to the `tm` structure described above. Each call to `localtime` overwrites static data.

Files

`/usr/lib/locale/`*`language`*`/LC_TIME` contains date and time information that is specific to a locale.

See Also

`getenv` (C), `mktime` (C), `printf` (S), `putenv` (C), `setlocale` (C), `strftime` (C), `cftime` (AT&T 1990m), `environ` (AT&T 1990m), `profile` (AT&T 1990m), `time` (Peterson 1991b), `timezone` (AT&T 1990m)

ctype (C) IDENTIFY A CHARACTER ctype (C)

Name

`ctype`: `isacii`, `isalnum`, `isalpha`, `iscntrl`, `isdigit`, `isgraph`, `islower`, `isprint`, `ispunct`, `isspace`, `isupper`, `isxdigit`—identify a character

Synopsis

```
#include <ctype.h>

int isalnum (int c);

int isalpha (int c);

int isascii (int c);

int iscntrl (int c);

int isdigit (int c);

int isgraph (int c);

int islower (int c);
```

```
int isprint (int c);

int ispunct (int c);

int isspace (int c);

int isupper (int c);

int isxdigit (int c);
```

Description

Each of the above macros classifies character-coded integer values.

Functions exist for each of these macros. In order to use the function form, undefine the macro name by using `#undef` *macro*.

The conversion functions and macros, as well as the character classification macros, use a table lookup approach.

The current locale affects the behavior of each of the above macros except `isascii` [see `setlocale` (C)]. To change this behavior, alter the LC_TYPE category by executing `setlocale (LC_TYPE,` *newlocale*`)`. Characters are classified by using the rules of the U.S. ASCII seven-bit coded character set if the locale is a C locale or is one in which character type data are not defined.

`isalnum` tests whether `isalpha` or `isdigit` is true for a character.

`isalpha` tests whether `isupper` or `islower` is true for a character, or whether the character is one of an implementation-defined set of characters for which neither `iscntrl` nor `isdigit` nor `ispunct` nor `isspace` is true. If the locale is the C locale, `isalpha` returns true only if `isupper` or `islower` is true.

`isascii` tests whether a character has an ASCII code between 0 and 0177 inclusive.

`iscntrl` tests whether a character is one of the control characters defined by the character set.

`isdigit` tests whether a character is any decimal digit character.

`isgraph` tests whether a character is any printing character except a space.

`islower` tests whether a character is a lowercase character or one among an implementation-defined set of characters such that neither `iscntrl` nor `isdigit` nor `ispunct` nor `isspace` nor `isupper` is true. If the locale is the C locale, `islower` returns true only for lowercase ASCII characters.

`isprint` tests whether a character is a printing character, including a space (" ").

`ispunct` tests whether a character is a printing character that is not a space and not a character for which `isalnum` is true.

`isspace` tests whether a character is a standard white-space character (space, tab, newline, carriage return, vertical tab) or one among an implementation-defined set of characters such that `isalnum` is false. If the locale is the C locale, `isspace` returns true only for standard white-space characters.

`isupper` tests whether a character is an uppercase character or one among an implementation-defined set of characters such that neither `iscntrl` nor `isdigit` nor `ispunct` nor `isspace` nor `islower` is true. If the locale is the C locale, `isupper` returns true only for uppercase ASCII characters.

`isxdigit` tests whether a character is any hexadecimal digit character, i.e., [0–9], [A–F], or [a–f].

Arguments

`c` specifies the character to be classified. For the `isascii` macro, `c` may be any integer value. For the other macros, `c` must be an `int` variable representable as an `usigned char` or as `EOF` (end-of-file, defined in `stdio.h`.)

Normal Completion: Value Returned

Each of the above macros returns nonzero for true and 0 for false.

Error Condition: Value Returned

The result produced by any of the above macros is undefined if its argument is not in the domain of the function.

Files

`/usr/lib/locale/`*`locale`*`/LC_CTYPE`

See Also

`setlocale` (C), `stdio` (C), `ascii` (AT&T 1990m), `chrtbl` (AT&T 1990o), `environ` (AT&T 1990m)

cuserid (S) GET USER LOGIN NAME cuserid (S)

Name

`cuserid`—get the character login name of the user

Synopsis

```
#include <stdio.h>

char *cuserid(char *string);
```

Description

`cuserid` creates a character string that represents the login name under which the owner of the current process is logged in.

Arguments

`string` may be a NULL pointer or a pointer to an array. If *`string`* is a NULL pointer, the character string which `cuserid` creates is placed in an internal static area that `cuserid` returns. If *`string`* is not NULL, it is assumed to point to an array of at least L_`cuserid` characters in which `cuserid` places the representation of the login name (L_`cuserid` is defined in `stdio.h`).

Normal Completion: Value Returned

If *`string`* is a NULL pointer, `cuserid` returns the address of the static array which contains the representation of the login name.

Error Condition: Value Returned

If `cuserid` cannot find the login name, it returns a NULL pointer. If *`string`* is not a NULL pointer, '\0' will be stored in *`string`*[0].

See Also

`getlogin` (C), `getpwent` (C)

decconv (C) DECIMAL/BINARY CONVERSION decconv (C)

Name

decconv: _d2dec, _dec2d, _dec2s, _s2dec—convert between binary and decimal values

Synopsis

```
#include <ieeefp.h>

void _d2dec (double *x, decimal *d, int p);

void _dec2d (decimal *d, double *x, int p);

void _dec2s (decimal *d, float *x, int p);

void _s2dec (float *x, decimal *d, int p);
```

Description

These functions convert values back and forth from binary floating point to decimal floating point.

Binary-to-Decimal Conversions

`_d2dec` converts a double-precision binary floating-point value to a decimal floating-point value.

`_s2dec` converts a single-precision binary floating-point number to a decimal floating-point value.

Decimal-to-Binary Conversions

`_dec2d` converts a decimal value to a double-precision binary floating-point value.

`_dec2s` converts a decimal value to a single-precision binary floating-point value.

Arguments

Some of the following function arguments vary, depending on the function.

Arguments of Binary-to-Decimal Functions

`_d2dec`

d points to a `decimal` structure defined in the `ieeefp` header file. The exponential component of the decimal will have three digits.

p tells how many of the digits in the output decimal mantissa string are to be to the right of the implicit decimal point. *p* may range from 0 to `ilen` inclusive. If *p* is outside the range, the function returns a `NaN`. `ilen`, a field in the decimal, can range from 1 to 17 inclusive. `ilen` should be set on input to tell what number of digits should be output in the mantissa for rounding purposes.

x points to a double-precision binary floating-point input value. If *x* is infinity or a `NaN`, the returned decimal *d* will be an infinity or a `NaN` with the correct sign.

`_s2dec`

d points to a `decimal` structure, as in `_d2dec` above.

p has the same meaning as in `_d2dec` above, except that the exponential component of the returned decimal value has two digits, and `ilen` can range from 1 to 9 inclusive.

x points to a single-precision binary floating-point value. As in `_d2dec` above, the returned decimal *d* will be an infinity or a `NaN` with the correct sign if *x* is infinity or a *NaN*.

Arguments of Decimal-to-Binary Functions

`_dec2d`

d points to the `decimal` structure that contains the decimal input value. Mantissa and exponent strings can have leading zero characters. After any leading zero characters are removed, the length of the mantissa string can range from 0 to 17 inclusive, and the exponent string should have no more than three digits. If the special case `d = 0` occurs, trailing zero characters in the string are not removed.

p tells how many digits in the mantissa string are to be to the right of the implicit decimal point. *p* can range between 0 and `ilen` inclusive. See `_d2dec` above.

x points to the double-precision binary floating-point value that `_dec2d` returns.

`_dec2s`

d points to the `decimal` structure that contains the decimal input value. Mantissa and exponent strings can have leading zero characters. After any leading zero characters are removed, the length of the mantissa string can range from 0 to 9 inclusive, and the exponent string should have no more than two digits. If the special case `d = 0` occurs, trailing zero characters in the string are not removed.

p tells how many digits in the mantissa string are to be to the right of the implicit decimal point. *p* can range between 0 and `ilen` inclusive. See `_s2dec` above.

x points to the single-precision binary floating-point value that `_dec2s` returns.

Normal Completion: Value Returned

None of the above functions returns a value.

Error Condition: Value Returned

Calling the above functions with the wrong arguments can result in overflow, underflow, an inexact result, or an invalid operation. In particular, conversion from decimal to binary formats may cause underflow or overflow because the decimal format can represent larger numbers than the binary format. When overflow or underflow occurs, the appropriate sticky bit is set and a signed infinity (signed zero) is returned.

See Also

`fpgetround` (C), "Floating Point Operations" (AT&T 1990g)

difftime (C) GET CALENDAR TIME DIFFERENCE difftime (C)

Name

`difftime`—calculate the difference between two calendar times

Synopsis

```
#include <time.h>

double difftime (time_t time1, time_t time0);
```

Description

`difftime` calculates the difference between two calendar times. `difftime` is provided because type `time_t` has no general arithmetic properties defined for it.

Arguments

time1 gives the time value from which *time0* is to be subtracted.

time0 gives the time value to subtract from *time0*.

Normal Completion: Value Returned

`difftime` returns the difference (*time1* – *time0*). The difference is of type `double`, expressed in seconds.

See Also

`ctime` (C)

directory (C) DIRECTORY OPERATIONS directory (C)

Name

`directory`: `closedir`, `opendir`, `readdir`, `rewinddir`, `seekdir`, `telldir`—do directory operations

Synopsis

```
#include <dirent.h>

int closedir (DIR *dirp);

DIR *opendir (const char *filename);

struct dirent *readdir (DIR *dirp);

void rewinddir (DIR *dirp);

void seekdir (DIR *dirp, long loc);

long telldir (DIR *dirp);
```

Description

`closedir` closes the specified directory stream and frees the associated `DIR` structure.

`opendir` opens the directory specified by *filename*. It also associates a directory stream with it. `opendir` positions the directory stream at the first entry.

`readdir` returns a pointer to the next active directory entry (contained in a structure of type `dirent`; see the `dirent.h` header file) and puts the directory stream at the next entry. It does not return any inactive directory entries.

It buffers several directory entries during each actual read operation. `readdir` also marks for update the `st_atime` field of the directory each time it actually reads the directory.

`rewinddir` resets the position of the specified directory stream to the start of the directory. Just as an `opendir` call would do, `rewinddir` makes the directory stream refer to the current state of the corresponding directory. The function address of `rewinddir` cannot be taken because `rewinddir` is implemented as a macro.

`seekdir` establishes the position of the next `readdir` operation to be executed on the directory stream. This position reverts to the position associated with the directory stream when the `telldir` operation that provided *loc* was executed.

`telldir` returns the current location that is associated with the specified directory stream.

Arguments

The arguments of the various functions are as follows:

`closedir`

dirp points to a directory stream which is to be closed.

`opendir`

filename specifies the directory which `opendir` is to open.

`readdir`

dirp points to a directory stream which is to be positioned at the next directory entry.

`rewinddir`

dirp points to a directory stream whose position is to be changed to the beginning of the directory.

`seekdir`

dirp points to a directory stream for which the position of the next `readdir` operation is to be set.

loc has a value provided by a `telldir` operation.

`telldir`

dirp points to a directory stream for which a current position is being sought.

Normal Completion: Value Returned

`opendir` returns a pointer that is used to identify the directory stream during later operations. It returns a NULL pointer if the specified *`filename`* is not a directory or cannot be accessed, or if not enough memory can be `malloc` (C) to contain a `DIR` structure or a buffer for the directory entries.

`readdir` returns a pointer to the next active entry in the directory. It returns NULL when it reaches the end of a directory.

`seekdir` will return an invalid value if the directory has changed because of expansion or compaction. This problem may happen with file system types other than System V.

`telldir` returns the current location that is associated with the specified directory stream.

Error Condition: Value Returned

Possibilities for error conditions depend on the specific function as follows:

`closedir`

If `closedir` fails, it returns −1 and sets `errno` to indicate the following error condition:

9 EBADF Bad file number

The file descriptor specified by the `DIR` stream is no longer valid. The `DIR` stream has been closed.

`opendir`

If `opendir` fails, it returns NULL and sets `errno` to indicate one of the following error conditions:

2 ENOENT No such file or directory

This error occurs if some component of *`filename`* does not exist or is a NULL pathname.

13 EACCES Permission denied

The protection system forbids the kind of file access that was attempted because

- Some component of *`filename`* denies search permission or
- Read permission on the specified directory is denied.

14 EFAULT Bad address

The system encountered a hardware fault because *`filename`* points outside the allocated address space.

20 ENOTDIR Not a directory

A directory is required, but *`filename`* is not a directory.

23 ENFILE File table overflow

Temporarily, no more opens can be executed because the system table is full, i.e., the maximum number of files, SYS_OPEN, are already open.

24 EMFILE Too many open files

An attempt was made to open more than OPEN_MAX file descriptors at one time.

78 ENAMETOOLONG The filename is too long

Either the *filename* argument length is greater than {PATH_MAX}, or {_POSIX_NO_TRUNC} is in effect and the length of a path component is greater than {NAME_MAX} [see limits (AT&T 1990o)].

90 ELOOP Symbolic links error

The number of symbolic links met while *filename* was being translated is greater than MAXSYMLINKS.

readdir

If readdir fails, it returns NULL and sets errno to indicate one of the following errors:

2 ENOENT No such file or directory

The current file pointer for this directory does not point to a valid entry.

9 EBADF Bad file number

The file descriptor specified by the DIR stream is no longer valid. The DIR stream has been closed.

seekdir *and* telldir

If seekdir or telldir fails, it returns −1 and sets errno to indicate the following error:

9 EBADF Bad file number

The file descriptor specified by the DIR stream is no longer valid. The DIR stream has been closed.

See Also

dirent (AT&T 1990m), getdents (Peterson 1991b)

div (C) GET QUOTIENT AND REMAINDER div (C)

Name

div, ldiv—calculate a quotient and remainder

Synopsis

```
#include <stdlib.h>

div_t div (int numer, int denom);

ldiv_t ldiv (long int numer, long int denom);
```

Description

`div` calculates the quotient and the remainder obtained by dividing the numerator *numer* by the denominator *denom*.

The sign of the quotient is the same as that of the algebraic quotient. If the division is inexact, the resulting quotient has a magnitude that is the largest integer that is smaller than the magnitude of the algebraic quotient. The value of (*quotient* * *denom* + *remainder*) equals *numer* unless the result of the division cannot be represented. Unlike the implementation semantics of built-in division operations, `div` and `ldiv` give well-defined semantics for both signed integral division and remainder operations.

See the "Arguments" and "Normal Completion: Value Returned" sections below for the differences between the `div` and `ldiv` functions.

Arguments

The arguments `div` are of type `int`, and the arguments `ldiv` are of type `long`.

denom specifies the value of the denominator.

numer specifies the value of the numerator.

Normal Completion: Value Returned

`div` returns a structure of type `div_t`. This structure contains both the quotient and the remainder as follows:

```
typedef struct div_t {
        int quot; /* quotient */
        int rem; /* remainder */
} div_t;
```

`ldiv` returns a structure of type `ldiv_t`. This structure contains both the quotient and the remainder as follows:

```
typedef struct ldiv_t {
        long quot; /* quotient */
        long rem; /* remainder */
} ldiv_t;
```

The values returned by `div` are of type `int`, and the values returned by `ldiv` are of type `long`.

Error Condition: Value Returned

If the result of division cannot be represented, the behavior is undefined.

drand48 (C) GENERATE RANDOM NUMBERS drand48 (C)

Name

`drand48`, `erand48`, `jrand48`, `lcong48`, `lrand48`, `mrand48`, `nrand48`, `seed48`, `srand48`—generate uniformly distributed random numbers

Synopsis

```
#include <stdlib.h>

double drand48 (void);

double erand48 (unsigned short xsubi[3]);

long jrand48 (unsigned short xsubi[3]);

void lcong48 (unsigned short param[7]);

long lrand48 (void);

double mrand48 (void);

long nrand48 (unsigned short xsubi[3]);

unsigned short *seed48 (unsigned short seed16v[3]);

void srand48 (long seedval);
```

Description

These functions use the linear congruential algorithm and 48-bit arithmetic to generate pseudorandom numbers. The linear congruential algorithm creates a sequence of 48-bit integer values, X_i, according to the formula

$$X_{n+1} + (aX_n + c)_{\text{mod } m} \quad n>=0$$

where the parameter m = 2**48. Thus 48-bit integer arithmetic is executed. The multiplier value a and the addend value c are as follows:

a = 5DEECE66D hexadecimal = 273673163155 octal
c = B hexadecimal = 13 octal

The value returned by any of the `drand48`, `erand48`, `jrand48`, `lrand48`, `mrand48`, or `nrand48` functions below is calculated by first getting the next 48-bit X_i in the sequence produced by the congruential algorithm. Next, the correct number of bits, depending on the type of value to be returned, are copied from the highest-order (i.e., leftmost) bits of X_i and converted into the returned value.

Floating-Point Random Numbers

`drand48` and `erand48` return nonnegative, double-precision, floating-point values. These values are uniformly distributed over the interval [0.0, 1.0].

An initialization entry point (see below) should be invoked before `drand48` is called. Constant default initializer values will be supplied automatically if `drand48` is called without an earlier call to an initialization entry point. Don't let this happen. It introduces nonrandomness. `drand48` stores the last 48-bit X_i created in an internal buffer. Also, X_i must be initialized before being invoked.

`erand48` does not require that an initialization entry point be called first. Instead, the calling program must place an initial value of X_i in an array that is supplied as an argument to `erand48` by the calling program (`erand48` also requires the calling program to supply storage for all of the successive X_i values in that array). Because the initial value of X_i is provided by the program, the `erand48` function, like the `nrand48` and `jrand48` functions below, allows a program to generate several independent streams of pseudorandom numbers. The sequence of numbers in each stream will not depend on how many times `erand48` (or `nrand48` or `jrand48`) have been called to generate numbers for the other streams.

Nonnegative Long Integer Random Numbers

`lrand48` and `nrand48` return nonnegative long integers. These integers are uniformly distributed over the interval [0, 2**31].

An initialization entry point (see below) should be invoked before `lrand48` is called. Constant default initializer values will be supplied automatically if `lrand48` is called without an earlier call to an initialization entry point. Don't let this happen. It introduces nonrandomness. `lrand48` stores the last 48-bit X_i created in an internal buffer. Also, X_i must be initialized before being invoked.

`nrand48` does not require that an initialization entry point be called first. Instead, the calling program must place an initial value of X_i in an array that is supplied as an argument to `mrand48` by the calling program. `mrand48` also requires the calling program to supply storage for all of the successive X_i values in that array. See `erand48` above for additional details.

Signed Long Integer Random Numbers

`mrand48` and `jrand48` return signed long integers. These integers are randomly distributed over the interval [−2**31, 2**31].

An initialization entry point (see below) should be invoked before `mrand48` is called. Constant default initializer values will be supplied automatically if `mrand48` is called without an earlier call to an initialization entry point. Don't let this happen. It introduces nonrandomness. `mrand48` stores the last 48-bit X_i created in an internal buffer. Also, X_i must be initialized before being invoked.

`jrand48` does not require that an initialization entry point be called first. Instead, the calling program must place an initial value of X_i into an array that is supplied as an argument to `jrand48` by the calling program. `jrand48` also requires the calling program to supply storage for all of the successive X_i values in that array. See `erand48` above for additional details.

Initialization Entry Points

`lcong48`, `seed48`, and `srand48` are initialization entry points.

`lcong48` enables the user to specify three values: the initial X_i, the multiplier value, `a`, and the addend value, `c` (see the descriptions of `a` and `c` above).

`seed48` sets X_i to the 48-bit value specified in the argument array. It also copies the previous value of X_i into an internal array which it maintains. The pointer which `seed48` returns (see below) permits a program to be restarted from the same point at some later time. In this case, the pointer can be used to retrieve and store the last value of X_i and use this value of X_i to reinitialize by means of `seed48` when the program is restarted.

If `seed48` is called after a call to `lcong48`, it will restore the standard multiplier and addend values, `a` and `c`, described above.

`srand48` sets the high-order 32 bits of X_i equal to the 32 bits contained in its argument. The lowest-order 16 bits of X_i are set equal to the arbitrarily chosen value of 330E hexadecimal. If `srand48` is called after a call to `lcong48`, it will restore the standard multiplier and addend values, `a` and `c`, described above.

Arguments

The arguments of the various functions are as follows:

`drand48`
None

`erand48`
`xsubi` specifies an initial value of *`Xi`*.

`jrand48`
`xsubi` specifies an initial value of *`Xi`*.

`lcong48`
`param`[0–2] specifies the value of *`Xi`*.
`param`[3–5] specifies the multiplier `a`.
`param`[6] specifies the 16-bit addend `c`.

`lrand48`
None

`mrand48`
None

`nrand48`
`xsubi` specifies an initial value of *`Xi`*.

`seed48`
`seed16v`[3] specifies the 48-bit value to which *`Xi`* will be set.

`srand48`
`seedval` specifies the 32-bit value to which the high-order 32 bits of *`Xi`* will be set.

Normal Completion: Value Returned

`drand48` or `erand48` returns a nonnegative, double-precision, floating-point number in the interval [0.00, 1.0].

`lrand48` or `nrand48` returns a nonnegative integer in the interval [0, 2**31].

`jrand48` or `mrand48` returns a signed long integer in the interval [−2**31, 2**31].

`seed48` returns a pointer to an internal array which contains values of X_i.

See Also

`rand` (C)

dup2 (C) DUPLICATE AN OPEN FILE DESCRIPTOR dup (C)

Name

`dup2`—duplicate an open file descriptor

Synopsis

```
#include <unistd.h>

int dup2 (int fildscr, int fildscr1);
```

Description

`dupr2` causes *`fildscr1`* to refer to the same file as *`fildscr`*, the descriptor of an open file. If *`fildscr1`* already refers to another open file, it is closed first. If *`fildscr1`* already refers to *`fildscr`*, or if *`fildscr`* is not a valid file descriptor, *`fildscr1`* will not be closed first.

Arguments

`fildscr` specifies an open file descriptor.

`fildscr1` is a nonnegative integer that must be less than {OPEN_MAX}, the number of open files.

Normal Completion: Value Returned

If `dup2` succeeds, it returns a nonnegative file descriptor, the file descriptor.

Error Condition: Value Returned

If `dup2` fails, it returns -1 and sets `errno` to indicate one of the following errors:

4 `EINTR` Interrupted system call
A signal was caught during execution of `dup2`.
9 `EBADF` Bad file number

- *`fildscr`* is an invalid file descriptor.
- *`fildscr1`* is negative, or it is greater than or equal to {`OPEN_MAX`}.

24 `EMFILE` Too many open files
An attempt was made to open more than {`OPEN_MAX`} file descriptors at one time.

See Also

`lockf` (C), `close` (Peterson 1991b), `creat` (Peterson 1991b), `exec` (Peterson 1991b), `fcntl` (Peterson 1991b), `limits` (AT&T 1990m), `open` (Peterson 1991b), `pipe` (Peterson 1991b)

ecvt (C) FLOATING-POINT ↔ STRING ecvt (C)

Name

`ecvt`, `fcvt`, `gcvt`—convert a floating-point number to a string

Synopsis

```
include <stdlib.h>

char *ecvt (double value, int ndigit, int *decpt,
int *sign);

char *fcvt (double value, int ndigit, int *decpt,
int *sign);

char *gcvt (double value, int ndigit, char *buffer);
```

Description

`ecvt` converts a floating-point number, *`value`*, to a null-terminated string of digits. If *`value`* is not 0, the high-order digit is nonzero. The lowest-order digit is rounded.

`fcvt` has the same effect as `ecvt`, except that `fcvt` rounds the appropriate digit so that `printf %f` can output the number of digits specified by *`ndigit`*.

`gcvt` converts a floating-point number, *`value`*, to a null-terminated string and stores it in an array specified by `buffer`. `gcvt` tries to generate `ndigit` significant digits in `%f` format if possible. Otherwise, it uses `%e` format (scientific notation). If there is a minus sign or a decimal point, it will be included in the returned string. `gcvt` supresses any trailing zeros.

Arguments

The arguments of the various functions are as follows:

`ecvt`

`decpt` stores the position of the decimal point in relation to the beginning of the string. If `decpt` is negative, the decimal point is to the left of the returned digits.

`ndigit` specifies the number of digits in the null-terminated string of digits to which the floating-point number is converted. The high-order digit is nonzero unless the value of the result is 0. The decimal point is not included in the string.

`sign` points to a word which is negative if the sign of the result of the conversion is negative. Otherwise, it is 0.

`value` specifies the floating-point value which is to be converted.

`fcvt`

`decpt` has the same meaning as in `ecvt` above.
`ndigit` has the same meaning as in `ecvt` above.
`sign` has the same meaning as in `ecvt` above.
`value` has the same meaning as in `ecvt` above.

`gcvt`

`buffer` points to the array that receives the null-terminated string of digits generated by `gcvt`.

`ndigit` specifies the number of significant digits to be generated.

`value` specifies the floating-point value to be converted.

Normal Completion: Value Returned

`ecvt` returns a pointer to a null-terminated string of digits contained in a single static data array that is overwritten by each call. No decimal point is included in the returned string.

`fcvt` returns a pointer to a null-terminated string of digits contained in a single static data array that is overwritten by each call.

`gcvt` returns `buffer`, a pointer to the array that contains the null-terminated string generated by `gcvt`.

See Also

printf (S)

end (C) LAST ADDRESS IN PROGRAM end (C)

Name

end, edata, etext—address of last locations in program

Synopsis

```
extern edata;

extern end;

extern etext;
```

Description

Only the addresses of edata, end, and etext, are meaningful.

The address of edata is the first address that is greater than the greatest address of the initialized data area.

The address of end is the first address above the uninitialized data area.

The address of etext is the first address that is above the program text area.

The address of end coincides with the program break (the first address beyond the data) when program execution first begins. However, the program break can be changed by several routines: brk (Peterson 1991b), malloc (X), routines in the standard I/O library [see stdio (S)], and the -p (profile) option of the compiler cc. Use sbrk ((char *)0) to determine the current program break [see brk (Peterson 1991b)].

Arguments

None

Normal Completion: Value Returned

None

Error Condition: Value Returned

None

See Also

`brk` (Peterson 1991b), `cc` (Peterson 1991a), `malloc` (C), `stdio` (S)

fclose (S) CLOSE OR FLUSH STREAM fclose (S)

Name

`fclose`, `fflush`—close or flush a stream

Synopsis

```
#include <stdio.h>

int fclose (FILE *stream);

int fflush (FILE *stream);
```

Description

`fclose` writes any waiting buffered data to the specified stream, *`stream`*, and closes the stream. If the file is capable of seeking and if the file pointer is not already at the end of the file, `fclose` changes the file pointer so that the next operation on the open file pointer refers to the byte following the last byte that was written to or read from the file being closed. If `exit` is called, `fclose` is automatically executed.

`fflush` writes to the file any buffered data that are waiting to be written for the specified stream, *`stream`*, if *`stream`* points to an output stream or to an update stream upon which the most recent I/O operation was not an input. If there are any unread data buffered in *`stream`*, such data are discarded. If the stream is open for reading, and if the file is capable of seeking and the file pointer is not already at the end of the file, `fflush` changes the file pointer so that the next operation on the open file pointer refers to the byte following the last byte that was written to or read from the *`stream`*.

Arguments

`fclose`

`stream` specifies the stream to which any waiting buffered data are to be written.

`fflush`

`stream` specifies an output stream, or an update stream, or a stream open for reading. The specified *`stream`* remains open after a `fflush` operation.

If `fflush` is called, all files open for writing are flushed if *`stream`* is a null pointer.

Normal Completion: Value Returned

If `fclose` or `fflush` succeeds, it returns 0.

Error Condition: Value Returned

If `fclose` or `fflush` fails, it returns EOF.

See Also

`fopen` (C), `intro` (C), `setbuf` (C), `stdio` (C), `close` (Peterson 1991b), `exit` (Peterson 1991b)

ferror (S) GET STREAM STATUS ferror (S)

Name

`ferror`, `clearerr`, `feof`, `fileno`—inquire about stream status

Synopsis

```
#include <stdio.h>

void clearerr (FILE *stream);

int feof (FILE *stream);

int ferror (FILE *stream);

int fileno (FILE *stream);
```

Description

The following functions manage inquiries about the status of streams.

`clearerr` resets to 0 the error indicator and to EOF the indicator associated with a specified *`stream`*.

`feof` indicates whether an EOF was detected during a previous read of the specified *`stream`*.

`ferror` indicates whether or not an error has previously occurred during reading from or writing to a specified stream.

`fileno` gets the file descriptor associated with the specified *`stream`*.

Arguments

`stream`

Normal Completion: Value Returned

`feof` returns 0 if no EOF was detected.

`ferror` returns 0 if no read error has occurred.

`fileno` returns the file descriptor associated with the specified *`stream`* [see `open` (Peterson 1991b)].

Error Condition: Value Returned

`feof` returns a nonzero value if an EOF has previously occurred.

`ferror` returns a nonzero value if an error has previously occurred.

See Also

`fopen` (S), `stdio` (S), `open` (Peterson 1991b),

ffs (C) FIND FIRST SET BIT ffs (C)

Name

`ffs`—find the first set bit in an argument

Synopsis

```
#include <string.h>

int ffs (const int i);
```

Description

`ffs` gets the index of the first set bit in its argument. The index starts at 1 with the lowest-order bit.

Arguments

i specifies the integer variable for which the first set bit is to be found.

Normal Completion: Value Returned

ffs returns 0 if *i* is 0. Otherwise, it returns the index of the first bit set in *i*.

Error Condition: Value Returned

None

fmtmsg (C) DISPLAY AN ERROR MESSAGE fmtmsg (C)

Name

fmtmsg—display a message on stderr or the system console

Synopsis

```
#include <fmtmsg.h>

int fmtmsg (long classification, const char *label,
int severity, const char *text, const char *action,
const char *tag);
```

Description

fmtmsg writes a formatted message to the console, to stderr, or to both, depending on the value of *classification*. Other arguments of fmtmsg specify the formatted components of the message. fmtmsg can be used instead of printf to display messages on stderr.

When used in conjunction with gettxt, fmtmsg gives an interface for creating language-independent applications.

Environment Variables

In addition to the arguments of fmtmsg, two environment variables control fmtmsg. These are MSGVERB and SEV_LEVEL.

MSGVERB specifies the message components that fmtmsg selects when it writes messages to stderr, the standard error stream. The first time fmtmsg is called, it uses MSGVERB to select the message components to write to `stderr`. `fmtmsg` saves the values of MSGVERB that it finds when it is called the first time. It reuses these values of MSGVERB if it is called again.

MSGVERB selects the components to be displayed on `stderr`, not the components to be displayed on the console. See the descriptions of the arguments below for an explanation of another means for selecting components.

MSGVERB consists of a list of keywords separated by colons. These may appear in any order. The value of MSGVERB is set as follows:

```
MSGVERB=[keyword[:keyword]:...]]].
export MSGVERB
```

keyword can be `action`, `label`, `severity`, `tag`, or `text` (defined in the "Arguments" section below). `fmtmsg` includes a component in a message when writing it to `stderr` if MSGVERB contains a keyword for that component and the value of that component is not the null value for that component (see the "Arguments" section below). If the keyword that corresponds to a component does not appear in MSGVERB, `fmtmsg` does not display that component on `stderr`.

`fmtmsg` will include all message components if MSGVERB is undefined, if the content of MSGVERB consists of the null string, if it contains keywords other than those mentioned above, or if the value of MSGVERB is not in the correct format.

SEV_LEVEL provides one of three means of establishing the severity levels and associated print strings that `fmtmsg` uses. `addseverity` (C) also can define, redefine, or remove severity levels. It will overrule the effect of SEV_LEVEL if both of these define the same severity level. In addition to the severity levels that may be defined by SEV_LEVEL or `addseverity`, there are five standard severity levels which may not be changed. These are:

0	(no severity level will be used)
1	HALT
2	ERROR
3	WARNING
4	INFO

The value of SEV_LEVEL is set as follows:

```
SEV_LEVEL=[description[:description[:...]]]
export SEV_LEVEL
```

where *description* is a comma-separated list that has the following three fields:

level is a character string that evaluates to some positve integer other than 0, 1, 2, 3, or 4. The severity value passed to the fmtmsg function is *level* if the *severity_key* is used.

printstring is used by fmtmsg in the standard message format if *level* is the severity value used.

severity_key is a character string used as a keyword on the -s *severity* option of the fmtmsg (AT&T 1990q) command. The fmtmsg function does not use this field.

Any *description* that is not three fields separated by commas is ignored by fmtmsg. Also, if the second field of a *description* does not evaluate to a positive integer, fmtmsg ignores that *description*.

The first time fmtmsg is called, it determines whether SEV_LEVEL defines levels of severity in addition to those defined by addseverity or by the five standard severity levels. fmtmsg saves the values of SEV_LEVEL that it finds when it is called the first time. It reuses these values if it is called again.

Arguments

The arguments of fmtmsg specify up to five standard message components that comprise the formatted message. These message components (arguments of fmtmsg defined below) are *action*, *label*, *severity*, *tag*, and *text*.

action is a string that tells the user the first step in recovering from the error condition. fmtmsg always precedes the string with the prefix TO FIX:. The length of the *action* string has no specific limit. This component of the message can be omitted by using the null value of *text*. The null value of *text* is 0, and the identifier of the null value of *text* is MM_NULLSEV.

classification is a sixth component of fmtmsg that defines the source of a message and controls the display of the formatted message. This component can be omitted by using the null value of *classification*. The null value of *classification* is 0L, and the identifier of the null value of *classification* is MM_NULLMC.

classification consists of combinations of identifiers chosen from among major classifications, message source classifications, display subclassifications, and status subclassifications defined below. Combinations of identifiers can be formed by ORing identifiers chosen from the various subclasses. However, two or more identifiers from a single subclass should not be used together. There is one exception: both display subclass identifiers may be used together in order to display a message on the console and on stderr.

Major classifications identify the source of a condition. The possible sources are as follows:

MM_FIRM indicates that the source is firmware.

MM_HARD indicates that the source is hardware.

MM_SOFT indicates that the source is software.

Message source classifications identify the type of software in which the condition was discovered. The possible software types are as follows:

MM_APPL indicates that the type of software is application software.

MM_OPSYS indicates that the type of software is operating system software.

MM_UTIL indicates that the type of software is utility software.

Display subclassifications tell where the message is to be displayed. None, any, or all of the following identifiers may be used.

MM_CONSOLE causes the message to be displayed on the console.

MM_NRECOV says that the condition is unrecoverable.

MM_PRINT causes the message to be displayed on the standard error system.

Status subclassifications tell whether the application can recover from the condition.

MM_RECOVER says that the condition is recoverable.

No classification component is supplied for the message if MM_NULLMC is specified.

label identifies the message source. This argument of `fmtmsg` has two fields separated by a semicolon. The first field, which may be as long as 10 characters, should be used to identify the package in which an application or program resides. The second field, which may be as long as 14 characters, should be used to identify the program or application. For example, `UX:cat` identifies UNIX System V and the `cat` application. This component of the message can be omitted by using the null value of *label*. The null value of *label* is `(char*)` NULL, and the identifier of the null value of *label* is MM_NULLLBL.

severity indicates the relative seriousness of the condition that caused the message. This component of the message can be omitted by using the null value of *severity*. The null value of *severity* is 0, and the identifier of the null value of *severity* is MM_NULLSEV.

Severity level identifiers may be added to the following list of severity identifiers by executing `addseverity` (C):

MM_ERROR generates the print string ERROR to indicate that the application has detected a fault.

MM_HALT generates the print string HALT to indicate that the application is halting because it has encountered a severe fault.

MM_INFO generates the print string INFO to indicate that a condition is not an error.

MM_NOSEV indicates that the message has no severity identifier supplied.

MM_WARNING generates the print string WARNING to indicate that a condition is unusual and possibly a problem.

tag is an identifier that refers to on-line documentation for the message. *tag* should include the *label* (see *label* above) and a unique number, for example, UX:cat:200. This component of the message can be omitted by using the null value of *tag*. The null value of *tag* is (char*) NULL, and the identifier of the null value of *tag* is MM_NULLTAG.

text is a string that describes the condition that caused the message. The length of the *text* string has no specific limit. This component of the message can be omitted by using the null value of *text*. The null value of *text* is (char*) NULL, and the identifier of the null value of *text* is MM_NULLTXT.

Normal Completion: Value Returned

If fmtmsg succeeds, the exit code is MM_OK.

Error Condition: Value Returned

If fmtmsg fails completely, the exit code is MM_NOTOK.

If fmtmsg fails in generating a message on stderr but otherwise succeeds, the exit code is MM_NOTOK.

If fmtmsg fails in generating a console message but otherwise succeeds, the exit code is MM_NOTOK.

See Also

addseverity (C), gettxt (C), printf (S), fmtmsg (AT&T 1990q)

fopen (S) OPEN A STREAM fopen (S)

Name

fopen, fdopen, freopen—open a stream

Synopsis

```
#include <stdio.h>

FILE *fdopen (int fildscr, const char *type);

FILE *fopen(const char *filename, const char *type);
```

`FILE *freopen (const char *`*`filename`*`, const char *`*`type`*`, FILE *`*`stream`*`);`

Description

`fdopen` associates a specified stream with a file descriptor. The file descriptor is one that was obtained by a `creat`, `dup`, `open`, or `pipe`. These functions open files but do not return pointers to a `FILE` structure associated with a stream.

`fopen` opens the file specifed by *`filename`* and associates a stream, *`stream`*, with it.

`freopen` ordinarily is used to attach the preopened stream associated with `stderr`, `stdin`, and `stdout` to other files. In general, it substitutes the specified file for the open stream specified by *`stream`*. `freopen` first tries to flush buffers associated with the stream; then it closes the stream, whether or not the open operation eventually succeeds. If `freopen` fails to flush or close the stream, it ignores this. If `freopen` is used with `stderr`, it causes `stderr` to become buffered or line-buffered, although `stderr` is unbuffered by default.

When a stream is opened, its error and end-of-file indicators are cleared.

A stream is fully buffered if and only if the device to which it refers is not interactive.

Arguments

`fdopen`

`fildscr` specifies the file descriptor which is to be associated with the given stream. The file offset associated with *`fildscr`* indicates where the file position indicator of the associated stream is to be set.

`type` has the same meaning as the *`type`* argument of `fopen` below. The *`type`* of the stream must agree with the mode of the open file associated with *`fildscr`*.

`fopen`

`filename` points to a character string that holds the name of the file which is to be opened.

`type` is a character string that begins with one of the following character sequences:

`"a"` or `"ab"` opens the file for writing at the end of the file (appending) or creates it for writing.

`"a+"`, `"a+b"`, or `"ab+"` opens or creates a file for updating at the end of the file.

`"r"` or `"rb"` opens the file for reading.

`"r+"`, `"r+b"`, or `"rb+"`, opens the file for reading and writing (updating).

`"w"` or `"wb"` truncates the file to 0 length or creates it for writing.

`"w+"`, `"w+b"`, or `"w+b"` truncates the file or creates it for updating.

`b` is ignored in each of the above *`type`*s. The purpose of `b` in the above *`type`*s is to discriminate between binary files and text files. However, the UNIX system does not distinguish between these two kinds of files.

If a file is opened for updating, both input and output may be done on the stream that results. An output operation cannot be directly followed by an input operation unless there is an intervening `fflush`, `fseek`, `fsetpos`, or `rewind` operation. Also, an input operation cannot be directly followed by an output operation unless there is an intervening `fseek`, `fsetpos`, or `rewind`, or an input operation that results in an end-of-file condition.

If a file is opened for appending—that is, when *`type`* equals `"a"`, `"ab"`, `"a+"`, or `"ab+"`—information already in the file cannot be overwritten. Even if `fseek` is used to reposition the file pointer, the file pointer will be disregarded when data are written to the file. All output is written to the end of the file, and the file pointer is positioned at the end of the file. If two separate processes append data to the end of a file, output from the files will be interleaved in the order in which it is written, and each process may write to the file without overwriting data that are being written by the other.

`freopen`

`filename` specifies the file to be substituted for the open stream.

`stream` specifies the stream which is replaced by the file.

`type` has the same meaning as the *`type`* argument of `fopen` above.

Normal Completion: Value Returned

`fopen` returns a pointer to the `FILE` structure that is associated with the specified stream.

`freopen` returns a pointer to the `FILE` structure that is associated with the specified stream.

Error Condition: Value Returned

`fdopen` will fail if 254 file descriptors are already open.

`fdopen` returns a null pointer if *`type`* is invalid, or the file cannot be opened, or *`fildscr`* is not a valid file descriptor.

`fdopen` or `fopen` will fail and not set `errno` to an error number if no `stdio` streams are free.

`fopen` and `freopen` return a null pointer if *`type`* is invalid, or the file cannot be opened, or the path cannot be accessed.

See Also

`fclose` (S), `fseek` (S), `setbuf` (S), `stdio` (S), `close` (Peterson 1991b), `creat` (Peterson 1991b), `dup` (Peterson 1991b), `open` (Peterson 1991b), `pipe` (Peterson 1991b), `write` (Peterson 1991b)

fpgetround (C) FLOATING-POINT ENVIRONMENT fpgetround (C)

Name

`fpgetround`, `fpgetmask`, `fpgetsticky`, `fpsetmask`, `fpsetround`, `fpsetsticky`—control the IEEE floating-point environment

Synopsis

```
#include <ieeefp>

fp_except fpgetmask (void);

fp_rnd fpgetround (void);

fp_except fpgetsticky (void);

fp_except fpsetmask (fp_except mask);

fp_rnd fpsetround (fp_rndrnd_dir);

fp_except fpsetsticky (fp_except sticky);
```

Description

These six functions manage responses to five floating-point exceptions: divide-by-zero, overflow, underflow, invalid operation, and inexact (imprecise) result. These functions enable the user to alter the program behavior on the occurrence of any of these five exceptions or to change the rounding mode used with floating-point operations.

If a floating-point exception occurs, the sticky bit corresponding to the exception is set (1) and, if the mask bit is enabled (1), the trap occurs. In order to proceed, the sticky bit first must be cleared. Otherwise, a wrong exception type may be signaled when the next trap occurs.

The following flags are defined:

Exception Sticky Bits

`FP_X_DZ` /* divide-by-zero exception sticky bit */
`FP_X_IMP` /* loss of precision sticky bit */
`FP_X_INV` /* invalid operation sticky bit */
`FP_X_OFL` /* overflow exception sticky bit */
`FP_X_UFL` /* underflow exception sticky bit */

Rounding Mode

`FP_RM` /* round to minus infinity */
`FP_RN` /* round to the nearest representative number */
`FP_RP` /* round to plus infinity */
`FP_RZ` /* round to zero */

The rounding mode has no effect on C language conversions from floating-point numbers to integers. (C requires rounding to 0—truncation—during such conversions.)

The default environment is to have all traps disabled and the rounding mode set to the nearest rounding mode, i.e., `FP_RN`.

`fpsetmask` sets the exception masks and clears the sticky bit that corresponds to any exception that is being enabled.

`fpsetround` sets the rounding mode.

`fpsetsticky` alters all sticky bits.

The values returned by `fpgetmask`, `fpsetmask`, `fpgetround`, `fpsetround`, `fpgetsticky`, and `fpsetsticky` are described in the "Normal Completion: Value Returned" section below.

Arguments

`mask` specifies the mask which is to be altered.
`rnd_dir` sets the rounding mode.
`sticky` specifies the sticky flags to be altered.

Normal Completion: Value Returned

`fpgetmask` returns the current exception masks.
`fpsetmask` returns the previous setting of the exception masks.
`fpgetround` returns the current rounding mode.

fpsetround returns the previous setting of the rounding mode.
fpgetsticky returns the current exception sticky bit flags.
fpsetsticky returns the previous setting of the exception sticky bit flags.

See Also

isnan (C)

fread (S) BINARY I/O fread (S)

Name

fread, fwrite—perform binary I/O

Synopsis

```
#include <stdio.h>

size_t fread (void *pointr, size_t size, size_t nitems, FILE *stream);
size_t fwrite (const void *pointr, size_t size, size_t nitems, FILE *stream);
```

Description

fread reads one or more sequences of bytes (data items) from a stream into a specified array. The data items are not necessarily terminated by a null byte. fread stops reading bytes when it has read the specified number of data items or if it finds an end-of-file condition or an error condition while reading the stream. fread does not alter the contents of the stream. However, fread increments the data pointer of the stream to point to the byte that follows the last byte that was read.

fwrite writes one or more data items from a specified array to a given stream. The data items are not necessarily terminated by a null byte. fwrite stops writing bytes when it has written the specified number of data items or if it finds an error condition while writing to the stream. fwrite increments the data pointer of the stream to point to the byte that follows the last byte that was written.

Arguments

nitems specifies the number of sequences of bytes (data items) which fread is to read from the stream or which fwrite is to write to the stream.

pointr points to the array in which `fread` stores the data items it reads from the stream or from which `fwrite` gets data items to write to the stream.

size specifies the number of bytes in a data item.

stream specifies the stream from which `fread` reads data items or to which `fwrite` writes data items.

Normal Completion: Value Returned

`fread` returns the number of data items it reads. It returns 0 if *size* or *nitems* is zero. In this case, `fread` does not affect the stream.

`fwrite` returns the number of data items it writes. It returns 0 if *size* or *nitems* is zero. In this case, `fwrite` does not affect the stream.

Error Condition: Value Returned

If an error occurs during an `fread` or `fwrite`, the error indicator for the stream is set. The `ferror` or `feof` routines must be used in order to discriminate between an error condition and an end-of-file condition.

See Also

`abort` (C), `fclose` (S), `fopen` (S), `getc` (S), `gets` (S), `printf` (S), `putc` (S), `puts` (S), `scanf` (S), `stdio` (S), `exit` (Peterson 1991b), `lseek` (Peterson 1991b), `read` (Peterson 1991b), `write` (Peterson 1991b)

frexp (C) MANIPULATE FLOATING-POINT NUMBERS frexp (C)

`frexp`, `ldexp`, `logb`, `modf`, `modff`, `nextafter`, `scalb`—manipulate components of floating-point numbers

Synopsis

```
#include <math.h>

double frexp (double value, int *eptr);

double ldexp (double value, int exp);

double logb (double value);
```

```
double modf (double value, double *iptr);

double modff (float value, float *iptr);

double nextafter (double value1, double value2);

double scalb (double value, double exp);
```

Description

Any nonzero number can be uniquely represented as a fraction (mantissa) `x` times an exponent consisting of an `n`th power of 2, where the absolute value of `x` ranges from less than or equal to 0.5 to less than 1.0 and `n` is an integer. The following functions manipulate such numbers:

`frexp` computes the mantissa of a type `double` value.

`ldexp` computes the product of a specified number, *`value`*, times 2 raised to the exponent *`exp`*.

`logb` computes the unbiased exponent of its floating-point argument.

`modf` gets the integer part of its argument and stores it in the location to which *`iptr`* points. It returns the signed fractional part of its argument.

`modff` is the single-precision version of `modf`.

`nextafter` computes the next representable double-precision floating-point value that follows *`value1`* in the direction of *`value2`*.

`scalb` computes the product of a specified number, *`value`*, times 2 raised to the exponent *`exp`*. `scalb` differs from `ldexp` only in that the `scalb` of a `NaN` will cause the invalid operation exception to be raised.

Arguments

`frexp`

`eptr` points to the location where the exponent *`n`* is to be stored.

`value` specifies a type `double` value whose mantissa is to be returned by `frexp`.

`ldexp`

`exp` specifies the power to which 2 is to be raised.

`value` specifies the value which is to be multipled by a power of 2.

`logb`

`value` specifies the floating-point value whose unbiased exponent is to be computed.

`modf`

`iptr` points to the location where `modf` stores the integer part of its argument.

`value` specifies the value which is to be split into an integer and a fractional part.

`modff`

`iptr` points to the location where `modff` stores the integer part of its argument.

`value` specifies the value which is to be split into an integer and a fractional part.

`nextafter`

`value1` specifes the floor (or ceiling) of an interval.

`value2` specifies the ceiling (or floor) of an interval.

`scalb`

`exp` specifies the power to which 2 is to be raised.

`value` specifies the value which is to be multiplied by a power of 2.

Normal Completion: Value Returned

`frexp` returns a value of 0 for the mantissa of *`value`* if *`value`* is 0. Otherwise, `frexp` returns the manissa of a type `double` value.

`ldexp` returns the product of *`value`* times the 2 to the *`exp`* power.

`logb` returns a double-precision floating-point value representing the unbiased exponent of its floating-point argument.

`modf` returns the signed fractional part of its double-precision argument, *`value`*.

`modf` returns the signed fractional part of its single-precision argument, *`value`*.

`nextafter` returns the largest representable double-precision floating-point number that is less than *`value1`* if *`value2`* is less than *`value1`*. If *`value2`* is greater than *`value1`*, `nextafter` returns the largest representable double-precision floating-point number that is greater than *`value1`*.

`scalb` returns the product of *`value`* times the 2 to the *`exp`* power.

Error Condition: Value Returned

Some of the above functions return −HUGE or +HUGE under certain circumstances. If the program was compiled with the `cc` options `-Xc` or `-Xa`, these functions return HUGE_VAL instead of HUGE under those circumstances.

The values returned by these functions when error conditions occur are as follows:

`ldexp` *Errors*

33 EDOM Math argument out of domain of function

If *`value`* is NaN or infinity, `ldexp` returns *`value`* and sets `errno` to EDOM.

34 ERANGE Result too large

- If `ldexp` would cause overflow if it were executed, it returns +HUGE or -HUGE (defined in the `math.h` header file), depending on the sign of *`value`*, and sets `errno` to ERANGE.
- If `ldexp` would cause underflow if it were executed, it returns 0 and sets `errno` to ERANGE.

`logb` *Errors*

33 EDOM Math argument out of domain of function

- If *`value`* is NaN, `logb` returns NaN and sets `errno` to EDOM.
- If *`value`* is infinity, `logb` returns positive infinity and sets `errno` to EDOM.
- If *`value`* is 0, `logb` returns negative infinity, causes the divide-by-zero exception to be raised, and sets `errno` to EDOM.

`nextafter` *Errors*

33 EDOM Math argument out of domain of function

If *`value1`* is positive or negative infinity, `nextafter` returns that input and sets `errno` to EDOM.

34 ERANGE Result too large

- If *`value1`* is finite but `nextafter`(*`value1`*, *`value2`*) is not, the overflow and inexact exceptions are signaled and `nextafter` sets `errno` to ERANGE.
- If `nextafter(`*`value1`*, *`value2`*) lies strictly between -2 to the minus 1022 power and $+2$ to the minus 1022 power, the underflow and inexact exceptions are raised and `nextafter` sets `errno` to ERANGE.

`scalb` *Errors*

33 EDOM Math argument out of domain of function

- If *`value`* is infinity, `scalb` returns infinity and sets `errno` to EDOM.
- If *`value`* is NaN, `scalb` returns NaN, causes the invalid operation exception to be raised, and sets `errno` to EDOM.

34 ERANGE Result too large

- If `scalb` would cause overflow if it were executed, it returns +HUGE or -HUGE (defined in the `math.h` header file), depending on the sign of *value*, and sets `errno` to ERANGE.
- If `scalb` would cause underflow if it were executed, it returns 0 and sets `errno` to ERANGE.

See Also

`intro` (M), `cc` (Peterson 1991a)

fseek (S) REPOSITION STREAM FILE POINTER fseek (S)

Name

`fseek`, `ftell`, `rewind`—change the file pointer position in the stream

Synopsis

```
#include <stdio.h>

int fseek (FILE *stream, long offset, int pointrnm);

long ftell (FILE *stream);

void rewind (FILE *stream);
```

Description

`fseek` establishes the position of the next I/O operation on the specified stream. `fseek` permits the file position indicator to be set past the end of the existing data in the file, but `fseek` does not extend the size of the file by itself. If data are written at a point past the end of the file, any subsequent reads of data from the gap between the old end of file and the new data will return 0 until data are actually written in the gap.

`ftell` returns the offset of the current byte in relation to the beginning of the file that is associated with the specified stream. On the UNIX system the offset that `ftell` returns is measured in bytes, so it is possible to seek to positions in relation to the offset. However, if portability to non-UNIX systems is required, the offset should be used by `fseek` directly because the offset is not necessarily measured in bytes on a non-UNIX system.

rewind may be thought of as a special case of fseek. In fact, rewind (*stream*) is equivalent to

```
(void) fseek (stream, 0L, SEEK_SET);
```

Both fseek and rewind undo the effects of any ungetc performed on the stream. They also clear the EOF indicator. They cause unwritten data to be written to the file if buffered data have not been written to the underlying file and the stream is writable.

If a file is open for updating, the next operation after an fseek or rewind can be either an input or an output operation.

Arguments

offset specifies the signed distance of the new file position, in bytes, from the beginning of the file, from the current file position, or from the end of the file, depending on the value of *pointrnm*.

pointrnm is one of the following values defined in stdio.h:

SEEK_CUR sets the file position equal to the current location plus *offset* bytes.

SEEK_END sets the file position equal to EOF plus *offset* bytes.

SEEK_SET sets the file position equal to *offset* bytes.

stream specifies the stream on which fseek, ftell, or rewind is to perform an operation.

Normal Completion: Value Returned

fseek returns 0 if it succeeds.
ftell returns the offset of a byte in relation to the beginning of the file.
rewind returns nothing.

Error Condition: Value Returned

If an improper seek is specified, fseek returns −1. Examples of improper seeks are a seek on a stream that has been closed, a seek on a file that has not been opened by using fopen, or a seek on a terminal or a file that has been opened by a popen.

See Also

fopen (S), popen (S), stdio (S), ungetc (S), lseek (Peterson 1991b), write (Peterson 1991b)

fsetpos (C) — REPOSITION FILE POINTER IN STREAM — fsetpos (C)

Name

fsetpos, fgetpos—change file pointer position in stream

Synopsis

```
#include <stdio.h>

int fgetpos (FILE *stream, fpos_t *posit);

int fsetpos (FILE *stream, const fpos_t *posit);
```

Description

fgetpos stores the current value of the file position for the specified stream in the object to which *pos* points. This value can be used by fsetpos to reposition the stream to the position it had at the time fgetpos was called.

fsetpos uses the value at which *pos* points to set the position of the next I/O operation on the stream. The value at which *pos* points must be one which was returned by an earlier call to fgetpos. After an fsetpos, the next operation performed on a file that is open for updating may be either an input or an output operation. fsetpos undoes the effects of any ungetc operation on the same stream. It also clears the end-of-file indicator for the stream.

Arguments

pos points to an object which tells the value of the file position.

stream is the stream whose current file position is managed by fsetpos and fgetpos.

Normal Completion: Value Returned

If fgetpos or fsetpos succeeds, it returns 0.

Error Condition: Value Returned

If fgetpos or fsetpos fails, it returns a nonzero value.

See Also

fseek (S), ungetc (S), lseek (Peterson 1991b)

ftw (C) MANAGE TREES ftw (C)

Name

`ftw`, `nftw`—walk a file tree

Synopsis

```
#include <ftw.h>

int ftw (const char *path, int (*fnc) (const char *,
const struct stat, int), int depth);

int nftw (const char *path, int (*fnc) (const char*,
const struct stat, int, struct FTW*), int depth, int
flags);
```

Description

`ftw` recursively travels the directory tree whose root is in *path*. For each object in the tree, `ftw` calls the user-defined function *fnc* and passes *fnc* three arguments: a pointer to a null-terminated character string that contains the name of the object, a pointer to a `stat` structure, and an integer that gives additional information about the object. In traversing the tree, `ftw` visits a directory before visiting any of its descendants. `ftw` continues its traversal until one of three things happens: the tree is exhausted, an invocation of *fnc* returns a nonzero value, or some error occurs in `ftw`—for example, an I/O error.

Because `ftw` is recursive, it may terminate with a memory fault if the file structure it traverses is very deep.

During its execution, `ftw` uses `malloc` (C) to allocate dynamic storage. That storage will remain permanently allocated if `ftw` is forceably terminated, for example, by an interrupt routine or by the execution of `longjmp`. To handle interrupts, store an indication that an interrupt has occurred and have *fnc* return a nonzero value the next time it is invoked.

`ftw`, like `nftw` below, uses one file descriptor at each level of the directory tree (see the *depth* argument below). When `ftw` (or `nftw`) returns, it closes any file descriptors that it may have opened, but it does not close any file descriptors that *fnc* may have opened.

Arguments

`ftw`

`ftw` has three arguments: *depth*, *fnc*, and *path*. One of these arguments, the function *fnc*, takes three arguments of its own.

depth limits the number of file descriptors used in describing the directory tree. *depth* cannot be greater than the number of file descriptors currently available. If *depth* is either negative or 0, it is treated as a 1. `ftw` will execute faster if *depth* is at least as large as the number of directory tree level.

fnc is a user-defined function to which `ftw` passes the following arguments at each file and directory in the tree:

* points to a null-terminated character string that contains the name of an object in the directory tree.

`int` is one of four values defined in the `ftw.h` header file:

FTW_D indicates that the object is a directory.

FTW_DNR indicates that the object is a directory that cannot be read. No descendents of the directory will be processed.

FTW_F indicates that the object is a file.

FTW_NS indicates that `stat` failed on the object because the appropriate permission was lacking or because the object is a symbolic link pointing to a non-existent file. The `stat` buffer that was passed to *fnc* is not defined.

path contains the root of the directory tree.

`stat` is a structure [see `stat` (Peterson 1991)] that contains information about an object in the directory tree.

nftw

`nftw` calls *fnc* with four arguments at each file and directory in the tree.

depth takes one of the following values:

FTW_CHDIR indicates that the walk will change to each directory before reading it.

FTW_D indicates that the object is a directory.

FTW_DEPTH indicates that all subdirectories will be visited before the directory itself.

FTW_DNR indicates that the object is a directory that cannot be read. No descendants of the directory will be processed.

FTW_DP indicates that the object is a directory and that subdirectories have been visited.

FTW_F indicates that the object is a file.

FTW_MOUNT indicates that the walk will not cross a mount point.

FTW_NS indicates that `stat` failed on the object because the appropriate permission was lacking. The `stat` buffer that was passed to *fnc* is not defined.

FTW_PHYS indicates that the walk is a physical walk; it does not follow symbolic links. Otherwise, `nftw` will follow such links but will not walk down any path that crosses itself.

FTW_SLN indicates that the object is a symbolic link that points to a nonexistent file.

flags specifies the following:

fnc is similar to *fnc* in `ftw` above, except that it takes four arguments, as follows:

`*` is the same as in `ftw` above.

`stat` is the same as in `ftw` above.

`int` is the same as in `ftw` above.

`FTW` is a structure that has the following members:

`int base;` /* the offset into the pathname of the base name of the object */

`int level;` /* the depth relative to the rest of the walk—where the root level is zero */

path is the same as in `ftw` above.

Normal Completion: Value Returned

`ftw` returns 0 if it exhausts the directory tree.

Error Condition: Value Returned

If `ftw` detects an error other than an `EACCES` error, it returns −1 and sets `errno` to indicate the error type.

If *fnc* returns a nonzero value, `ftw` halts its directory tree traversal and returns whatever value *fnc* returned.

`nftw` returns −1 if `stat` fails for any reason other than lack of permission (EACCES).

See Also

`malloc` (C), `stat` (Peterson 1991b)

getc (S) GET DATA FROM A STREAM getc (S)

Name

`getc`, `fgetc`, `getchar`, `getw`—get a character or word from a stream

Synopsis

```
#include <stdio.h>

int getc (FILE *stream);

int getchar (void);
```

```
int fgetc (FILE *stream);

int getw (FILE *stream);
```

Description

getc is a macro that returns the next byte from an input stream. getc advances the file pointer one character in the specified stream if the file pointer is defined. getc(stdin) is the same as getchar. Use fgetc instead of getc with arguments like *f++ because getc evaluates a stream argument more than once; getc thus may treat side effects incorrectly.

fgetc, a function, works the same way as getc, except that fgetc executes more slowly than getc. However, fgetc takes less space per invocation and the name fgetc can be passed as an argument to a function.

getw returns the next word (integer) from the specified stream and increments the file pointer associated with the stream (if the file pointer is defined) so that it points to the next integer. getw does not assume any special alignment in the file, but the size of an integer is the size of a word on a particular machine. This size may vary from machine to machine.

Differences in word length and byte order from machine to machine may make it impossible for getw to read files written by putw on another machine.

Accurate comparison of the integer constant EOF with the integer returned by getc, getchar, or fgetc may be impossible because of implementation-dependent differences in the sign extension of a character when it is widened to an integer.

In order to get the function version of any of the macros above, undefine the macro name by using a directive such as #undef getc.

Arguments

stream specifies the stream upon which fgetc, getc, or getw operates.

Normal Completion: Value Returned

fgetc returns the next character (byte) from the specified input stream as an unsigned char converted to a type int variable.

getc returns the next character (byte) from the specified input stream as an unsigned char converted to a type int variable.

getw returns the next word (integer) from the specified input stream.

Error Condition: Value Returned

If an error occurs during the execution of one of the above functions, it sets the error indicator of the stream. If one of the above functions encounters an end-of-file condition, it sets the EOF of the stream. Since EOF is a valid integer, use `ferror` to detect `getw` errors.

See Also

`fclose` (S), `ferror` (S), `fopen` (S), `fread` (S), `gets` (S), `putc` (S), `scanf` (S), `stdio` (S), `ungetc` (S)

getcwd (C) GET DIRECTORY PATHNAME getcwd (C)

Name

`getcwd`—get the pathname of the current directory

Synopsis

```
#include <unistd.h>

char *getcwd (char *buffer, int size);
```

Description

`getcwd` gets the pathname of the current directory.

Arguments

`buffer` causes `getcwd` to get *`size`* bytes of space by using `malloc` (C) if *`buffer`* is a NULL pointer. If *`buffer`* is not a NULL pointer, the pathname will be stored in the space to which *`buffer`* points.

`size` specifies the size of storage for the pathname. *`size`* must specify at least one byte more than the number of bytes in the pathname.

Normal Completion: Value Returned

`getcwd` returns a pointer to the pathname of the current directory. The pointer to be used as the argument in a subsequent call to `free` (C) if *`buffer`* is a NULL pointer.

Error Condition: Value Returned

If *size* is not positive, getcwd fails, returns NULL, and sets errno to indicate an EACCES error.

13 EACCES Permission denied

The protection system forbids the kind of file access that was attempted.

If *size* is greater than 0 but less than the length of the pathname plus 1, getcwd fails, returns NULL, and sets errno to indicate an EINVAL error.

22 EINVAL Invalid argument

A math function was supplied with an invalid argument, or an invalid argument was supplied to some other function.

If the parent directory cannot be read to get its name, getcwd fails, returns NULL, and sets errno to indicate an ERANGE error.

34 ERANGE Result too large

The value returned by a math function cannot be represented within the precision permitted by the machine.

If an error occurs in a lower-level function, getcwd returns NULL and sets errno.

See Also

malloc (C)

getdate (C) CONVERT DATA AND TIME getdate (C)

Name

getdate—convert the user format of date and time

Synopsis

```
#include <time.h>

struct tm *getdate (const char *string);

extern int getdate_err
```

Description

getdate uses the macros described in ctype (C) to convert user-definable date and/or time specifications to a tm structure.

The `tm` structure is declared in the `time.h` header file. See `ctime` (C) for a detailed description of `tm`.

`getdate` uses templates supplied by the user to parse and interpret the input string. Templates consist of text files. Each template is identified by means of the variable DATEMSK. Each line in a template uses some of the same field descriptors used by the `date` (AT&T 1990q) command. Field descriptors are used to represent an acceptable date and/or time specification. The first template line that matches the input specification is used to convert the date and/or time specification to an internal format.

These are the available field descriptors:

`%%` has the same effect as `%`.
`%a` designates an abbreviated weekday name.
`%A` designates a full weekday name.
`%b` designates an abbreviated month name.
`%B` designates a full month name.
`%c` expresses the locale's date and time representation.
`%d` designates the day of month (01–31; with optional leading 0).
`%D` has the same effect as `%m/%d/%y`.
`%e` has the same effect as `%d`.
`%h` designates an abbreviated month name.
`%H` designates the hour (00–23).
`%I` designates the hour (00–12).
`%m` designates the month number (01–12).
`%M` designates the minute (00–59).
`%n` has the same effect as `n`.
`%p` designates the locale's equivalent of AM or PM.
`%r` has the same effect as `%I:%M:%S %p` (time).
`%R` has the same effect as `%H:%M` (time).
`%S` designates seconds (00–59).
`%t` inserts a tab.
`%T` expresses time as `%H:%M:%S`.
`%w` designates weekday number (0–6, where Sunday is 0).
`%x` designates date representation appropriate to a locale.
`%X` designates time representation appropriate to a locale.
`%y` expresses the year with the century (00–99).
`%Y` expresses year as *ccyy* (e.g., 1990)
`%Z` expresses the time zone name (no characters if no name exists).

Names of months and weekdays can be formed from any combination of upper- and lowercase letters. The user can set the categories `LC_TIME` and `LC_CTYPE` of `setlocale` in order to request that the input specifications for date or time be in a given language.

`getdate` supports local date and time specifications. Local date and time specifications can be defined in the templates as follows:

The invocation `getdate("Sunday 12:00:00")` corresponds to the line `%y-%m-%d` in the template.

The invocation `getdate("12/31/90")` corresponds to the line `%m/%d/%y` in the template.

The invocation `getdate("90-12-31")` corresponds to the line `%y-%m-%d` in the template.

The invocation `getdate("31.12.90")` corresponds to the line `%d.%m.%y` in the template.

Input specifications are converted into the internal format according to the following rules:

- The current hour, minute, and second are assumed if no hour, minute, and second are given.
- Today is assumed if only the weekday is given and the given day is equal to the current day.
- Today is assumed if no date is given and the given hour is greater than the current hour.
- Tomorrow is assumed if no date is given and the given hour is less than the current hour.
- Next week is assumed if only the weekday is given and the given day is less than the current day.
- The current month is assumed if only the month is given and the given month is equal to the current month.
- Next year is assumed if only the month is given and the given month is less than the current month.

Arguments

`string` points to a user-definable date and/or time specification which is to be converted by `getdate`.

Normal Completion: Value Returned

If `getdate` succeeds, it returns a pointer to the `tm` structure that holds the converted user-definable date and/or time specification.

Error Condition: Value Returned

If `getdate` fails, it returns NULL and sets the type `extern int` variable `getdate_err` to a value whose meaning is one of the following:

1 means that the `DATEMSK` variable is null or undefined.
2 means that the template file cannot be opened for reading.
3 means that `getdate` failed to get file status information.
4 means that the template file is not a regular file.
5 means that `getdate` encountered an error while reading the file.
6 means that `malloc` failed because not enough memory is available.
7 means that no line in the template matches the input.
8 means that the input specification is invalid (e.g., September 31). Dates before 1970 and after 2037 are illegal.

Any subsequent call to `getdate` will change the contents of `getdate_err`.

Files

`/usr/lib/locale/<locale>/LC_TIME` contains printable files that are specific to a natural language.

`/usr/lib/locale/<locale>/LC_TYPE` contains printable files that are specific to a code set.

See Also

`ctype` (C), `setlocale` (C), `environ` (AT&T 1990m)

getenv (C) MANAGE ENVIRONMENTAL VARIABLES getenv (C)

Name

`getenv`—get the value of an environment name

Synopsis

```
#include <stdlib.h>

char *getenv (const char *name)
```

Description

`getenv` searches for a string of the form *`name`*`=`*`value`* in the environment list. [See `environ` (AT&T 1990m) for a description of the environment list].

Arguments

`name` points to the environment string for which `getenv` is to search.

Normal Completion: Value Returned

`getenv` returns a pointer to *`value`* in the current environment if the string *`name`*=*`value`* is present in the current environment.

`getenv` returns a null pointer if the string is not present.

See Also

`putenv` (C), `environ` (AT&T 1990m), `exec` (Peterson 1991b)

getgrent (C) GET GROUP FILE ENTRY getgrent (C)

Name

`getgrent`, `endgrent`, `fgetgrent`, `getgrgid`, `getgrnam`, `setgrent`—get a group file entry

Synopsis

```
#include <grp.h>

void endgrent (void);

struct group *getgrent (void);

struct group *fgetgrent (FILE *stream);

struct group *getgrid (gid_t gid);

struct group *getgrnam (const char name);

void *setgrent (void);
```

Description

The `getgrent`, `getgrgid`, and `getgrnam` functions find objects that hold the separate fields of a line in the `/etc/group` file. Each line of the file contains a structure defined in the `grp.h` header file. The structure has the following members:

```
char **gr_mem        /* vector of pointers to member names */
char *gr_name;       /* name of the group */
char *gr_passwd;     /* encrypted group password. */
gid_t gr_gid;        /* numerical group id. */
```

`endgrent` is used to close a group file when processing of the file is finished.

`fgetgrent` finds the next group structure in the stream *`stream`* whose format matches that of `/etc/group`.

`getgrent` is used to search an entire file by returning a pointer to the *n*th group structure of the file on the *n*th call to the function.

`getgrgid` searches from the beginning of a group file until it finds a numerical group ID that matches its argument, *`gid`*.

`getgrnam` searches from the beginning of a group file until it finds a group name that matches its argument, *`name`*.

`setgrent`, in effect, rewinds a group file. This permits repeated searches of the file.

Arguments

`gid` specifies a group ID.

`name` specifies a group name.

`stream` specifies a stream containing a group structure.

Normal Completion: Value Returned

The information gathered by the following functions is contained in a static area, so it must be copied to another location if it must be saved.

`fgetgrent` returns a pointer to the next group structure in the stream *`stream`* whose format matches that of `/etc/group`.

`getgrent` returns a pointer to the first group structure in the file on the first call. On the *n*th call to `getgrent`, it returns a pointer to the *n*th group structure in the file.

`getgrgid` returns a pointer to the structure in which it finds a numerical group ID that matches *`gid`*.

`getgrnam` returns a pointer to the structure in which it finds a group name that matches *`name`*.

Error Condition: Value Returned

If `fgetgrent`, `getgrent`, `getgrgid`, or `getgrnam` encounters an end-of-file condition or an error, it returns a null pointer.

Files

`/etc/group` is described above.

See Also

`getlogin` (C), `getpwent` (C), `group` (AT&T 1990o)

getitimer (C) GET/SET INTERVAL TIMER getitimer (C)

Name

`getitimer`, `setitimer`—get or set the interval timer value

Synopsis

```
#include <sys/time.h>

int getitimer (int which, struct itimerval *value);

int setitimer (int which, struct itimerval *value,
itimerval *ovalue);
```

Description

`getitimer` stores the current value of a specified interval timer of a process in an `itimerval` structure.

An `itimerval` structure defines a timer value. The structure includes the two following `timeval` structures as members [see `getttimeofday` (C) for details about `timeval` structures]:

`struct timeval it_interval;` /* `it_interval` specifies a value to use in reloading `it_val` if the timer expires and the initial value of `it_interval` is 0. If `it_interval` is 0, it disables the timer following its next expiration if `it_value` is nonzero. */

`struct timeval it_value;` /* `it_value` indicates the time until the timer next expires. If `it_value` is set to 0, it disables the timer, no matter what the value of `it_interval`. */

The microseconds field should be less than one second. Any time values that are smaller than the resolution of the system clock are rounded up to the resolution of the system clock.

The UNIX system supplies three interval timers for each process. These are defined in the `sys/time.h` header file. The three timers are as follows:

`ITIMER_PROF` causes the `SIGPROF` signal to be delivered when this timer expires. Programs that use this timer must be able to restart interrupted system calls because this signal can interrupt system calls that are in progress. This timer decrements in process virtual time and while the system is executing in behalf of the process. This timer is meant to be used by interpreters that are statistically profiling the execution of interpreted programs.

`ITIMER_REAL` causes a `SIGALRM` signal to be delivered when this timer expires. This timer decrements in real time.

ITIMER_VIRTUAL causes a SIGVTALRM signal to be delivered when this timer expires. This timer decrements in process virtual time. It runs only while the process actually is executing.

settimer sets the value of a specified interval timer to the value stored in a specified structure. setitimer is separate from and independent of the alarm system call.

If sleep is executed after setitimer, it will eliminate any knowledge of the user signal handler. Therefore, do not use sleep and setitimer together.

Arguments

getitimer

value points to the itimerval structure in which getitimer is to store the current value of the specified timer.

which specifies the current value of an interval timer which is to be stored in a specified itimerval structure.

setitimer

ovalue points to the itimerval structure in which setitimer stores the previous value of the timer if *ovalue* is not NULL .

value specifies an itimerval structure.

which specifies the interval timer whose value is to be set to the value in the specified itimerval structure.

Normal Completion: Value Returned

If getitimer or setitimer succeeds, it returns 0.

Error Condition: Value Returned

If getitimer or setitimer fails, it returns −1 and sets the global variable errno to indicate the following error:

22 EINVAL Invalid argument

The number of seconds specified exceeds 100,000,000 or the number of microseconds specified exceeds 1,000,000, or the *which* parameter is not recognizable.

See Also

gettimeofday (C), alarm (Peterson 1991b)

getlogin (C) GET LOGIN NAME getlogin (C)

Name

getlogin—get the login name

Synopsis

```
#include <stdlib.h>

char *getlogin(void);
```

Description

getlogin gets the login name as it found the name in /var/adm/utmp. getlogin can be used with getpwnam to find the correct password file entry when several login names share the same user ID.

Arguments

None

Normal Completion: Value Returned

getlogin returns a pointer to the login name as it found the name in /var/adm/utmp. The pointer points to static data which are overwritten by the next call to getlogin.

Error Condition: Value Returned

getlogin returns a NULL pointer if it does not find the login name. getlogin returns a NULL pointer if it is called from within a process that is not attached to a terminal.

Files

/var/adm/utmp

See Also

cuserid (S), getgrent (C), getpwent (C), utmp (AT&T 1990m), utmp (AT&T 1990o)

getmntent (C) GET `mnttab` FILE ENTRY getmntent (C)

Name

`getmntany`, `getmntent`—get an `mnttab` entry

Synopsis

```
#include <stdio.h>
#include <sys/mnttab>

int getmntent (FILE *fptr, struct mnttab *mp);

int getmntent (FILE *fptr, struct mnttab *mp, struct
mnttab *mpref);
```

Description

`getmntent` fills a specified `mnttab` structure with fields from a line in the `/etc/mnttab` file. Successive calls to `getmntent` can search an entire `/etc/mnttab` file, accessing successive lines by using a pointer to the next line.

Each line of the `/etc/mnttab` file consists of an `mnttab` structure, as defined in the `sys/mnttab.h` header file. `mnttab` is declared as follows:

```
struct mnttab {
        char *mnt_special;
        char *mnt_mountp;
        char *mnt_fstype;
        char *mnt_mntopts;
        char *mnt_time;
};
```

`getmntany`, like `getmntent`, fills a specifed `mnttab` structure with the fields from a line in the `/etc/mnttab` file. `getmntany` also searches the file specified by *`fptr`* until it finds a match between a line in that file and the `mnttab` structure to which *`mpref`* points. The `mnttab` structure to which *`mpref`* points matches a line in the `/etc/mnttab` file if all of the nonnull entries in the `mnttab` structure match corresponding fields in the `/etc/mnttab` file.

Neither `getmntent` nor `getmntany` opens, closes, or rewinds the `/etc/mnttab` file.

Arguments

fptr points to an /etc/mnttab file.
mp points to an mnttab structure which is to be filled with the contents of fields in a line of the /etc/mnttab file.
mpref points to an mnttab structure whose contents are to be compared with fields in lines of an /etc/mnttab file.

Normal Completion: Value Returned

If getmntany succeeds in finding a match, it returns 0.
If getmntent succeeds in reading a file entry, it returns 0.
The mnttab structure members point to data in static areas, so the data must be copied if they must be saved.

Error Condition: Value Returned

If getmntent or getmntany encounters an end-of-file condition during reading, it returns −1.
If getmntent or getmntany encounters an error, it returns one of the following positive values:
MNT_TOOFEW means that a line in the file has too few fields.
MNT_TOOLONG means that a line in the file exceeds the internal buffer size or limit, MNT_LINE_MAX.
MNT_TOOMANY means that a line in the file has too many fields.

Files

/etc/mnttab

See Also

mnttab (AT&T 1990o)

getopt (C) GET OPTION LETTER FROM VECTOR getopt (C)

Name

getopt—get an option letter from an argument vector

Synopsis

```
#include <stdlib.h>

int getopt (int argc, char * const *argv, const char
*optstring);
```

```
extern char *optarg;

extern int optind, opterr, optopt;
```

Description

`getopt` finds the next option letter in *argv* that is the same as a letter in *optstring*.

`getopt` supports all of the rules of the UNIX command syntax standard as described in (Peterson 1991a). New commands adhere to the UNIX command syntax standard and should use `getopt`, `getopts` (AT&T 1990q), or `getsubopts` (C) to check for legal options and parse positional parameters.

The checking that `getopt` does when it looks for mandatory arguments is not exhaustive. For example, if `getopt` is given an option string `a:b` and an input string `-a -b`, it assumes that `-b` is the mandatory option associated with the option `-a`. It does not assume that `-a` is missing an argument.

Do not group options that have arguments together with other options. That is, *cmd* `-aboyy` *filename*, in which `a` and `b` are options without arguments and in which `o` is an option that the argument `yy` should not be used even though such usage now is permitted. Future releases may not support such usage. Use the syntax *cmd* `-ab -oyy` *filename* instead.

External Variables

`optarg` points to an option string.

`opterr` will, if it is set to 0, disable the error message that will be output by `getopt` if it encounters an unexpected character. See the "Error Condition: Value Returned" section below.

`optind` holds the *argv* index of the next argument that is to be processed by `getopt`. `optind` is initialized to 1 before the first call to `getopt`.

`optopt` contains the value of a character if the character causes an error in `getopt`. See the "Error Condition: Value Returned" section below.

Arguments

argc contains a count of the number of arguments in *argv*.

argv contains option letters to be matched with letters in *optstring*. Two hyphens (`--`) can be used as a special option to mark the end of options. When `getopt` encounters this special option, it returns `EOF` and skips the two hyphens. This permits demarcation of nonoption arguments that begin with a single hyphen.

optstring contains all of the option letters that the command using `getopt` will recognize. `getopt` expects any option letter that is followed by a colon to have either an argument or a group of arguments following the colon, possibly separated from the colon by white space.

Normal Completion: Value Returned

`getopt` returns `EOF` when it has processed all options up to the first nonoption argument.

Error Condition: Value Returned

If `getopt` encounters an option letter in *`argv`* that is not in *`opstring`*, it prints an error message on `stderr` and returns a question mark (?). It also prints an error message on `stderr` and returns a question mark (?) if it finds no argument after an option where it expects one. See the `optopt` and `opterr` external variables above.

See Also

`getsubopt` (C), `getopts` (AT&T 1990q), `intro` (AT&T 1990q)

getpass (C) READ A PASSWORD getpass (C)

Name

`getpass`—read a password

Synopsis

```
#include <stdlib.h>

char *getpass (const char *prompt);
```

Description

`getpass` reads from the file `/dev/tty` until it encounters a newline or an EOF after sending the *`prompt`* string to `stderr` and disabling echoing.

If an interrupt occurs, `getpass` will terminate input and send an interrupt signal to the calling program before returning.

Arguments

`prompt` contains a prompt string to be output on `stderr`.

Normal Completion: Value Returned

If `getpass` succeeds, it returns a pointer to a null-terminated string of at most eight characters. The string is in a static area that is overwritten by each call to `getpass`.

Error Condition: Value Returned

If `/dev/tty` cannot be opened, `getpass` returns a NULL pointer.

Files

`/dev/tty`

getpw (C) SEARCH PASSWORD FILE FOR USER ID getpw (C)

Name

`getpw`—get a name from UID

Synopsis

```
#include <stdlib.h>

int petpw (uid_t uid, char *buffer);
```

Description

`getpw` searches the password file for a specified user ID. If it finds the user ID, it copies the line of the password file in which it found the user ID into the specified buffer.

Use routines from `getpwent` (C) instead of `getpw` because `getpw` is included only for compatibility with earlier versions of the system.

Arguments

`buffer` specifies a buffer into which a line of the password file is to be copied if a user ID in the line is equal to the specified user ID number.

`uid` specifies a user ID number for which `getpw` searches the password file.

Normal Completion: Value Returned

If `getpw` finds the specified user ID in the password file, it returns 0.

Error Condition: Value Returned

If `getpw` fails, it returns a nonzero value.

Files

`/etc/passwd`

See Also

`getpwent` (C), `passwd` (AT&T 1990o)

getpwent (C) MANAGE PASSWORDS getpwnt (C)

Name

`getpwent`, `endpwent`, `fgetpwent`, `getpwnam`, `getpwuid`, `setpwent`—manipulate a password entry

Synopsis

```
#include <pwd.h>

struct passwd *getpwent (void);

void endpwent (void);

struct passwd *fgetpwent (FILE *strm);

struct passwd *getpwnam (const char *name);

struct passwd *getpwuid (uid_t uid);

void setpwent (void);
```

Description

`getpwent` returns a pointer to the `passwd` structure that contains the separate fields of a line in the `/etc/passwd` file (password file). Each line in the password file holds a `passwd` structure. Because `getpwent` returns a pointer to the next `passwd` structure in the file, successive calls to `getpwent` can search the entire file.

The passwd structure is defined in the pwd.h header file as follows:

```
struct passwd {
        char *pw_name
        char *pw_passwd;
        uid_t pw_uid;
        gid_t pw_gid;
        char *pw_age;
        char *pw_comment;
        char *pw_gecos;
        char *pw_dir;
        char *pw_shell;
};
```

endpwent can be used to close the password file when processing is finished.

fgetpwent finds the next passwd structure in the specified stream, *stream*, which matches the format of the password file.

getpwnam searches from the beginning of the password file until it finds a login name that matches *name*.

getpwuid searches from the beginning of the password file until it finds a numerical user ID that matches the user ID specified by its argument, *uid*.

setpwent, in effect, rewinds the password file to enable repeated searches of the file.

Arguments

name specifies the login name for which getpwname is to search.

stream specifies the stream in which fgetpwent is to search for the next passwd structure that matches the format of /etc/passwd.

uid specifies the user ID for which getpwuid is to search.

Normal Completion: Value Returned

getpwent returns a pointer to the next passwd structure in the /etc/passwd file.

getpwnam returns a pointer to the passwd structure in which it finds a login name that matches *name*.

getpwuid returns a pointer to the passwd structure in which it finds a specified user ID.

Error Condition: Value Returned

If fgetpwnt, getpwent, getpwnam or getpwnid, encounters an error or an EOF, it returns a NULL pointer.

Files

/etc/passwd

See Also

getgrent (C), getlogin (C), passwd (AT&T 1990o)

gets (S) GET STRING FROM STREAM gets (S)

Name

gets, fgets—get a string from a stream

Synopsis

```
#include <stdio.h>

char *fgets (char *string, int n, FILE *stream);

char *gets (char *string);
```

Description

fgets reads characters from a specified stream until one of three things occurs: *n* − 1 characters have been read, fgets has encountered a newline and has transferred it to *string*, or fgets has encountered an end-of-file condition. fgets next terminates the string with a null character.

gets reads characters from the standard input stream, stdin, into the character array to which *string* points. It continues to read until it encounters a newline or an end-of-file condition. If the length of the input line is longer than the length of *string*, undefined behavior may occur. Therefore, use fgets instead of gets.

Arguments

n tells fgets to read *n* − 1 characters from the stream.
stream specifies the stream from which fgets is to read characters.

string is a string that contains *n* characters: *n* − 1 characters followed by a null character.

Normal Completion: Value Returned

If fgets or gets succeeds in reading characters, it returns a pointer to the string of characters that it transferred.

Error Condition: Value Returned

If fgets or gets encounters a read error, as when trying to read a file that has not been opened, it returns a NULL pointer and sets the error indicator for the stream.

If fgets or gets encounters an end-of-file condition, it sets the EOF indicator for the stream.

If fgets or gets encounters an end-of-file condition and no characters have been read, it returns a NULL pointer and transfers no characters to *string*.

See Also

ferror (S), fopen (S), fread (S), getc (S), scanf (S), stdio (S), ungetc (S), lseek (Peterson 1991b), read (Peterson 1991b)

getspent (C) MANAGE PASSWORDS getspent (C)

Name

getspent, endspent, fgetspent, getspnam, lckpwdf, setspent, ulckpwdf—manipulate an entry in a shadow password file

Synopsis

```
#include <shadow>

void endspent (void);

struct spwd *fgetspent (FILE *fptr);

struct spwd *getspent (void);

struct spwd *getspnam (const char *name);
```

```
int lckpwdf (void);

void setspent (void);

int ulckpwdf (void);
```

Description

getspent and its associated functions are for internal use only. Compatibility is not guaranteed.

On the *n*th call to getspent, it returns a pointer to the *n*th spwd structure whose members contain fields from a line in the /etc/shadow file. Thus, successive calls to getspent can be used to search the entire /etc/shadow file.

Each line in the /etc/shadow file holds a shadow password structure, as declared in the shadow.h header file:

```
struct spwd {
        char *sp_namp;
        char *sp_pwdp;
        long sp_lstcgg;
        long sp_min;
        long sp_max;
        long sp_warn;
        long sp_inact;
        long sp_expire;
        insigned long sp_flag;
};
```

endspent closes the shadow password file when processing is finished.

fgetspent finds the next spwd structure in the specified stream which matches the format of /etc/shadow.

getspnam searches from the beginning of the /etc/shadow file until it finds the login name that matches the login name specified by *name*. getspnam, like getspent, puts −1 in any of the sp_expire, sp_flag, sp_inact, sp_lstchg, sp_max, sp_min, and sp_warn fields of the spwd structure for which the corresponding field in /etc/shadow is empty.

lckpwdf uses the lockfile /etc/.pwd.lock to lock a password file (/etc/shadow or /etc/passwd), thereby gaining the exclusive right to modify the password file. lckpwdf tries to lock /etc/.pwd.lock within

15 seconds. `lckpwdf` prevents simultaneous modifications of the password files.

`setspent`, in effect, rewinds the shadow password file, thereby enabling repeated searches of the file.

`ulckpwdf` attempts to unlock the lockfile `/etc/.pwd.lock`. `ulckpwdf` should release the lock on the lockfile as soon as file modifications are completed.

Arguments

`fptr` specifies a stream in which `fgetspent` searches for an `spwd` structure that matches the format of `/etc/shadow`.

`name` specifies a login name for which `getspnam` is to search the `/etc/shadow` file.

Normal Completion: Value Returned

All information is stored in a static area. If it must be saved, it must be copied.

On the *n*th call to `getspent`, it returns a pointer to the *n*th `spwd` structure in the `/etc/shadow` file.

If `getspnam` finds a login name in the `/etc/shadow` file that matches the login name specified by *`name`*, it returns a pointer to the particular structure in which it was found.

If `lckpwdf` succeeds in locking lockfile `/etc/.pwd.lock`, it returns a value other than -1.

Error Condition: Value Returned

If `fgetspent`, `getspent`, `getspnam`, `lckpwdf`, or `ulckpwdf` encounters an error or end-of-file, it returns a NULL pointer.

If `getspent` or `getspnam` encounters an end-of-file condition, a format error in a file, or a read error, it returns a NULL pointer and sets `errno` to EINVAL.

22 EINVAL

A function was supplied with an invalid argument, or an invalid argument was supplied to some other function.

Files

`/etc/passwd` is a password file.

`/etc/.pwd.lock` is the lock file. It helps coordinate modification access to `/etc/passwd` and `/etc/shadow`.

`/etc/shadow` is a password file.

See Also

getpwent (C), putpwent (C), putspent (C)

getsubopt (C) PARSE STRING getsubopt (C)

Name

getsubopt—parse suboptions from a string

Synopsis

```
#include <stdlib.h>

int getsubopt (char **optionp, char * const *tokens,
char **valuep);
```

Description

getsubopt parses the suboptions contained in a flag argument (*optionp*) that was first parsed by getopt (C).

Arguments

optionp is the address of a pointer to an option string. Suboptions in the option string are separated by commas if there is more than one option. A suboption can consist of a single token or a token-value pair separated by an equals (=) sign. Because commas delimit the suboptions of an option string, they cannot be part of a suboption or part of the value of a suboption. Thus, during parsing, any commas that appear in the option input string are changed to null characters. Any white space in tokens or in token-value pairs must be enclosed in quotation marks in order to protect it from the shell.

If the option string holds only one suboption, getsubopt updates *optionp* so that it points to the null character at the end of the string. Otherwise, it isolates the suboption by substituting a null character for the comma separator, and updates *optionp* so that it points to the beginning of the next suboption.

Upon return from getsubopt, *optionp* points to the next option that is to be parsed or (if there are no more tokens) to a null character.

tokens points to a vector of possible tokens. The vector consists of a series of pointers to null strings. A null pointer marks the end of the vector.

valuep is the address of a value string pointer. If getsubopt finds a suboption that has an associated value, `getsubopt` updates *`valuep`* so that it points to the first character of the value. Otherwise, `getsubopt` sets *`valuep`* equal to NULL. If *`valuep`* is not NULL when `getsubopt` returns, it means that the last suboption processed included a value. The presence (or absence) of such a value may indicate an error which the calling program may need to examine. If `getsubopt` fails to recognize an option, the variable to which *`valuep`* points contains a pointer to the first character of the token that was not recognized, not to a pointer to a value for that token.

Normal Completion: Value Returned

If `getsubopt` finds a match between a token and a suboption in its input string, it returns an index of the token. See the *`valuep`* and *`optionp`* arguments above.

Error Condition: Value Returned

If the token that `getsubopt` is scanning is not in the token vector, `getsubopt` returns −1. If this happens, the calling program needs to decide whether this is an error or if the (unrecognized) option should be passed to another program.

See Also

`getopt` (C)

gettimeofday (C) GET/SET DATA AND TIME gettimeofday (C)

Name

`gettimeofday`, `settimeofday`—get or set the date and time

Synopsis

```
#include <sys/time.h>

int gettimeofday (struct timeval *tptr);

int settimeofday (struct timeval *tptr);
```

Description

gettimeofday gets the system clock's current time expressed in seconds and microseconds elapsed since 00:00 UTC, January 1, 1970.

settimeofday sets the system clock's current time. Only the superuser may execute settimeofday.

The resolution of the system clock depends on hardware. The system may update time continuously or in clock ticks.

Arguments

tptr points to a timeval structure that includes the following members:

long tv_sec /* seconds since 1/1/70 */

long tv_usec /* microseconds in addition to tv_sec */

The tv_sec field is not used by settimeofday. If accuracy greater than 1 second is required in setting the time, use settimeofday to set the seconds and use adjtime to adjust the time for greater accuracy.

The current time information is neither returned nor set if *tptr* is a null pointer.

Normal Completion

See *tptr* above.

Error Condition: Value Returned

If gettimeofday or settimeofday fails, it returns −1 and sets errno to indicate one of the following errors:

1 EPERM Not superuser

A user other than the superuser tried to set the time or the time zone.

22 EINVAL Invalid argument

tptr specifes an invalid time zone.

Files

/etc/TIMEZONE sets and exports TZ, the environmental variable that contains time zone information [see ctime (C)]. /etc/TIMEZONE is dotted into other files that need to know the time zone.

See Also

ctime (C), adjtime (Peterson 1991b), profile (AT&T 1990o), rc2 (AT&T 1990o)

Name

gettxt—retrieve a text string

Synopsis

```
#include <unistd.h>

char *gettxt (const char *msgid, const char
*dflt_str);
```

Description

getttxt gets a text string (message) from a file previously created by the mkmsgs (AT&T 1990q) utility and installed in directories in /usr/lib/locale/<*locale*>/LC_MESSAGES. The <*locale*> directory can be thought of as the language in which messages are written.

An application may have a separate message database for each of several natural languages. For example, an application may have one message database with Italian messages and another message database with Spanish messages.

The user can call setlocale (C) to change the language in which messages are displayed. Alternatively, the user can set the environment variable LC_MESSAGES to specify the language in which messages are to be displayed. The LANG environment variable will be used to specify the language of messages if LC_MESSAGES is not set. If neither LC_MESSAGES nor LANG is set, the files containing message strings are in /usr/lib/locale/C/LC_MESSAGES.

Arguments

dflt_str points to a default message string to be used if the text string retrieval fails. See the "Error Condition: Value Returned" section below.

msgid specifies a message. The syntax of *msgid* must be

<*msgid*> = <*msgfilename*>:<*msgnumber*>

where *msgfilename* specifies the file that contains the message. The length of the message filename must be 14 characters or less selected from any character values except a null (\0), an ASCII code for a slash (/), or a colon (:). The message file name must be the same as the names of files that were created by mkmsgs and installed in /usr/lib/locale/<*locale*>/LC_MESSAGES. The *msgnumber* field specifies the sequence number of the message in the file. These messages are numbered from 1 to *n*, where *n* is the number of messages in the file.

Normal Completion: Value Returned

If gettxt succeeds, it returns a pointer to a text string.

Error Condition: Value Returned

If gettxt fails to retrieve a message in the specified language, it will try to retrieve the same message in U.S. English. If gettext fails to retrieve a message and *dflt_str* is not null, gettxt returns a pointer to *deflt_str*. If gettext fails and *dflt_str* is null, gettxt returns a pointer to the text string "Message not found!!\n". If gettxt is passed an incorrect *msgid* or an incorrect message number, it returns a pointer to the text string "Message not found!!\n".

Example

gettxt("UX:20", "helloworld\n") specifies message number 20 in the UX file.

Files

/usr/lib/locale/C/LC_MESSAGES/* holds default message files. These files are created by mkmsgs

/usr/lib/locale/<*locale*>/LC_MESSAGES holds message files for different languages (locales). These files are created by mkmsgs.

See Also

fmtmsg (C), setlocale (C), environ (AT&T 1990m), exstr (AT&T 1990q), mkmsgs (AT&T 1990q), srchtxt (AT&T 1990q)

getut (C) ACCESS utmp FILE ENTRY getut (C)

Name

getut: endutent, getutent, getutid, getutline, pututline, setutent, utmpname—access a utmp file entry

Synopsis

```
#include <utmp.h>

void endutent (void);

struct utmp *getutent (void);

struct utmp *getutid (const struct utmp *id);

struct utmp *getutline (const struct utmp *line);

struct utmp *pututline (const struct utmp *utmp);

void setutent (void);

int utmpname (const char *filename);
```

Description

`endutent` closes the currently open `utmp` file.

`getut` routines access entries in a `utmp` file. The most current `utmp` file entry is saved in a static `utmp` stucture described below. Except for `pututline`, these routines use standard I/O for input.

`getutent` reads the next entry from a `utmp` file. It opens the file if it is not already open. If `getutent` succeeds in reading the next entry, it returns a pointer to a `utmp` structure (defined in the `<utmp.h>` header file) that has the following members:

```
struct  utmp {
        char ut_user[8]; /* user login name */
        char ut_id[4]; /* /sbin/inittab ID created by the
process that puts the entry in utmp */
        char ut_line[12]; /* device name (console, lnxx), a string
consisting of 11 or fewer characters, including a null character. The string may
have one of the following special strings or formats when accounting is for
something other than a process:
                #define RUNLVL_MSG "run-level %c"
                #define BOOT_MSG "system boot"
                #define OTIME_MSG "old time"
                #define NTIME_MSG "new time" */
        short  ut_pid; /* process ID */
```

```
        short  ut_type;  /* entry type, one of the following types:
            #define EMPTY            0
            #define RUN_LVL          1
            #define BOOT_TIME        2
            #define OLD_TIME         3
            #define NEW_TIME         4
            #define INIT_PROCESS     5
            #define LOGIN_PROCESS    6
            #define USER_PROCESS     7
            #define DEAD_PROCESS     8
            #define ACCOUNTING       9
            #define UTMAXTYPE        ACCOUNTING */
/* ACCOUNTING is the maximum legal value for ut_type */
    struct exit_status {
        short e_termination;  /* termination status of a process
*/
        short e_exit;  /* exit status of process */
    } ut_exit;  /* exit status of a process marked as DEADPRO-
CESS  */
    time_t ut_time;  /* time when an entry was made */
  };
```

getutid searches forward from the current position in the utmp file, looking for an entry that matches criteria specified by *id* (see the description of the *id* argument of getutid below for details). The current entry that getutid finds is saved in the utmp structure (a static structure). On each call to getutid, it examines the utmp structure before doing another I/O operation. If the contents of the structure match what getutid is searching for, it looks no further. If getutid must access the utmp file more than once and the contents of the structure must be saved, the contents must be copied to another location before getutid is called again.

getutline searches forward from the current position in the utmp file until it locates an entry whose ut_type field equals LOGIN_PROCESS or USER_PROCESS and whose ut_line field matches the *id*->ut_id string. See the description of the *line* argument of getutline below for details. Because the structure that getutline returns is static, it is necessary to zero out the static area if getutline is to be used to search for multiple occurences. Otherwise, getutline will find the same structure again and again.

pututline writes the specified utmp structure to the utmp file. If pututline finds that it is not already at the correct utmp file position, it uses getutid to search forward until it reaches the correct position. If it does not find such a position, it adds a new entry to the end of the file. If `pututline` has to search forward in the file, the implicit read that it performs will not damage the contents of any static structure that was returned by `getutent`, `getutid`, or `getutline` immediately before calling `pututline`. Normally, a `getut` routine should be used to search for the correct entry before `pututline` is called. If so, `pututline` will not need to search for a file entry.

`pututline` uses an unbuffered, nonstandard write operation in order to avoid race conditions between processes that are trying to modify `utmp` and `wtmp` files.

`setutent` resets the input string to the beginning of the file. If the entire file is to be examined, `setutent` must be executed before each search for a new entry.

`utmpname` enables the user to change the name of the file examined from `/var/adm/utmp` to some other file, usually `/var/adm/wtmp`. If the file is nonexistent, this will become apparent only when the first attempt is made to refer to the file. `utmpname` does not open the new file. It merely closes the old file if it is open and saves the new file name.

Arguments

`endutent`

None

`getutent`

None

`getutid`

id specifies the kind of match for which `getutid` searches in its forward search of the `utmp` file. If *id* specifies RUN_LVL, BOOT_TIME, NEW_TIME, or OLD_TIME, (see the `ut_type` member of the `utmp` structure above), `getutid` searches until it finds an entry that has a `ut_type` value that matches *id*->`ut_type`. If *id* specifies DEAD_PROCESS INIT_PROCESS, LOGIN_PROCESS, or USER_PROCESS, `getutid` searches for the first entry whose `ut_type` field matches one of these four values and whose `ut_id` field matches *id*->`ut_id`, and returns a pointer to the first such entry that it finds.

`getutline`

line specifies a *line*->`ut_line` value that must equal the `ut_line` field of a `utmp` entry as one of two criteria that determine whether a match has occurred.

`pututline`
utmp specifies the `utmp` structure which is to be written to a `utmp` file.

`setutent`
None

`utmpname`
filename specifies a file other than the `/var/adm/utmp` file which is to be examined by `getut` routines. Often the other file will be `/var/adm/wtmp`.

Normal Completion: Value Returned

If `getutent` succeeds, it returns a pointer to a static `utmp` structure. See the description of `getutent` above for details.

If `getutid` finds the matching entry for which it searches, it returns a pointer to a static `utmp` structure. See the description of the *id* argument of `getutid` for details.

If `getutline` finds the matching entry for which it searches, it returns a pointer to a static `utmp` structure. See the description of `getutline` above for details.

If `pututline` succeeds in writing a `utmp` structure, it returns a pointer to the structure.

`utmpname` returns 0 if the specified *filename* is longer than 79 characters. Otherwise, it returns 1.

Error Condition: Value Returned

If `getutent` reaches the end of the file while trying to read the next entry, it fails.

If `getutid` reaches the end of the file without finding the entry for which it searches, it fails.

If `getutline` reaches the end of the file without finding the entry for which it searches, it fails.

If any of the above functions fails during a read operation (either because of an end-of-file condition or because of a lack of permission), it returns a null pointer. If it fails during a write operation, it returns a null pointer.

Files

`/var/adm/utmp`
`/var/adm/wtmp`

See Also

ttyslot (C), utmp (AT&T 1990m)

getutx (C) ACCESS utmpx FILE ENTRY getutx (C)

Name

getutx: endutxent, getutmp, getutmpx, getutxent, getutxid, getutxline, pututxline, setutxent, updwtmp, updwtmpx, utmpxname—access a utmpx file entry

Synopsis

```
#include <utmpx.h>

void endutxent (void);

void getutmp (struct utmpx *utmpx, struct utmp *utmp);

void getutmpx (struct utmp *utmp, struct utmpx *utmpx);

struct utmpx *getutxent (void);

struct utmpx *getutxid (const struct utmpx *id);

struct utmpx *getutxline (const struct utmpx *line);

struct utmpx *pututxline (const struct utmpx *utmpx);

void setutxent (void);

void updwtmp (char *wfile, struct utmp *utmp);

void updwtmpx (char *wfilex, struct utmpx *utmpx);

int utmpxname (const char *filename);
```

Description

endutxent closes the currently open utmpx file.

getutmp copies data in fields of the utmpx structure to corresponding fields of the utmp structure. Any data in a utmpx field that do not fit into the corresponding utmp field will be truncated.

getutmpx copies data in fields of the utmp structure to corresponding fields of the utmpx structure.

getutx routines access entries in an utmpx file. The most current utmpx file entry is saved in a static utmpx stucture described below (see getutxent). Except for pututxline, these routines use standard I/O for input.

getutxent reads the next entry from an utmpx file. It opens the file if it is not already open. If getutxent succeeds in reading the next entry, it returns a pointer to a utmpx structure (defined in the <utmpx.h> header file) that has the following members:

```
struct utmpx {
        char utuser[32]; /* user login name */
        char ut_id[4]; /* /sbin/inittab ID created by the
process that puts the entry in utmpx */
        char ut_line[12]; /* device name (console, lnxx), a string
consisting of 11 or fewer characters, including a null character. The string may
have one of the following special strings or formats when accounting is for
something other than a process:
                #define RUNLVL_MSG "run-level %c"
                #define BOOT_MSG "system boot"
                #define OTIME_MSG "old time"
                #define NTIME_MSG "new time" */
        pid_t ut_pid; /* process ID */
        short ut_type; /* entry type, one of the following types:
                #define EMPTY           0
                #define RUN_LVL         1
                #define BOOT_TIME       2
                #define OLD_TIME        3
                #define NEW_TIME        4
                #define INIT_PROCESS    5
                #define LOGIN_PROCESS   6
                #define USER_PROCESS    7
                #define DEAD_PROCESS    8
                #define ACCOUNTING      9
                #define UTMAXTYPE       ACCOUNTING */
/* ACCOUNTING is the maximum legal value for ut_type */
/* INIT_PROCESS indicates a process spawned by init */
```

/* LOGIN_PROCESS indicates a "getty" process that is waiting for login */
/* USER_PROCESS indicates a user process */

```
    struct exit_status {
        short e_termination; /* termination status of process */

        short e_exit; /* exit status of the process */

    } ut_exit;
    struct timeval ut_tv; /* time when an utmpx file entry was made */
    long ut_session; /* Session ID, for windowing purposes */

    long pad[5]; /* Reserved */

        short ut_syslen; /* Length of ut_host, including terminating null character */
        char ut_host[257]; /* Name of remote host */
     };
```

getutxid searches forward from the current position in the utmpx file, looking for an entry that matches criteria specified by *id* (see the description of the *id* argument of getutxid below for details). The current entry that getutxid finds is saved in the utmpx structure (a static structure). On each call to getutxid, it examines the utmpx structure before doing another I/O operation. If the contents of the structure are what getutxid is searching for, it looks no further. If getutxid must access the utmpx file more than once and the contents of the structure must be saved, the contents must be copied to another location before getutxid is called again.

getutxline searches forward from the current position in the utmpx file until it locates an entry whose uttype field equals LOGIN_PROCESS or USER_PROCESS and whose ut_line field matches the *id*->ut_id string. See the description of the *line* argument of getutxline below for details. On each call to getutxline, it examines the utmpx structure before doing another I/O operation. If the contents of the structure are what getutxline is searching for, it looks no further. Because the structure that getutxline returns is static, it is necessary to zero out the static area if getutxline is to be used to search for multiple occurrences. Otherwise, getutxline will find the same structure again and again.

pututxline writes the specified utmpx structure to the utmpx file. If pututxline finds that it is not already at the correct utmpx file position, it uses getutxid to search forward until it reaches the correct position. If it does not find such a position, it adds a new entry to the end of the file. If pututxline has to search forward in the file, the implicit read that it performs will not damage the contents of any static structure that was returned by getutxent, getutxid, or getutxline immediately before calling pututxline. Normally, a getutx routine should be used to search for the correct entry before pututxline is called. If so, pututxline will not need to search for a file entry. pututxline uses an unbuffered, nonstandard write operation in order to avoid race conditions between processes that are trying to modify utmpx and wtmpx files.

setutent resets the input string to the beginning of the file. If the entire file is to be examined, setutent must be executed before each search for a new entry.

updwtmp determines whether *wfile* and its parallel file, *wfile*x, exist. The name of the parallel file is gotten by appending an "x" to *wfile*. If only one of these files exists, updwtmp creates and initializes it to the state of the existing file. udwtmp writes the utmp structure to *wfile* and writes the corresponding utmpx structure to the parallel file.

updwtmpx determines whether *wfilex* and its parallel file, *wfile*, exist. The name of the parallel file is gotten by removing the final "x" character from *wfilex*. If only one of these files exists, updwtmp creates and initializes it to the state of the the existing file. udwtmp writes the utmpx structure to *wfilex* and writes the corresponding utmpx structure to the parallel file.

utmpxname enables the user to change the name of the file examined from /var/adm/utmpx to some other file, usually /var/adm/wtmpx. If the file is nonexistent, this will become apparent only when the first attempt is made to refer to the file. utmpxname does not open the new file. It merely closes the old file if it is open and saves the new file name.

Arguments

endutxent

None

getutmp

utmp specifies the utmp structure whose fields are to receive data from corresponding fields of the utmpx structure.

utmpx specifies the utmpx structure whose data fields are to be copied to corresponding fields of the utmp structure.

getutmpx

utmp specifies the utmp structure whose data fields are to be copied to corresponding fields of the utmpx structure.

utmpx specifies the utmpx structure whose fields are to receive data from corresponding fields of the utmp structure.

getutxent
None

getutxid
id specifies the kind of match for which getutid searches in its forward search of the utmp file. If *id* specifies RUN_LVL, BOOT_TIME, NEW_TIME, or OLD_TIME (see the ut_type member of the utmp structure above), getutxid searches until it finds an entry that has a uttype value that matches id->ut_type. If *id* specifies DEAD_PROCESS, INIT_PROCESS, LOGIN_PROCESS, or USER_PROCESS, getutxid searches for the first entry whose ut_type field matches one of these four values and whose ut_id field matches id->ut_id, and returns a pointer to the first such entry that it finds.

getutxline
line specifies a *line*->ut_line value that must equal the ut_line field of a utmpx entry as one of two criteria that determine whether a match has occurred. See the description of getutxline above for an explanation of the other criterion.

pututxline
utmpx specifies the utmpx structure which is to be written to a utmpx file.

setutxent
None

updwtmp
utmp specifies the utmp structure from which data are to be written to *wfile*.
wfile specifies the file which is to receive data written from a utmp structure.

updwtmpx
utmpx specifies the utmpx structure from which data are to be written to *wfilex*.
wfilex specifies the file which is to receive data written from a utmpx structure.

`utmpxname`
`filename` specifies a file other than `/var/adm/utmpx` as the file which is to be examined by `getutx` routines. Often the other file will be `/var/adm/wtmpx`. The new filename must end with an "`x`" character so that the name of the corresponding `utmp` file is easily obtainable.

Normal Completion: Value Returned

If `getutxent` succeeds, it returns a pointer to a static `utmpx` structure. See the description of `getutxent` above for details.

If `getutxid` finds the matching entry for which it searches, it returns a pointer to a static `utmpx` structure. See the description of the *`id`* argument of `getutxid` for details.

If `getutxline` finds the matching entry for which it searches, it returns a pointer to a static `utmpx` structure. See the description of `getutxline` above for details.

If `pututxline` succeeds in writing a `utmpx` structure, it returns a pointer to the structure.

Error Condition: Value Returned

If `getutxent` reaches the end of the file while trying to read the next entry, it fails.

If `getutxid` reaches the end of the file without finding the entry for which it searches, it fails.

If `getutxline` reaches the end of the file without finding the entry for which it searches, it fails.

`utmpxname` returns 1 as an error code if its argument does not end with an "`x`" character.

If any of the above functions fails during a read operation (either because it has reached the end of the file or because of a lack of permission), it returns a null pointer. If it fails during a write operation, it returns a null pointer.

Files

`/var/adm/utmp`, `/var/adm/utmpx`, `/var/adm/wtmp`, `/var/adm/wtmpx`

See Also

`ttyslot` (C), `utmp` (AT&T 1990m), `utmpx` (AT&T 1990m)

getvfsent (C) GET vfstab FILE ENTRY getvfsent (C)

Name

getvfsent, getvfsfile, getvfsany, getvfsspec—get vfstab file entry

Synopsis

```
#include <stdio.h>
#include <sys/vfstab.h>

int getvfsany (FILE *, struct vfstab *vptr, vfstab
*vref);

int getvfsent (FILE *fptr, struct vfstab *vptr);

int getvfsfile (FILE *fptr, struct vfstab *vptr, char
*file);

int getvfsspec (FILE *, struct vfstab *vptr, char *
spec);
```

Description

The above functions each fill the members of a vfstab structure (defined in the sys/vfstab.h header file) with the contents of corresponding fields of a line in the /etc/vfstab file. Each line in the /etc/vfstab file consists of a vfstab structure that has the following members [see (AT&T 1990m)]:

```
char *vfs_
char *vfs_
char *vfs_
char *vfs_
char *vfs_
char *vfs_
char *vfs_
```

The members of the vfstab structure point to information contained in a static area. If this information needs to be saved, it must be copied elsewhere.

None of the routines for getting the contents of lines from the /etc/vfstab file are able to open, close, or rewind a file. Other routines must be used to do this.

`getvfsany` searches the *`vfptr`* file until it finds a match between a line in the file and the contents of the `vfstab` structure referenced by *`vref`*. If all nonnull entries in *`vref`* match corresponding fields of a line in *`vfptr`*, the match occurs.

`getvfsent` returns a pointer to the next `vfstab` structure in the file specified by *`fptr`*. Successive calls to `getvfsent` can be used to search the entire file from beginning to end.

`getvfsfile` searches the *`fptr`* file until it finds a mount point that matches *`file`*. It then fills the `vfstab` structure referenced by *`vptr`* with the fields from a line in the *`fptr`* file.

`getvfsspec` searches the *`fptr`* file until it finds a special device that matches *`spec`*. If it finds a match, it fills the `vfstab` structure specified by *`vptr`* with fields from a line in the *`fptr`* file. `getvfsspec` tries to match on device type (block device or character special device) and on major and minor device numbers. If it cannot match in this way, it tries to match by comparing strings.

Arguments

`getvfsent`

`fptr` specifies a file containing `vfstab` structures.

`vptr` points to a `vfstab` structure.

`getvfsfile`

`file` specifies a mount point which is to be matched.

`fptr` specifies a file that is to be searched for a mount point.

`vptr` specifies a `vfstab` structure whose members are to be filled by corresponding fields from a line in the specified file.

`getvfsspec`

`spec` specifies a special device.

`vptr` specifies a `vfstab` structure whose members are to be filled by corresponding fields from a line in the specified file.

`getvfsany`

`vptr` specifies a `vfstab` structure whose members are to be filled by corresponding fields from a line in the specified file.

`vref` specifies a `vfstab` structure whose members are to be compared with the contents of corresponding fields from a line in the specified file.

Normal Completion: Value Returned

If `getvfsent` reads the next entry, it returns 0.

If `getvfsany`, `getvfsfile`, or `getvfsspec`, finds a match, it returns 0.

Error Condition: Value Returned

If any of the above functions encounters an end-of-file condition, it returns −1.

If any of the above functions encounters an error, it returns a positive number equal to one of the following constants:

VFS_TOOFEW means that a line in the file has too few fields.

VFS_TOOLONG means that a line in the file was too long for the internal buffer size specified by VFS_LINE_MAX.

VFS_TOOMANY means that a line in the file has too many fields.

Files

/etc/vfstab

hsearch (C) HASH SEARCH TABLES hsearch (C)

Name

hsearch, hcreate, hdestroy—manage hash search tables

Synopsis

```
#include <search.h>

ENTRY *hsearch (ENTRY item, ACTION action);

int hcreate (size_t nel);

void hdestroy (void);
```

Description

hcreate uses malloc (C) to allocates space for a hash table which is to be searched by hsearch. hcreate must be called before hsearch is called.

hdestroy destroys the hash table, after which hcreate can be called to allocate space for another hash table. No more than one hash table can be active at one time.

hsearch is a hash-table search routine based on Knuth's Algorithm D. It uses the strcmp (C) function to make comparisons. If necessary, hsearch uses malloc (C) to allocate more hash table space.

Arguments

`hcreate`

nel estimates the maximum number of elements that the hash table will contain. The Knuth (6.4) Algorithm D may adjust this number upward.

`hdestroy`

None

`hsearch`

action is a member of the ACTION enumeration type defined in `search.h`. It indicates one of two possibilities for the disposition of an entry if `hsearch` cannot find it in the hash table:

ENTER specifies that the item should be inserted in the hash table at an appropriate point. If the item is a duplicate of an existing item, `hsearch` does not insert the new item. Instead, `hsearch` returns a pointer to the existing item.

FIND specifies that no entry should be made.

item is a structure of type ENTRY (defined in `search.h`) that contains two pointers:

item.key points to the comparison key.

item.data points to any other data which are to be associated with the comparison key. Pointers to data types other than void should be cast to pointer-to-void.

Normal Completion: Value Returned

`hsearch` returns a pointer to a location in a hash table where an entry can be found. See the ENTER value of the *action* argument of `hsearch`.

Error Condition: Value Returned

If `hcreate` cannot allocate enough space for the hash table, it returns 0.

If `hsearch` cannot find an item and the disposition of an entry is FIND, it returns a null pointer.

If the action is ENTER and the hash table is full, `hsearch` returns a null pointer.

See Also

`bsearch` (C), `lsearch` (C), `malloc` (C), `malloc` (X), `string` (C), `tsearch` (C)

Name

`initgroups`—initialize the supplementary group access list

Synopsis

```
#include <grp.h>
#include <sys/types.h>

int initgroups (const char *name, gid_t basegid);
```

Description

`initgroups` uses `getgrent` (C) to read the group file in order to get the group membership for a specified user. Next, `initgroups` uses `setgroups` (Peterson 1991b) to initialize the supplementary group access list of the calling process.

If `initgroups` encounters more than {NGROUPS_MAX} groups (including *`basegid`*) while scanning the group file, it ignores subsequent group entries.

Arguments

`basegid` causes the *`basegid`* group ID to be included in the supplementary group access list. *`basegid`* usually is the real group ID from the password file.

`name` specifies the user whose group membership is to be found by `initgroups`.

Normal Completion: Value Returned

If `initgroups` succeeds in changing the supplementary group access list, it returns 0.

Error Condition: Value Returned

If `initgroups` fails to change the supplementary group access list, it returns -1 and sets `errno` to indicate the following error:

1 EPERM
The effective user is not the superuser.

See Also

getgrent (C), setgroups (Peterson 1991b)

insque (C) MANAGE QUEUES insque (C)

Name

insque, remque—insert or remove an element from a queue

Synopsis

```
#include <search>

void insque (struct qelem *elem, struct qelem *pred);

void remque (struct qelem *elem);
```

Description

inseque inserts a specified element immediately after another specified element in a queue built from doubly linked lists.

remque removes a specified element from a queue built from doubly linked lists.

Each element in the queue must have the following form:

```
struct qelem {
        struct  qelem *q_forw;
        struct  qelem *q_back;
        char  q_data[];
};
```

Arguments

inseque
elem specifies the element to be inserted in the list.
pred specifies the element after which *elem* is to be inserted.

remseque
elem specifies the element to be removed from the list.

isnan (C) MANAGE FLOATING-POINT NUMBERS isnan (C)

Name

`isnan`, `finite`, `fpclass`, `isnand`, `isnanf`, unordered—determine the type of a floating-point number

Synopsis

```
#include <ieeefp>

int isnand (double dsrc);

int isnanf (float fsrc);

int finite (double dsrc);

fpclass_t fpclass (double dsrc);

int unordered (double dsrc1, double dsrc2);

#include <math.h>

int isnan (double dsrc);
```

Description

`isnan` returns true (1) if its type `double` argument is a NaN. Otherwise, it returns false (0). This routine has the same functionality as `isnand`.

`isnand` returns true (1) if its type `double` argument is a `NaN`. Otherwise, it returns false (0).

`isnanf` returns true (1) if its type `float` argument is a `NaN`. Otherwise, it returns false (0). `isnanf` is implemented as a macro and is included in the `ieeefp.h` header file.

`finite` returns true (1) if its type `double` argument is neither infinity nor a `NaN`. Otherwise, `finite` returns false (0).

`fpclass` returns one of 10 possible classes to which its type `double` argument belongs. These 10 classes are as follows:

`FP_NINF`	negative infinity
`FP_PINF`	positive infinity
`FP_NZERO`	negative zero

`FP_PZERO`	positive zero
`FP_QNAM`	quiet `NaN`
`FP_SNAN`	signaling `NaN`
`FP_NDENORM`	negative denormalized nonzero
`FP_PDENORM`	positive denormalized nonzero
`FP_NNORM`	negative normalized nonzero
`FP_PNORM`	positive normalized nonzero

`unordered` returns true (1) if one of its two arguments is not ordered with respect to the other, i.e., if one of its two arguments is a NaN. If neither of the two arguments is a NaN, `unordered` returns false (0).

Arguments

`isnan`
`dsrc` is a type `double` argument whose NaN status is to be determined.

`isnand`
`dsrc` is a type `double` argument which is to be compared with NaN.

`isnanf`
`fsrc` is a type `float` argument which is to be compared with NaN.

`finite`
`dsrc` is a type `double` argument which is to be compared with NaN or infinity.

`fpclass`
`dsrc` is a type `double` argument whose class membership is to be determined.

`unordered`
`dsrc1` is a type `double` argument which is to be compared with the *`dsrc2`* argument.
`dsrc2` is a type `double` argument which is to be compared with the *`dsrc1`* argument.

Normal Completion: Value Returned

See the descriptions above.

Error Condition: Value Returned

These routines generate no exceptions, even for signaling NaNs.

See Also

fpgetround (C), intro (M)

l3tol (C) INTEGER/LONG INTEGER CONVERSION l3tol (C)

Name

l3tol, ltol3—convert between three-byte integers and long integers

Synopsis

```
#include <stdlib.h>

void l3tol (long *lptr, const char *cptr, int n);

void ltol3 (char *cptr, const long *lptr, int n);
```

Description

l3tol and ltol3 are useful for maintaining file systems in which block numbers are three bytes long.

l3tol converts a list of three-byte integers in a character string to a list of long integers.

ltol3 converts a list of long integers to a list of three-byte integers in a character string (the reverse of the l3tol conversion).

The numerical values of the long integers are machine dependent because byte ordering may vary from machine to machine.

Arguments

cptr points to a list of three-byte characters.

lptr points to a list of long integers.

n specifies how many three-byte integers are packed into the character string at which *cptr* points.

See Also

fs (AT&T 1990o)

Name

`localeconv`—get numeric formatting information

Synopsis

```
#include <locale.h>

struct lconv *localeconv (void);
```

Description

`localeconv` fills the members of an `lconv` structure (defined in the `locale.h` header file) with values needed to format numeric quantities according to the rules of the current locale [see `setlocale` (C)].

Members of the `lconv` structure have type `char *` or type `char`. Members with type `char *` are strings, any of which can (except for `char * decimal_point`) point to `""` to indicate that the value either is not available in the current locale or has zero length. `lconv` members that have type `char` are nonnegative. Any of these nonnegative members can be equal to CHAR_MAX (defined in `limits.h`) to indicate that the value corrsponding to that member is not available in the current locale.

The definition of the `lconv` structure is as follows, with values for fields in the C locale given in comments:

`char *decimalpoint;` /* `"."` formats nonmonetary quantities. */

`char *thousands_sep;` /* `""` (zero-length string) separates groups of digits to the left of the decimal point character in formatted nonmonetary quantities. */

`char *grouping;` /* `""` encloses a string in which each element is an integer that tells how many digits comprise the current group in the formatted nonmonetary quantity. The grouping elements are interpreted as follows:

CHAR_MAX means that no further grouping is to be performed.

0 means that the previous element is to be used repeatedly for the remainder of the digits.

`other` specifies the number of digits that comprise the current group. The next element determines the size of the next group of digits to the left of the current group. */

`char *int_curr_symbol;` /* `""` encloses the international currency symbol that is applicable to the current locale (left-justified within a four-character, space-padded field). The permissible character sequences are specified in *ISO 427 Codes for the Representation of Currency and Funds*. */

`char *currency_symbol;` /* "" encloses the local currency symbol that is applicable to the current locale. */

`char *mon_decimal_point;` /* "" encloses the decimal point that is used to format monetary quantities. */

`char *mon_thousands_sep;` /* "" encloses the separator for groups of digits that are to the left of the decimal point in formatted monetary quantities. */

`char *mon_grouping;` /* "" encloses a string in which each element is an integer that tells how many digits comprise the current group in a formatted monetary quantity. */

`char *positive_sign;` /* "" encloses a string that is used to indicate a nonnegative monetary quantity. */

`char *negative_sign;` /* "" encloses a string that is used to indicate a negative-valued monetary quantity. */

`char int_frac_digits;` /* Indicates the number of fractional digits (digits to the right of the decimal point) to be displayed in an internationally formatted monetary quantity. Otherwise, it is CHAR_MAX. */

`char frac_digits;` /* indicates the number of fractional digits (digits to the right of the decimal point) to be displayed in a formatted monetary quantity. Otherwise, it is CHAR_MAX. */

`char p_cs_precedes;` /* is set to 1 or 0 if the `currency_symbol` respectively precedes or follows the value for a nonnegative monetary quantity. Otherwise, it is CHAR_MAX. */

`char p_sep_by_space;` /* is set to 1 if the `currency_symbol` is separated by a space from the value of a nonnegative formatted monetary quantity or to 0 if `currency_symbol` is not separated from the value. Otherwise, it is CHAR_MAX. */

`char n_cs_precedes;` /* is set to 1 if the `currency_symbol` respectively precedes or follows the value for a negative formatted monetary value. Otherwise, it is CHAR_MAX. */

`char n_sep_by_space;` /* is set to 1 if the `currency_symbol` is separated by a space from the value of a negative formatted monetary quantity or to 0 if the symbol is not separated from the value. Otherwise, it is CHAR_MAX. */

`char p_sign_posn;` /* is set to CHAR_MAX if this field is not used. Otherwise, it is set to one of the following four values that indicate the position of the `positive_sign` string for a nonnegative formatted monetary quantity, where

0 means that parentheses enclose the quantity and `currency_symbol` string.
1 means that the sign string precedes the quantity and `currency_symbol` string.
2 means that the sign string follows the quantity and `currency_symbol` string.
3 means that the sign string immediately precedes the quantity and `currency_symbol` string.
4 means that the sign string immediately follows the quantity and `currency_symbol` string. */

`char n_sign_posn;` /* is set to CHAR_MAX if this field is not used. Otherwise, it is set to one of four values that indicate the position of the `negative_sign` for a negative formatted monetary quantity. These four values are described under `char_p_sign_posn` above.

Arguments

None

Normal Completion: Value Returned

`localeconv` returns a pointer to the filled-in `lconv` structure. A subsequent call to `localeconv` may overwrite the `lconv` structure.

Files

/usr/lib/locale/*locale*/LC_MONETARY contains the LC_MONETARY database for the *locale*.

/usr/lib/locale/*locale*/LC_NUMERIC contains the LC_NUMERIC database for the *locale*.

See Also

`setlocale` (C), `chrtbl` (AT&T 1990o), `montbl` (AT&T 1990o)

lockf (C) RECORD LOCKING ON FILES lockf (C)

Name

`lockf`—lock sections of a file

Synopsis

```
#include <unistd.h>

int lockf (int fildscr, int function, long size);
```

Description

`lockf` enables a process to put advisory or mandatory write locks on sections of a file, depending on the mode bits of the file [see `chmod` (Peterson 1991b)].

If another process tries to lock the locked file sections, that process will return an error code or be put to sleep until the file sections are unlocked. If a process that controls a locked resource such as a locked file section requests a resource that has been locked by another process, a potential for deadlock exists. Therefore, calls to `lockf` [or `fnctl` (Peterson 1991b)] search for a deadlock before sleeping on a locked resource (see `EDEADLCK` error below).

Any signal interrupts a process sleeping on a resource. The `alarm` (Peterson 1991b) can provide a timeout capability for any application that needs it.

The standard I/O package can be a source of unexpected buffering operations when processes do buffering in the user address space and portions of the user address space are locked. The process may later read or write data that are or were locked. For example, when a process terminates, all of its locks are removed and data are output.

Arguments

`fildscr` is an open file descriptor. It must have `O_WRONLY` or `O_RDWR` permission in order for `lockf` to establish locks.

`function` may have one of the four values defined in the `unistd.h` header as follows:

```
#define F_ULOCK  0
#define F_LOCK   1
#define F_TLOCK  2
#define F_TEST   3
```

Other values of *`function`* are reserved for future extensions to `lockf`. Until then, any other value will cause `lockf` to return an error code.

The action specified by each value of *`function`* is as follows:

`F_LOCK` locks a specified section of a file if the section is not already locked by another process. `F_LOCK` and `F_TLOCK` differ only in the action they take if a resource is not available: `F_LOCK` puts the calling process to sleep until the resource is available. F_TLOCK causes `lockf` to return −1 and set `errno` to EACCES if another process has already locked the resource (see the EAGAIN error below). File sections locked by F_LOCK (or F_TLOCK) can contain (either in whole or in part) a section previously locked by the same process. F_LOCK (or F_TLOCK) will unlock sections beginning at the point of the offset and extending through *size* bytes or (if *size* equals `(off_t)` 0) to the end of the file. If a previous lock has occurred in this section or in an adjacent section, the sections are combined into one section. If such a F_LOCK (or F_TLOCK) request requires a new element to be added to the table of active locks and the table is full, `lockf` returns an error and does not lock the new section (see the ENOLCK error below).

F_TEST tests whether another process has locked the file section specified by *fildscr* and *size*.

F_TLOCK has the same effect as F_LOCK, except as noted in the description of F_LOCK above.

F_ULOCK removes locks from a section of the file specified by *fildscr* and *size*. F_ULOCK may cause `lockf` to release (in whole or in part) locks on one or more locked sections controlled by the process. If some parts of a section are not released, the remaining parts remain locked by the process. If the center part of a locked section is released, the table of active locks must have an additional element (see the ENOLCK error below).

size specifies the number of contiguous bytes to be locked or unlocked. The bytes to be locked or unlocked start at the current offset in the file and extend forward in the file if *size* is positive and backward if *size* is negative. If *size* is negative, the bytes can extend backward to, but not including, the current offset. If *size* is 0, `lockf` locks the section from the current offset to the largest possible future end of file. Because locks can extend beyond the end of a file, an area need not not be allocated to the file in order to be locked.

Normal Completion: Value Returned

If `lockf` succeeds, it returns 0.

Error Condition: Value Returned

If `lockf` fails, it returns −1 and sets `errno` to indicate one of the following error conditions:

9 EBADF

fildscr is an invalid file descriptor.

11 EAGAIN

`lockf` failed because *cmd* is F_TLOCK or F_TEST and the section is already locked by another process. Early releases of System V set `errno` to

EACCES when this error occurs. In this release and in future releases, `errno` will be set to EAGAIN instead of to EACCES when a section of a file is already locked by another process; applications should expect (and test for) either value of `errno`.

45 EDEADLK
cmd is F_LOCK, and a deadlock is possible.

46 ENOLCK
cmd is F_LOCK, T_LOCK, or F_ULOCK, and the number of lock table entries would exceed the number allocated on the system if the command is executed.

70 ECOMM
fildscr is on a remote machine, and the link to that machine is inactive. This error is specific to Remote File Sharing (RFS).

See Also

`alarm` (Peterson 1991b), `chmod` (Peterson 1991b), `close` (Peterson 1991b), `creat` (Peterson 1991b), `fcntl` (Peterson 1991b), `intro` (Peterson 1991b), `open` (Peterson 1991b), `read` (Peterson 1991b), `write` (Peterson 1991b)

lsearch (C) SEARCH A TABLE lsearch (C)

Name

`lsearch`, `lfind`—do a linear search of a table and update the pointer

Synopsis

```
#include <search.h>

void *lfind (const void *key, void *base, size_t
*nelp, size_t width, int (*compar) (const void *, const
void *));

void *lsearch (const void *key, void *base, size_t
*nelp, size_t width, int (*compar) (const void *, const
void *));
```

Description

`lfind` has the same effect as `lsearch` except that if `lfind` does not find its datum, it does not add it to the table but returns a null pointer instead.

`lsearch` uses a linear search procedure based on Knuth (6.1) Algorithm S to search a table for a specified datum. The pointer that `lsearch` returns tells where a sought-for datum may be found. If the datum is not found, `lsearch` adds it to the table.

Arguments

`base` points to the first element of the table which is to be searched by `lsearch` or `lfind`. This pointer may be of any type.

`compar` points to a comparison function to be supplied by the user, for example, `strcmp` (C). *`compar`* has two arguments that point to the elements that are to be compared. If the elements are equal, *`compar`* must return 0. Otherwise, it must return a nonzero value. Because *`compar`* does not compare every byte, arbitrary data can be contained in the data elements in addition to the values that are compared.

`key` points to the datum for which `lsearch` or `lfind` is to search. This pointer may be of any type.

`nelp` points to an integer that specifies the current number of elements in the table. If `lsearch` adds an element to the table, the integer is incremented.

`width` specifies the number of bytes in an element of the table.

Normal Completion: Value Returned

If `lfind` finds the datum for which it searches, it returns a pointer to the datum. The pointer should be cast to type pointer-to-element. If `lfind` does not find its datum, it returns a null pointer.

If `lsearch` finds the datum for which it searches, it returns a pointer to the datum. Otherwise, `lsearch` returns a pointer to the newly added element of the table. The pointer should be cast to type pointer-to-element.

Error Condition: Value Returned

If there is insufficient room for `lsearch` to add a new element to the table, undefined results can occur.

See Also

`bsearch` (C), `hsearch` (C), `string` (C), `tsearch` (C)

makecontext (C) **SWITCH BETWEEN CONTROL THREADS** **makecontext (C)**

Name

makecontext, swapcontext—manipulate user contexts

Synopsis

```
#include <ucontext.h>

void makecontext (ucontext_t *ucp, (void (*)
())func, int argc, ...);

int swapcontext (ucontext_t *oucp, ucontext_t
*ucp);
```

Description

makecontext and swapcontext can be used in implementing user-level context switching between multiple threads of control within a process.

makecontext modifies the specified context after the context has first been initialized by getcontext (Peterson 1991b). When the newly modified context is resumed by using swapcontext or setcontext (see getcontext), program execution continues by calling the function *func* and passing *func* the arguments that follow *argc* in the makecontext call.

swapcontext stores the current context in the ucontext_t context structure at which *oucp* points and gets a new context from the ucintext_t structure at which *ucp* points.

Always use makecontext or getcontext to create new instances of the ucontext_t structure because future releases of System V may change the size of the ucontext_t.

Arguments

makecontext

argc is an integer that specifies the number of arguments that follow *argc* in the makecontext call. If the number of arguments does not agree with *argc*, makecontext behavior is undefined.

func is the function that will be executed when the context is resumed.

ucp specifies the context which makecontext is to modify.

`swapcontext`

oucp points at the `ucontext_t` structure where the current context is to be saved.

ucp points at the structure from which the new context is to be gotten.

Normal Completion: Value Returned

If `swapcontext` succeeds, it returns 0.

Error Condition: Value Returned

If `makecontext` or `swapcontext` fails, it returns −1 and sets `errno` to indicate one of the following errors:

12 ENOMEM
ucp has insufficient stack space to complete the operation.

14 EFAULT
ucp or *oucp* points to an invalid address.

See Also

`exit` (Peterson 1991b), `getcontext` (Peterson 1991b), `sigaction` (Peterson 1991b), `sigprocmask` (Peterson 1991b), `ucontext` (AT&T 1990m)

makedev (C) DEVICE NUMBERS makedev (C)

Name

`makedev`, `major`, `minor`—manage a device number

Synopsis

```
#include <sys/mkdev.h>
#include <sys/types.h>

major_t major (dev_t device);

dev_t makedev (major_t maj, minor_t min);

minor_t minor (dev_t device);
```

Description

`major` gets the major number component of a device number.

`makedev` gets a formatted device number and can be used to create a device number for input to `mknod` (Peterson 1991b).

`minor` gets the minor number component of a device number.

Arguments

`device` is a device number.

`maj` is the major number of a device number.

`min` is the minor number of a device number.

Normal Completion: Value Returned

If `major` succeeds, it returns the major number component from *`device`*.

If `makedev` succeeds, it returns a formatted device number.

If `minor` suceeds, it returns the minor number component from *`device`*.

Error Condition: Value Returned

On failure, NODEV is returned.

If `major` fails, it sets `errno` to indicate one of the following two errors:

22 EINVAL

- *`device`* equals NODEV.
- The major number component of the *`device`* argument is too big.

If `makedev` fails, it sets `errno` to indicate one of the following two errors:

22 EINVAL

- *`maj`* or *`min`* or both are too large.
- NODEV is the device number created from *`maj`* and *`min`*.

If `minor` fails, it sets `errno` to indicate the following error:

22 EINVAL

`device` equals NODEV.

See Also

`mknod` (Peterson 1991b), `stat` (Peterson 1991b)

malloc (C) MEMORY ALLOCATION malloc (C)

Name

`malloc`, `calloc`, `free`, `memalign`, `realloc`, `valloc`—memory allocator

Synopsis

```
#include <stdlib.h>

void *calloc (size_t nelem, size_t elsize);

void free (void *ptr);

void *malloc (size_t size);

void *memalign (size_t alignment, size_t size);

void *realloc (void *ptr, size_t size);

void *valloc (size_t size);
```

Description

`calloc` allocates space for the elements of an array and initializes the elements to 0.

`free` frees a specified block of memory.

`malloc`, together with `free`, is part of a general-purpose memory allocation package. It allocates a block of memory of the specified size or more.

`memalign` allocates a specified number of bytes on a specified alignment boundary.

`realloc` changes the size of a specified block to a specified size. The contents of the block will remain unchanged up to the lesser of the new and old sizes.

`valloc(`*`size`*`)` has the same effect as `memalign(sysconf (_SC_PAGESIZE),` *`size`*`)`. See `sysconf` (C).

Arguments

`calloc`

`elsize` specifies the size of the elements of an array.

`nelem` specifies the number of elements in an array.

free

ptr points to a block of memory previously allocated by `malloc`, `calloc`, or `realloc`. `free` performs no action if *ptr* is NULL. Otherwise, `free` makes the specified block of memory available for further allocation.

malloc

size specifies the size, in bytes, of a block of memory to be allocated by `malloc`.

memalign

alignment specifies the alignment boundary for a block. It has a value equal to a power of 2 and greater than or equal to the size of a word.

size specifies the number of bytes of memory which `memalign` is to allocate.

realloc

ptr specifies the block of memory whose size is to be changed by `realloc`. If `pter` is NULL, `realloc` has the same effect as `malloc` for the specified size.

size specifies the size to which `realloc` is to change the specified block of memory. If *size* is 0 and *ptr* is not NULL, `realloc` frees the object to which *ptr* points.

valloc

size specifies the size, in bytes, of the block to be allocated on a page size alignment boundary.

Normal Completion: Value Returned

Each of the allocation routines returns a pointer to space that is suitably aligned for storage of any type of object. If necessary, the pointer will be coerced.

If *size*, *nelem*, or *elsize* is 0, a unique pointer to the memory area is returned.

If `malloc` succeeds, it returns a pointer to a block of memory suitably aligned for any use.

If `memalign` succeeds, it returns an address that is guaranteed to be an even multiple of *alignment*.

If `realloc` succeeds, it returns a pointer to the block whose size it has changed. The block may have been moved. If `realloc` returns a null pointer, the block to which *ptr* points remains intact.

Error Condition: Value Returned

If `free` is given some random number as an argument, undefined results will occur.

If the space assigned by `malloc` is overrun, undefined results will occur.

If `calloc`, `malloc`, `memalign`, `realloc`, or `valloc` is called and insufficient memory is available, the function will fail and return a null pointer.

See Also

`malloc` (X)

mbchar (C) HANDLE MULTIBYTE CHARACTERS mbchar (C)

Name

`mbchar`: `mblen`, `mbtowc`, `wctomb`—handle multibyte characters

Synopsis

```
include <stdlib.h>

int mblen (const char *s, size_t n);

int mbtowc (wchar_t *pwc, const char *s, size_t n);

int wctomb (char *s, wchar_t *wchar);
```

Description

The character sets of some locales are too large to be represented by using eight bits per character. Characters in these extended character sets must be represented by multibyte characters.

The `mblen`, `mbtowc`, and `wctomb` multibyte character-handling functions can translate multibyte characters into wide characters and back again.

Wide characters have type `wchar_t` (defined in `stdlib.h`). Type `wchar_t` is an integer type that has a large enough range of values that a unique code can be assigned to each character in the largest character set specified among any of the locales that System V supports.

Each locale supports a maximum of three extended character sets. The `LC_TYPE` [see `setlocale` (C)] category of each locale specifies the number of bytes in an extended character set. MB_LEN_MAX (defined in `stdlib.h`) specifies the maximum number of bytes that any multibyte character can have. The macro MB_CUR_MAX, also defined in `stdlib.h`, specifies the maximum number of bytes that any character in an extended character set in the current locale can have.

The value of a wide character that corresponds to a null character is 0.

`mblen` determines how many bytes comprise the multibyte character at which *s* points. `mblen (`*s*`,` *n*`)` has the same effect as

```
mbtowc ((wchar_t *)0, s, n);
```

`mbtowc` determines how many bytes comprise a multibyte character to which *s* points. Unless *pwc* is a null pointer, `mbtowc` converts the multibyte character into a wide character and stores it in the location to which *pwc* points.

`wctomb` determines how many bytes are needed to represent the multibyte character corresponding to the wide character whose value is *wchar*. Unless *s* is a null pointer, `wctomb` converts *wchar* to a multibyte character and stores it in the location to which *s* points. `wctomb` stores at most MB_CUR_MAX characters.

Arguments

`mblen`

n specifies the number of characters which `mblen` is to examine.

s points to a multibyte character that `mblen` is to examine.

`mbtowc`

n specifies the number of characters that `mbtowc` will examine, starting at the character to which *s* points.

pwc points to the object that receives the wide character that results from `mbtowc`'s conversion.

s points to the multibyte character that `mbtowc` is to convert to a wide character.

`mctomb`

s points to the array that receives the result of the conversion from *wchar* to a multibyte character if *s* is not a null pointer.

wchar specifies the character code which is to be converted to a multibyte character.

Normal Completion: Value Returned

`mblen`

`mblen` returns the same values as `mbtowc` below.

`mbtowc`

`mbtowc` returns 0 if *s* is a null pointer. `mbtowc` returns 0 if *s* is not a null pointer but points to the null character. If the next *n* bytes (or fewer) comprise a valid multibyte character, `mbtowc` returns the number of bytes that comprise the converted multibyte character. If none of the above conditions are true, *s* does not point to a valid multibyte character (see the error conditions below).

`wctomb`

`wctomb` returns 0 if *s* is a null pointer. If *s* is not a null pointer and *wchar* corresponds to a valid multibyte character, `wctomb` returns the number of bytes in the multibyte character that correspond to *wchar*.

Error Condition: Value Returned

`mblen`

`mblen` returns −1 if *s* does not point to a valid multibyte character.

`mbtowc`

`mbtowc` returns −1 if *s* does not point to a valid multibyte character.

`wctomb`

`wctomb` returns −1 if *s* is not a null pointer and *wchar* is does not correspond to a valid multibyte character.

See Also

`mbstring` (C), `setlocale` (C), `chrtbl` (AT&T 1990o), `environ` (AT&T 1990m)

mbstring (C) HANDLE MULTIBYTE STRINGS mbstring (C)

Name

`mbstring`: `mbstowcs`, `wcstombs`—handle multibyte strings

Synopsis

```
#include <stdlib.h>

size_t mbstowcs (wchart *pwcs, const char *s,
size_t n);
```

```
size_t wcstombs (wchar_t *pwcs, const wchar_t
*pwcs, size_t n);
```

Description

`mbstowcs` converts a sequence of multibyte characters from the array specified by *s* into a sequence of corresponding wide character codes, stores these codes in an array specified by *pwcs*, and stops after it stores *n* codes or after it stores a code whose value is 0 (a converted null character).

`wcstombs` converts a sequence of wide character codes from the array specified by *pwcs* into a sequence of corresponding multibyte characters, stores these multibyte characters in an array specified by *s*, and stops if a multibyte character would exceed the limit of *n* total bytes or if it stores a null character.

Arguments

n specifies the number of wide character codes which `mbstowcs` stores or the total number of bytes that `wcstombs` stores.

pwcs points to the array where `mbstowcs` stores wide character codes or from which `wcstombs` gets the wide character codes that it converts.

s points to the array from which `mbstowcs` gets the multibyte characters that it converts to wide character codes, or in which `wcstombs` stores the multibyte characters that result from its conversion of wide character codes.

Normal Completion: Value Returned

`mbstowcs` returns the number of array elements modified, not including any terminating 0 code.

`wcstombs` returns the number of bytes modified, not including any terminating null character.

Error Condition: Value Returned

`mbstowcs` returns `(size_t) - 1` if it encounters an invalid multibyte character.

`wcstombs` returns `(size_t) - 1` if it encounters a wide character code that does not correspond to a valid multibyte character.

See Also

`mbchar` (C), `setlocale` (C), `chrtbl` (AT&T 1990o), `environ` (AT&T 1990m)

memory (C) STRINGS memory (C)

Name

memory: memccpy, memchr, memcmp, memcpy, memmove, memset—memory operations

Synopsis

```
#include <string.h>

void *memccpy (void *s1, const void *s2, int c, size_t n);

void *memchr (const void *s1, int c, size_t n);

int *memcmp (const void *s1, const void *s2, size_t n);

void *memcpy (void *s1, const void *s2, size_t n);

void *memmove (void *s1, const void *s2, size_t n);

void *memset (void *s, int c, size_t n);
```

Description

These functions manipulate memory areas that consist of arrays of bytes that are bounded by a count, not terminated by a null character. None of these functions tests for overflow in any receiving memory area.

`memccpy` copies bytes from memory area *s2* to memory area *s1* and stops after it has copied *n* bytes or after the first occurrence of *c* (converted to an `unsigned char`), whichever occurs first.

`memchr` searches for the first occurrence of *c* (converted to an `unsigned char`) in the first *n* bytes (each is interpreted as an `unsigned char`).

`memcmp` makes a lexicographical comparison of the first *n* bytes (converted to `unsigned char`) of *s1* with *s2*.

`memcpy` copies *n* bytes from *s2* to *s1*.

`memmove` copies *n* bytes from *s2* to *s1*. `memmove` can copy correctly when *s1* overlaps *s2*.

`memset` puts *c* (converted to an `unsigned char`) in the first *n* bytes of the memory area at which *s* points.

Arguments

`memccpy`

c specifies an `unsigned char` for which `memccpy` is to search.

n specifies the maximum number of bytes which `memccpy` is to copy if it does not find *c* in the first *n* bytes.

s1 specifies the destination of bytes copied from *s2*.

s2 specifies the source of bytes copied to *s1*.

`memchr`

c specifies an `unsigned char` for which `memchr` is to search.

n specifies the maximum number of bytes which `memccpy` searches while it is looking for the first occurrence of *c*.

s specifies the string which `memchr` examines while it searches for the first occurrence of *c*.

`memcmp`

n specifies how many bytes of *s1* will be lexicographically compared with *s2*.

s1 points to the memory area whose contents are to be lexicographically compared with *s2*.

s2 points to the memory area to which the contents of *s1* are to be compared.

`memcpy`

n specifies the number of bytes to be copied from *s2* to *s1*.

s1 points to the memory area which is the destination of bytes copied from *s2*.

s2 points to the memory area which is the source of bytes copied to *s1*.

`memmove`

n specifies the number of bytes to be copies from *s2* to *s1*.

s1 points to the memory area which is the destination of bytes copied from *s2*.

s2 points to the memory area which is the source of bytes copied to *s1*.

`memset`

c specifies the `unsigned char` that is to be put in the first *n* bytes of the memory area to which *s* points.

n specifies how many bytes of *s* are to be set to the value of *c*.

s points to the memory area whose first *n* bytes are set to *c*.

Normal Completion: Value Returned

If `memccpy` finds *c* in the first *n* bytes of *s2*, it returns a pointer to the first byte after *c* in *s1*.

If `memchr` finds *c* in the first *n* bytes of *s*, it returns a pointer to the first occurrence of *c*.

`memcmp` returns an integer that is less than, equal to, or greater than 0 if *s1* is respectively less than, equal to, or greater than *s2*.

`memcpy` returns *s1*.

`memmove` returns *s1*.

`memset` returns *s*.

Error Condition: Value Returned

If `memccpy` fails to find *c* in the first *n* bytes of *s2*, it returns a NULL pointer.

If `memchr` fails to find *c* in the first *n* bytes of *s*, it returns a NULL pointer.

See Also

`string` (C)

mkfifo (C) MAKE A FIFO FILE mkfifo (C)

Name

`mkfifo`—make a new FIFO

Synopsis

```
#include <sys/stat.h>
#include <sys/types.h>

int mkfifo (const char *pathname, mode_t mode);
```

Description

`mkfifo` uses the `mknod` (Peterson 1991b) system call to create a new FIFO special file that is named by the pathname at which *pathname* points.

`mkfifo` sets the owner ID of the FIFO to the effective user ID of the process. It sets the group ID of the FIFO to the effective group ID of the process, or the FIFO inherits its group ID from the parent if the S_ISGID bit is set in the parent directory.

Arguments

mode initializes the mode of the new FIFO file. The file creation mask [see umask (Peterson 1991b)] of the process modifies the file permission bits of *mode*. Bits of *mode* other than the file permission bits are ignored.

pathname points to the name of the new FIFO file.

Normal Completion: Value Returned

If mkfifo succeeds, it returns 0.

Error Condition: Value Returned

If mkfifo fails, it returns −1 and sets errno to indicate the error.

See Also

chmod (Peterson 1991b), exec (Peterson 1991b), fs (AT&T 1990m), mkdir (AT&T 1990q), mknod (Peterson 1991b), stat (AT&T 1990m), umask (Peterson 1991b)

mktemp (C) CREATE A UNIQUE FILENAME mktemp (C)

Name

mktemp—create a unique filename

Synopsis

```
#include <stdlib.h>

char *mktemp(char *template);
```

Description

mktemp converts the string to which *template* points into a character string that can be used to make a unique filename and returns *template*.

Arguments

`template` points to a string which `mktemp` is to convert into a unique filename. The contents of the string should look like a filename with six trailing Xs. `mktemp` replaces the Xs with a character string that can be used in forming a unique filename. Each unique value of the string to which `template` points permits `mktemp` to create 26 unique filenames per process.

Normal Completion: Value Returned

If `mktemp` succeeds, it returns `template`, which points to a unique filename.

Error Condition: Value Returned

If `mktemp` cannot create a unique filename, it assigns the empty string "" to `template`.

See Also

`tmpfile` (S), `tmpnam` (S)

mktime (C) TIME AND DATE mktime (C)

Name

`mktime`—converts a `tm` structure to a calendar time

Synopsis

```
#include <time.h>

time_t mktime (struct tm *timeptr);
```

Description

`mktime` converts the time in the `tm` structure to which `timeptr` points to a calendar time that is expressed as the number of seconds since 00:00:00 UTC, January 1, 1970.

`mktime` also normalizes the `tm` structure as described below. It uses local time zone information as if it had called `tzset` [see `ctime` (C)].

Arguments

timeptr points to a tm structure that has the following format:

struct tm{

int tm_sec; /* Seconds after the minute [0, 61]. */

int tm_min; /* Minutes after the hour [0, 59]. */

int tm_hour; /* Hours since midnight [0, 23]. The original value of tm_hour (and other components) may be greater or less than the specified range. For example, if tm_hour is −2, it means 2 hours before midnight. If mktime succeeds, it forces the value of tm_hour to be within the specified range and to represent the specified calendar time. */

int tm_mday; /* Day of the month [1, 31]. The original value of tm_day may be greater or less than the specified range. For example, if tm_day is 0, it means the day before the current month. The final value of tm_mday is not determined until the values of tm_mon and tm_year are determined. If mktime succeeds, it forces the value of tm_mday to be within the specified range and to represent the specified calendar time. */

int tm_mon; /* Months since January. The original value of tm_mon may be greater or less than the specified range. For example, if tm_mon is −3, it means 3 months before January of tmyear. If mktime succeeds, it forces the value of tm_mday to be within the specified range and to represent the specified calendar time. See tm_mday above. */

int tm_year; /* Must be the year 1970 or later. See tmmday above. */

int tm_wday; /* Days since Sunday [0, 6]. mktime ignores the original value of tm_wday. If mktime succeeds, it sets the value of tm_wday appropriately. See tm_mday above. */

int tm_yday; /* Days since January 1 [0, 365]. mktime ignores the original value of tmyday. If mktime succeeds, it sets the value of tm_yday appropriately. */

int tm_isdst; /* tm_isdst is a daylight savings time flag that can be negative, 0, or positive. If it is positive, original time values are assumed to be in the alternate time zone. The tm components are adjusted to be in the main time zone if the alternate time zone is not valid for the computed calendar time. If tm_isdst equals 0, the original tm values are assumed to be in the main time zone; they are converted to the alternate time zone if the main time one is invalid. If tm_isdst is negative, the correct time zone is determined; the tm components are not adjusted.

};

Normal Completion: Value Returned

If mktime succeeds, it returns the specified calendar time.

Error Condition: Value Returned

If `mktime` fails because the calendar time cannot be represented, it returns `(time_t) - 1`. No calendar times before 00:00:00 UTC, January 1, 1970, or after 03:14:07, January 19, 2038, can be represented. See the `tm_year` member of the `tm` structure above.

See Also

`ctime` (C), `getenv` (C), `timezone` (AT&T 1990m)

mlock (C) LOCK/UNLOCK MEMORY PAGES mlock (C)

Name

`mlock`, `munlock`—lock or unlock memory pages

Synopsis

```
#include <sys/types.h>

int mlock (caddr_t addr, size_t len);

int munlock (caddr_t addr, size_t len);
```

Description

`mlock` locks pages into memory. It uses memory mappings established for the address range from *addr* to *addr* + *len* inclusive to identify the pages to be locked. The effect of `mlock(`*addr*`, `*len*`)` is the same as the effect of `memcntl(`*addr*`, `*len*`, MC_LOCK, 0, 0, 0)`.

Locks that `mlock` establishes are not inherited by a child process, nor are they nested.

`munlock` can remove locks that are established by `mlock`.

Arguments

addr specifies the beginning of an address space.
len specifies the length of an address space.

Normal Completion: Value Returned

If `mlock` or `munlock` succeeds, it returns 0.

Error Condition: Value Returned

If `mlock` or `munlock` fails, it returns −1 and sets `errno` to indicate the error. See `memcntl` (Peterson 1991b).

See Also

`mlockall` (C), `sysconf` (C), `fork` (Peterson 1991b), `memcntl` (Peterson 1991b), `mmap` (Peterson 1991b), `plock` (Peterson 1991b)

mlockall (C) LOCK/UNLOCK ADDRESS SPACE mlockall (C)

Name

`mlockall`, `munlockall`—lock or unlock an address space

Synopsis

```
#include <sys/man>

int mlockall (int flags);

int munlockall (void);
```

Description

`mlockall` locks into memory all pages mapped by an address space. `mlockall(`*`flags`*`)` has the same effect as

```
memcntl(0, 0, MC_LOCKAS, flags, 0, 0)
```

See `memcntl` (Peterson 1991b).

The locks that `mlockall` establishes are not inherited by a child process after a `fork`, nor are the locks nested.

`munlockall` removes address space locks. It also removes locks on mappings in address space. `munlockall` has the same effect as

```
memcntl(0, 0, MC_UNLOCKAS, 0, 0, 0)
```

Arguments

`flags` specifies whether the pages to be locked are those currently mapped by the address space, those that will be mapped in the future, or both kinds of pages:

MCL_CURRENT locks pages that are currently mapped.
MCL_FUTURE locks pages that will be mapped in the future.

Normal Completion: Value Returned

If `mlockall` or `munlockall` succeeds, it returns 0.

Error Condition: Value Returned

If `mlockall` or `munlockall` fails, it returns −1 and sets `errno` to indicate the error [see `memcntl` (Peterson 1991b)].

See Also

`sysconf` (C), `fork` (Peterson 1991b), `memcntl` (Peterson 1991b), `mlock` (C), `mmap` (Peterson 1991b), `plock` (Peterson 1991b)

monitor (C) EXECUTION PROFILE monitor (C)

Name

`monitor`—prepare an execution profile

Synopsis

```
#include <mon.h>

void monitor(int (*lowpc)(), int (*highpc)(), WORD *buffer, size_t bufsize, size_t nfunc);
```

Description

`monitor` is an interface to `profil` (Peterson 1991b), the execution-time profiler. `cc -p` inserts two calls to `monitor` in each program that it compiles, so it is not necessary to call `monitor` explicitly, except to establish more control over profiling.

The first call to `monitor` starts the recording of two kinds of information about the execution profile: a function call count and execution distribution data. `profil` generates the execution distribution data, and `cc -p` supplies code to object file(s) that generates the function call counts. The last call to `monitor` writes the function call counts and execution distribution data to the output file `mon.out` (see "Files" below).

The default call to `monitor` is

```
monitor (&eprol, &etext, wbuf, wbufsize, 600);
```

It establishes the computation of an execution-time distribution histogram that uses `profil` for the entire program. It provides enough histogram cells to generate usable results of distribution measurements. The parameters of the default call to `monitor` have the following meanings:

`eprol` is the beginning of the user program when it is linked using `cc -p` [see `end` (C)].

`etext` is the beginning of the user program.

`wbuf` is a type WORD array that contains *`wbufsize`* elements.

`wbufsize` is computed as shown in the description of the *`bufsize`* argument below, with BARSIZE equal to 8.

600 is the number of call count cells initially reserved in *`buffer`*.

If additional calls to `monitor` are inserted after the call to `main` but before the call to `exit`, they will add to the capacity to count function calls, but such calls will restart the `profil` histogram computation.

The following call stops execution and writes the results to a file:

```
monitor ((int (*) () )0, (int (*) () )0, (WORD *)0, 0,
0);
```

Use `prof` (Peterson 1991a) to examine `monitor` results.

Arguments

`buffer` specifies the address of a user-supplied array where `monitor` stores call counts and the histogram that `profil` generates. The data type of the array is WORD (defined in the `mon.h` header file).

`bufsize` specifies the number of array elements in *`buffer`*. See `profil` (Peterson 1991b) for information about the effects of *`bufsize`* on execution-distribution measurements. *`bufsize`* should be computed as follows:

```
buffer_size =
         sizeof(struct hdr) +
         nfunc * sizeof(struct cnt) +
         ((highpc - lowpc)/BARSIZE) * sizeof(WORD) +
          sizeof(WORD) - 1 ;
bufsize = buffer_size / sizeof(WORD);
```

where

- *highpc*, *lowpc*, and *nfunc* are arguments of `monitor`,
- `BARSIZE` specifies the number of bytes that correspond to each bar of the profile histogram or to each cell of the profile buffer,
- `hdr` and `cnt` are structures defined in `mon.h`, and
- `WORD` is a data type defined in `mon.h`.

  highpc is the ending address of the area to be profiled.

  lowpc is the beginning address of the area to be profiled.

  nfunc specifies the number of function call count cells that have been reserved in the specified *buffer*. `monitor` will allocate additional call count cells as needed.

Files

`mon.out` is an output file that is automatically created in the current directory by `monitor` if the environment variable `PROFDIR` does not exist. If `PROFDIR` exists but has no value, `monitor` neither profiles the program nor creates an output file. If `PROFDIR` equals *dirname* and `monitor` is automatically called by compilation with `cc -p`, the name of the output file created by `monitor` is *dirname/pid.program*.

See Also

`end` (C), `cc` (Peterson 1991a), `prof` (Peterson 1991a), `profil` (Peterson 1991b)

msync (C) MEMORY CONTROL msync (C)

Name

`msync`—synchronize memory with physical storage

Synopsis

```
#include <sys/mman.h>
#include <sys/types.h>

int msync (caddr_t addr, size_t len, int flags);
```

Description

`msync` writes to backing storage copies of all pages that have been modified over the address range from *addr* to *addr* + *len*.

The effect of `msync(addr, len, flags)` is the same as the effect of

`memcntl(addr, len, MC_SYNC, flags, 0, 0)`

`msycn` (or `memcntl` with the appropriate parameter values) should be used by any program that must have a memory object in a known state, as when transaction facilities are being built.

Optionally, `msync` invalidates a copy so that if a further reference is made to that copy, the system will retrieve it from backing storage.

If the address mapping is a modified `MAP_SHARED` mapping, backing storage for a page is the file to which the page is mapped. If the address mapping is a modified `MAP_PRIVATE` mapping, backing storage for a page is its swap area.

Arguments

addr specifies, together with *len*, the memory address space from which pages are to be copied to storage.

flags is a bit pattern built from one or more of the following three values:

`MS_ASYNC` causes `msync` to return immediately after all write operations are scheduled (if `MS_ASYNC` is set).

`MS_INVALIDATE` invalidates mappings. All cached copies of data that are in memory are invalidated; further references to pages cause them to be retrieved from their backing storage locations.

`MS_SYNC` causes synchronous writes to be performed; `msync` does not return until all write operations are completed.

len specifies the length of the address space from which page copies are to be made.

Normal Completion: Value Returned

If `msync` succeeds, it returns 0.

Error Condition: Value Returned

If `msync` fails, it returns −1 and sets `errno` to indicate the error number.

See Also

`sysconf` (C), `memcntl` (Peterson 1991b), `mmap` (Peterson 1991b)

nl_langinfo (C) LOCALE INFORMATION nl_langinfo (C)

Name

`nl_langinfo`—get locale information

Synopsis

```
#include <langinfo.h>

#include <nl_types.h>

char *nl_langinfo (nl_item item);
```

Description

nl_langinfo uses the gettxt (C), localeconv (C), or strftime (C) function to get a pointer to a specified language information constant (native language datum) of the locale of a program. If possible, use the appropriate one of these three functions directly instead of calling nl_langinfo.

The names and values of the constants which nl_langinfo gets are defined in the langinfo.h header file, as described in the following section.

Language Constants

AM/PM Constants

AM_STR is the locale's equivalent of 'AM'. nl_langinfo uses strftime to get this constant.

PM_STR is the locale's equivalent of 'PM'. nl_langinfo uses strftime to get this constant.

nl_langinfo is based on the gettxt, localeconv, and strftime functions. Whenever possible, use these functions as interfaces to the required data instead of using nl_langinfo.

Currency Constant

CRNCYSTR is the locale's currency symbol. nl_langinfo extracts this item from the currency_symbol field in the structure returned by localeconv.

Date and Time Formats

nl_langinfo uses gettxt (C) to extract date and time format information from a special message catalog, Xopen_info, previously installed in the appropriate directory by mkmsgs (AT&T 1990o). The Xopen_info catalog should have its messages in the order T_FMT, D_FMT, D_T_FMT, YESSTR, and NOSTR (see the descriptions of these variables below).

D_FMT is the locale's default date format.

T_FMT is the locale's default time format.

D_T_FMT is the locale's default date and time format.

Day Constants

`nl_langinfo` uses `strftime` to get day constants.

ABDAY_1 is the locale's equivalent of 'sun'
ABDAY_2 is the locale's equivalent of 'mon'
ABDAY_3 is the locale's equivalent of 'tue'
ABDAY_4 is the locale's equivalent of 'wed'
ABDAY_5 is the locale's equivalent of 'thur'
ABDAY_6 is the locale's equivalent of 'fri'
ABDAY_7 is the locale's equivalent of 'sat'
DAY_1 is the locale's equivalent of 'sunday'
DAY_2 is the locale's equivalent of 'monday'
DAY_3 is the locale's equivalent of 'tuesday'
DAY_4 is the locale's equivalent of 'wednesday'
DAY_5 is the locale's equivalent of 'thursday'
DAY_6 is the locale's equivalent of 'friday'
DAY_7 is the locale's equivalent of 'saturday'

Decimal Point Constant

RADIXCHAR is the locale's equivalent of '.' `nl_langinfo` extracts this item from the `decimal_point` field in the structure returned by `localeconv`.

Month Constants

`nl_langinfo` uses `strftime` to get month constants.

ABMON_1 is the locale's equivalent of 'jan'
ABMON_2 is the locale's equivalent of 'feb'
ABMON_3 is the locale's equivalent of 'mar'
ABMON_4 is the locale's equivalent of 'apr'
ABMON_5 is the locale's equivalent of 'may'
ABMON_6 is the locale's equivalent of 'jun'
ABMON_7 is the locale's equivalent of 'jul'
ABMON_8 is the locale's equivalent of 'aug'
ABMON_9 is the locale's equivalent of 'sep'
ABMON_10 is the locale's equivalent of 'oct'
ABMON_11 is the locale's equivalent of 'nov'
ABMON_12 is the locale's equivalent of 'dec'
MON_1 is the locale's equivalent of 'january'
MON_2 is the locale's equivalent of 'february'
MON_3 is the locale's equivalent of 'march'
MON_4 is the locale's equivalent of 'april'
MON_5 is the locale's equivalent of 'may'
MON_6 is the locale's equivalent of 'june'

MON_7 is the locale's equivalent of 'july'
MON_8 is the locale's equivalent of 'august'
MON_9 is the locale's equivalent of 'september'
MON_10 is the locale's equivalent of 'october'
MON_11 is the locale's equivalent of 'november'
MON_12 is the locale's equivalent of 'december'

No/Yes Constants

`nl_langinfo` uses `gettxt` (C) to extract no/yes constants from a special message catalog, `Xopen_info`, previously installed in the appropriate directory by `mkmsgs` (AT&T 1990o).

NOSTR is the locale's equivalent of 'no'.
YESSTR is the locale's equivalent of 'yes'.

Thousands Separator

THOUSEP is the locale's equivalent of ','. `nl_langinfo` extracts this item from the `decimal_point` field in the structure returned by `localeconv`.

Modes of Language Constants

The mode of each of the language information constants is defined in the `nl_types.h` header file. The file contains the following definitions:

DEF_NLSPATH specifies the default search path for locating message catalogs.

`nl_catd` is used by `catclose` (C), `catgets` (C), and `catopen` (C) to identify a message catalog.

`nl_item` is used by `nl_langinfo` to identify items of language information.

NL_MSGMAX specifies the maximum number of messages per set.

NL_SETD is used by `gencat` (AT&T 1990q) if no `$set` directive is specified in a message text source file. Subsequent calls to `catgets` can use NL_SETD as the value of the set identifier parameter

NL_SETMAX specifies the maximum number of sets per catalog.

NL_TEXTMAX specifies the maximum size of a message.

Arguments

`item` specifies a language information constant.

Normal Completion: Value Returned

If `nl_langinfo` succeeds, it returns a pointer to a null-terminated string that contains information about the language or cultural area that is defined in the program's locale. For example,

```
nl_langinfo(ABDAY_2);
```

will return a pointer to the string "mon" if the locale is English.

The value returned should not be modified by the calling program. Subsequent `nl_langinfo` calls will overwrite the string.

Error Condition: Value Returned

If `nl_langinfo` fails, as it will if *`item`* contains an invalid setting, it returns a pointer to an empty string. If the `setlocale` (C) call has not succeeded, language information for a native language is not available, or a specified *`item`* is not defined, `nl_langinfo` returns a pointer to the corresponding string in the C locale.

See Also

`gettxt` (C), `localeconv` (C), `setlocale` (C), `strftime` (C)

offsetof (C) MANIPULATE STRUCTURES offsetof (C)

Name

`offsetof`—get the offset of a structure member

Synopsis

```
#include <stddef.h>

size_t offsetof (type, member_designator);
```

Description

`offsetof` is a macro which expands to an integral constant expression whose value is the offset (in bytes) from the beginning of the specified structure *`type`* to its member *`member_designator`*. `offsetof` is defined in the `stddef.h` header file.

Arguments

`member_designator` specifies the structure member whose offset is sought.

`type` specifies the structure which contains *`member_designator`*.

perror (C) PRINT SYSTEM ERROR MESSAGE perror (C)

Name

`perror`—print system error messages

Synopsis

```
#include <stdio.h>

void perror (const char *string);
```

Description

`perror` prints a message on the standard error output file (file descriptor 2) that describes the last error that occurred during a call to a library function or system call.

`perror` prints its argument string *`string`*, followed by a colon, a blank, the error message, and a newline. If *`string`* is a null pointer or points to a null string, however, `perror` will not print the colon.

Arguments

`string` should include the name of the program that incurred the error and the error number, as taken from the external variable `errno`.

See Also

`fmtmsg` (C), `strerror` (C), `intro` (Peterson 1991b)

popen (S) PIPES popen (S)

Name

`popen`, `pclose`—initiate a pipe to or from a process

Synopsis

```
#include <stdio.h>

FILE *popen (const char *command, const char *type);

int pclose (FILE *stream);
```

Description

`pclose` should be used to close the file *`stream`* (see `intro`) opened by `popen`. `pclose` waits for the associated process to terminate and returns the exit status of the command.

`popen` creates a pipe between the calling program and a command which is to be executed.

Do not use buffered I/O if the original and `popen`ed processes concurrently read or write a common file. If buffered I/O is used, execute `fflush` [see `fclose` (C)] to flush buffers to prevent problems with an output filter (see *`type`* below).

The `IFS` and `PATH` environment variables provide a security hole. Use full pathnames or a `PATH` reset. Set `IFS` to space and tab `"\t"`.

Arguments

`command` points to a null-terminated string that comprises a shell command line.

`type` specifies an I/O mode; the mode is reading if *`type`* is `r` and writing if *`type`* is `w`. Because open files are shared, a command with an `r` mode can be used as an input filter, and one with a `w` mode can be used as an output filter.

Normal Completion: Value Returned

If `popen` succeeds, it returns a stream pointer that permits writing to the standard input of the command if *`type`* is `w` and reading from the standard output of the command if *`type`* is `r`.

Error Condition: Value Returned

If files or processes cannot be created, `popen` returns a null pointer.

If *`stream`* is not associated with a `popen`ed command, `pclose` returns −1.

See Also

`fclose` (C), `fopen` (C), `stdio` (C), `system` (C), `pipe` (Peterson 1991b), `wait` (Peterson 1991b)

printf (S) FORMATTED OUTPUT printf (S)

Name

printf, fprintf, sprintf—print formatted output

Synopsis

```
#include <stdio.h>

int fprintf (FILE *stream, const char *format, .../
* args */);

int printf (const char *format, .../* args */);

int sprintf (char *s, const char *format, .../* args
*/);
```

Description

fprintf places its formatted output on the specified *stream*.

printf places its formatted output on stdout, the standard output stream.

sprintf places its formatted output in consecutive bytes of memory starting at *s* and ending with a null character (\0). The user must allocate enough space to hold all characters.

These three functions permit insertion of a language-dependent decimal-point character in output. The decimal-point character is defined by the LC_NUMERIC category of the program's locale. The decimal point defaults to a period (.) in the C locale or in any locale in which the decimal point is not defined.

Characters printed by printf or fprintf are printed as though by the putc routine.

The output of fprintf, printf, or sprintf is [+|−]*nan*0*xm* if a floating-point value being converted is the internal representation of "not a number." *nan* is nan or NAN, depending on whether the conversion character is upper- or lowercase. 0*xm* represents the mantissa of the floating-point number, where x is x or X, depending on the conversion character, and *m* uses the letters abcdef or ABCDEF, again depending on the conversion character. See the "Arguments" section below for the rules governing printing the sign of the result.

The output of fprintf, printf, or sprintf is [+|−]*inf* if a floating-point value being converted is the internal representation of infinity, where *inf* is inf or INF, depending on the value of the conversion character. See the "Arguments" section below for the rules governing printing of the sign of the result.

Arguments

args If a *field_width_specifier* (see *format* below) is an asterisk (*) instead of a digit, *args* specifies the field width or precision. The *args* that specifies field width must appear before the *args* (if any) which is to be converted, because the *args* to be converted is not fetched until the *args* that specifies the field width is encountered. If the *N*th argument of a set of numbered argument specifications is specified in a format string (see *format*), all leading arguments, from the first through the ($N - 1$)th, must be present.

format is a character string that controls the conversion, formatting, and printing of the specified *args*. The string may contain three kinds of objects: *conversion specification*s, *escape sequence*s, and *plain character*s.

*conversion specification*s are preceded by the character %. If the character following % is not a conversion character, the resulting conversion is not defined. Each specification consists of as many as six kinds of fields, five of which are optional. The fields appear in the following order: *decimal_digit_string$*, zero or more *flag*s, *field_width_specifier*, *precision_specifier*, h-specifier, and *conversion_character*.

decimal_digit_string$ is an optional field that consists of a decimal digit string followed by $. It specifies the next *args* to be converted. If this field is not given, the next *args* to be converted will be the *args* that follow the last *args* converted. If a conversion specification contains **decimal_digit_string$*, either a field width or precision may also be specified by **decimal_digit_string$*, giving the position in the argument list of an *args* integer that contains the field width or precision. If the character that follows a *%decimal_digit_string$* sequence is not a valid conversion character, the conversion result is not defined.

flag is an optional field that modifies the action of the *conversion_character* as follows:

– left-justifies the result of the conversion within its field. Otherwise, the result is right-justified.

\+ prepends a sign (+ or –) to the result of a signed conversion. Otherwise, the result of a signed conversion will begin with a sign only when a negative value is converted.

space puts a space in front of the result of a signed conversion if the first character of the result is not a sign. The 'space' flag will be ignored if the both the + and the 'space' flags appear.

# indicates that *args* is to be converted to an alternate form. The effect of # depends on the value of *conversion_character* (see below) as follows:

- c, d, i, s, or u causes # to have no effect.
- o increases the precision to force the first digit of the conversion result to be 0 if # is specified.
- x or X causes 0x or 0X to be prepended to the conversion result if it is nonzero and # is specified.
- e, E, f, g, or G forces the conversion result to contain a decimal-point character if # is specified, even if no digits follow the point. Otherwise, a decimal point appears in the result only if a digit follows it.
- g or G causes all trailing zeroes in the result to be retained if # is specified.

0 is ignored if *flag* is - or if *conversion_character* is d, i, o, u, x, or X and *precision_specifier* is used. Otherwise, the behavior of 0 is undefined unless *conversion_character* is d, e, E, f, g, G, i, o, u, x, or X. If the character is d, e, E, f, g, G, i, o, u, x, or X, leading zeroes (following any sign or indication of the base) are used to pad the conversion result in its field. No spaces are used to pad the result.

field_width_specifier is an optional string of digits that specifies a minimum field width. If the result of the conversion has fewer characters than the field width, the field will be padded on the left unless the left-adjustment *flag* – (see above) is specified. If the left-adjustment flag is specified, the result will be padded on the right. If *field_width_specifier* is negative, it is treated as a - *flag* followed by a positive field width. A nonexistent or small field width never causes truncation of a field. The width of a field is expanded to contain the conversion result if it is wider than the field width.

precision_specifier is an optional field that takes the form of a period (.) followed by a decimal digit string. A null digit string is treated as zero. *precision_specifier* gives the following:

- The minimum number of digits to appear for the d, i, o, u, or X conversions (with padding by leading zeroes),
- The number of digits to appear after the decimal-point character for e, E, and f conversions,
- The maximum number of significant digits for the g and G conversions, or
- The maximum number of characters to be printed from a string in an s conversion.

If *precision_specifier* is negative, it will be changed to zero. If padding is specified by *precision_specifier*, it overrides the padding specified by *field_width_specifier*.

h-specifier is an optional character h that specifies that a following d, i, o, u, x, or X conversion specifier applies to a short int or unsigned short int argument.

conversion_character is a mandatory character that indicates the type of conversion to be performed. Each *conversion_character* causes zero or more *args* to be fetched. If there are too few *args* for the *format*, the results are undefined. If any *args* remain when *format* is exhausted, they are ignored. *conversion_character* can have one of the following values:

c converts a type int *args* to an unsigned char and prints the resulting character.

d, i, o, u, x, or X converts the integer *args* to signed decimal (d or i), unsigned octal (o), unsigned decimal (u), or unsigned hexadecimal (x or X). The x conversion uses the letters abcdef and the decimal digits. The X conversion uses the letters ABCDEF and the decimal digits. If the converted value can be represented in fewer digits than the specified minimum, it will be padded with leading zeroes. If the value to be converted is 0 and the specified precision is 0, no characters are converted. The default precision is 0.

e, E converts a type double *args* to the form [−] *d*.*ddd*e[+|−]*dd* if the conversion character is e or to the form [−] *d*.*ddd*E[+|−]*dd* if the conversion character is E. The exponent always contains two digits. No decimal-point character appears if the precision is 0 and *flag* is not #. One digit (nonzero if the argument is nonzero) precedes the decimal-point character and the number of digits after the decimal point character equals the precision. Six digits are output if no precision is specified. The value is rounded to the appropriate number of digits.

f converts a type double *args* to decimal notation having the form [−]*ddd*.*ddd*, where the number of digits after the decimal-point character [see setlocale (C)] equals the specified precision. If no precision is specified, six digits are output. If a decimal point appears, at least one digit is output before it. If the precision is 0, no digit appears if the value of *flag* is not #. The value is rounded to the appropriate number of digits.

g, G prints a type double *args* in the f or e style if the conversion character is g, or in the E style if the conversion character is G. Style e or E will be used only if the exponent that results from the conversion is less than −4 or is greater than or equal to the precision. The precision specifies the number of significant digits. If the precision is 0, it is treated as 1. The decimal-point character appears only if a digit follows it. Trailing zeroes are deleted from the fractional part of the result.

n requires *args* to be a pointer to an integer which contains a count of the number of characters so far written to the output standard I/O stream by the current call to `fprintf`, `printf`, or `sprintf`. No argument is converted.

p requires that *args* be a pointer to `void`. The value of the pointer is converted to a set of sequences of printable characters. The set is implementation defined and should be the same as the set that is matched by the `%p` conversion specifier of the `scanf` function.

s causes *args* to be treated as a pointer to a string of characters. Characters from the string are printed up to, but not including, the terminating null character. If no precision is specified, it is treated as infinite and all characters up to the first null character are printed. If a precision is specified, the number of characters printed will be less than or equal to the precision. If *args* is NULL, the result of an s conversion is undefined.

% prints a % character without converting any argument.

escape sequences produce the following kinds of action on display devices that are capable of such action:

\a rings the bell (alert).

\b moves the printing position to a position one character before the current printing position, unless the current position is the beginning of a line (backspace).

\f moves the printing position to the first printing position of the next logical page (formfeed).

\n moves the printing position to the first character position of the next line (newline).

\r moves the printing position to the start of the current line (carriage return).

\t moves the printing position to the next horizintal tab position on the current line (horizontal tab).

\v moves the printing position to the beginning of the next vertical tab position (vertical tab).

plain characters are simply copied to the output stream.

s specifies the string of characters where `sprintf` places its output.

stream specifies the stream where `fprintf` places its output.

Normal Completion: Value Returned

If `fprintf`, `printf`, or `sprintf` succeeds, it returns the number of characters that it transmitted. In the case of `sprintf`, this count does not include the null character that terminates the string.

Error Condition: Value Returned

If `fprintf`, `printf`, or `sprintf` encounters an error, it returns a negative value.

See Also

`abort` (C), `ecvt` (C), `putc` (S), `scanf` (S), `setlocale` (C), `stdio` (S), `exit` (Peterson 1991b), `lseek` (Peterson 1991b), `write` (Peterson 1991b)

psignal (C) SIGNALS psignal (C)

Name

`psignal`, `psiginfo`—produce a message describing a signal

Synopsis

```
#include <siginfo.h>

void psiginfo (siginfo_t *pinfo, char *s);

void psignal (int sig, const char *s);
```

Description

`psignal` and `psiginfo` create messages on the standard error output that describe a signal.

Arguments

`pinfo` points to a `siginfo` structure that may have been passed as the second argument to an enhanced signal handler [see `sigaction` (Peterson 1991b)].

`s` is a string that is printed followed by a colon, a blank, a message, and a newline.

`sig` is a signal that may have been passed as a first argument to a signal handler.

See Also

`perror` (C), `sigaction` (Peterson 1991b), `siginfo` (AT&T 1990m), `signal` (Peterson 1991b)

putc (S) OUTPUT TO A STREAM putc (S)

Name

putc, fputc, putchar, putw—put a character or word on a stream

Synopsis

```
#include <stdio.h>

int fputc (int c, FILE *stream);

int putc (int c, FILE *stream);

int putchar (int c);

int putw (int w, FILE *stream);
```

Description

putc is a macro that writes a character *c* (converted to type unsigned char) to the specified output *stream* [see intro] at the place specified by the file pointer if the file pointer is defined. It increments the file pointer appropriately. putc appends *c* to the output *stream* if *stream* was opened in the append mode or if the device cannot seek. Because putc is a macro, it evaluates its *stream* argument more than once. Accordingly, putc(c, *f++) will not produce the same result as fputc(c, *f++). Use fputc(c, *f++) instead of putc(c, *f++) if the use of putc(c, *f++) would result in a bug, not a feature, in your program.

putchar is a macro defined as putc (c, stdout).

fputc is a function that behaves like putc. It runs more slowly than putc but takes less space per invocation. Its name can be passed as an argument to a function. If fputc is to be used instead of putc, the putc macro must be undefined by using #undef putc.

putw is a function that writes the integer (word) *w* to the specified output *stream* at the place specified by the file pointer. The word size is the same as that of an integer, but this size is machine dependent. putw does not cause any special alignment of words in the file, nor does it assume any special alignment. Because byte order and word length can vary from machine to machine, getw cannot always be depended upon to read files created by putw on another machine.

Arguments

`c` specifies the character to be output by `fputc`, `putc`, or `putchar`.

`stream` specifies the stream which receives the output of `fputc`, `putc`, or `putw`.

`w` specifies the word that is output by `putw`.

Normal Completion: Value Returned

If any of these functions succeeds, it returns the value that it has written, except that `putw` returns `ferror (`*`stream`*`)` instead.

Error Condition: Value Returned

If any of these functions fails because the output file cannot grow, because the file *`stream`* is not open, or for any other reason, it returns `EOF`.

See Also

`abort` (C), `fclose` (S), `ferror` (S), `fopen` (S), `fread` (S), `printf` (S), `puts` (S), `setbuf` (S), `stdio` (S), `exit` (Peterson 1991b), `lseek` (Peterson 1991b), `write` (Peterson 1991b)

puts (S) OUTPUT TO A STREAM puts (S)

Name

`puts`, `fputs`—put a string to a stream

Synopsis

```
#include <stdio.h>

int fputs (const char *s, FILE *stream);

int puts (const char *s);
```

Description

`fputs` writes to the specified output *`stream`* the null-terminated string to which *`s`* points. `fputs` does not append a newline character to the string, nor does it write the terminating null character to the stream.

puts writes to stdout (the standard output stream) the character string to which *s* points. puts appends a newline to the string but does not write the terminating null character to stdout.

Arguments

s points to the string of characters that is to be output by fputs or puts.
stream points to the stream which receives the output of fputs.

Normal Completion: Value Returned

If either of these functions succeeds, it returns the number of characters written.

Error Condition: Value Returned

If either of these functions fails, it returns EOF.

See Also

abort (C), fclose (S), ferror (S), fopen (S), fread (S), printf (S), putc (S), stdio (S), exit (Peterson 1991b), lseek (Peterson 1991b), write (Peterson 1991b)

putenv (C) ENVIRONMENTAL VARIABLES putenv (C)

Name

putenv—change or add a value to an environment

Synopsis

```
#include <stdlib.h>

int putenv (char *string);
```

Description

putenv manipulates the environment to which *environ* points. It makes the value of the environment variable *name* equal to *value* (see *string* below) by changing an existing variable or by creating a new one. It does not change the value of *envp*, the third argument of main.

`putenv` can be used with `getenv` (C), a function which ascertains the particular value of *`value`*.

`putenv` uses `malloc` (C) to enlarge the environment.

Following a call to `putenv`, environmental variables are not in alphabetical order.

Arguments

`string` points to a string that has the form "*`name`*=*`value`*." The string to which string points becomes part of the environment, so any alteration of the string changes the environment. *`string`* should be declared `static` if it is declared within a function because the space occupied by *`string`* is no longer used after a new string that defines *`name`* is passed to `putenv`. If *`string`* is a pointer to an automatic variable and `putenv` exits to the calling function while *`string`* is still part of the environment, it can cause an error.

Normal Completion: Value Returned

`putenv` returns 0 if it obtains enough space for an expanded environment.

Error Condition: Value Returned

`putenv` returns a nonzero value if it fails to obtain enough space for an expanded environment. See *`string`* above.

See Also

`getenv` (C), `malloc` (C), `environ` (AT&T 1990m), `exec` (Peterson 1991b)

putpwent (C) PASSWORDS putpwent (C)

Name

`putpwent`—write a password file entry

Synopsis

```
#include <pwd.h>

int putpwent (const struct passwd *ptr, FILE *strm);
```

Description

`putpwent` writes a line on the specified stream. The line matches the format of `/etc/passwd`. `putpwent` is the inverse of `getpwent`.

Arguments

ptr points to a `passwd` structure that was created by `getpwent` (C), `getpwnam` (C), or `getpwuid` (C).

strm points to the stream upon which `putpwent` writes data from the `passwd` structure to which *ptr* points.

Normal Completion: Value Returned

If `putpwent` succeeds, it returns 0.

Error Condition: Value Returned

If `putpwent` fails, it returns a nonzero value.

Files

`/etc/passwd`

See Also

`getpwent` (C)

putspent (C) PASSWORDS putspent (C)

Name

`putspent`—write a shadow password entry

Synopsis

```
#include <shadow.h>

int putspent (const struct spwd *ptr, FILE *fptr);
```

Description

`putspent` writes a line on the *fptr* stream. The line matches the format of `/etc/shadow`. `putspent` is the inverse of `getspent` (C).

`putspent` is intended for internal use only. Its compatibility is not guaranteed.

Arguments

fptr points to the stream upon which `putspent` writes data from the `spwd` structure to which *ptr* points.

ptr points to a `spwd` that was created by `getspent` (C) or `getspnam` (C). If the `sp_expire`, `sp_inact`, `sp_lstchg`, `sp_max`, `sp_min`, or `sp_warn` field of the `spwd` structure is equal to −1 or if the `sp_flag` field of `spwd` is 0, the corresponding field of `/etc/shadow` is cleared.

Normal Completion: Value Returned

If `putspent` succeeds, it returns 0.

Error Condition: Value Returned

If `putspent` fails, it returns a nonzero value.

Files

`/etc/shadow`

See Also

`getpwent` (C), `getspent` (C), `putpwent` (C)

qsort (C) SORTING qsort (C)

Name

`qsort`—perform a quicker sort

Synopsis

```
#include <stdlib.h>

void qsort (void * base, size_t nel, size_t width,
int (*compar) (const void *, const void *));
```

Description

`qsort` sorts a table of data in place in ascending order. It implements the quicker-sort algorithm. The relative order of two items that are equal is unpredictable.

Arguments

`base` points to the element at the base of the table.

`compar` is the function used to compare table elements. It is called with two arguments that point to the elements that are to be compared. It must return an integer that is less than, equal to, or greater than 0 to tell whether the first argument is respectively less than, equal to, or greater than the second. *`compar`* need not compare every byte. This permits the table elements to contain arbitrary data in addition to the elements being compared.

`nel` specifies the number of elements in the table.

`width` gives the size of each table element.

See Also

`bsearch` (C), `lsearch` (C), `string` (C), `sort` (AT&T 1990q)

raise (C) SIGNALS raise (C)

Name

`raise`—send a signal to a program

Synopsis

```
#include <signal.h>

int raise (int sig);
```

Description

`raise` uses `kill(getpid(), sig)` to send a specified signal to an executing program [see `kill` and `getpid` (Peterson 1991b)]. See `signal` (Peterson 1991b) for a list of the signals that `raise` can send.

Arguments

`sig` specifies the signal that is to be sent to the program.

Normal Completion: Value Returned

If `raise` succeeds, it returns 0.

Error Condition: Value Returned

If `raise` fails, it returns −1 and sets `errno` to indicate the error. See `kill` (Peterson 1991b) for a list of the error conditions that can cause `raise` to fail.

See Also

`getpid` (Peterson 1991b), `kill` (Peterson 1991b), `signal` (Peterson 1991b)

rand (C) RANDOM NUMBERS rand (C)

Name

`rand`, `srand`—get a pseudorandom number

Synopsis

```
#include <stdlib.h>

int rand (void)

void srand (unsigned int seed);
```

Description

`rand` generates successive pseudorandom numbers in the range from 0 to RAND_MAX [defined in `<stdlib.h>`]. `rand` uses a multiplicative congruential random-number generator that has a 2^{32} period.

`srand` uses its *`seed`* argument as a seed for a new sequence of pseudorandom numbers that is to be returned by `rand`.

Use `drand48` instead of `rand` to generate pseudo-random numbers. `drand48` has less limited spectral properties than `rand`, although it has the drawback of being more elaborate than `rand`.

Arguments

`seed` specifies the seed that used `srand` for the new sequence of pseudorandom numbers which is to be returned by `rand`. If the same value of *`seed`*

is used by a subsequent call to `srand`, `rand` will generate the same sequence of pseudorandom numbers.

Normal Completion: Value Returned

`rand` returns successive pseudorandom numbers, as discussed above. If `rand` is called before `srand` is first called, `rand` will generate the same pseudorandom number sequence as when `srand` was called with *seed* equal to 1.

See Also

`drand48` (C)

realpath (C) FILES realpath (C)

Name

`realpath`—get the real pathname

Synopsis

```
#include <stdlib.h>
#include <sys/param.h>

char *realpath (char * filename, char * resolved
_name);
```

Description

`realpath` resolves all of the links and references to "." and ".." that appear in *filename* and stores the result in *resolved_name*. It can resolve both relative and absolute pathnames.

The user should have execution permission on all of the directories in the specified path and in the resolved path.

Arguments

filename is a null-terminated string that specifies the pathname which is to be resolved.

resolved_name receives the resolved pathname. *resolved_name* must be large enough to hold the fully resolved pathname. MAXPATHLEN specifies the maximum size of *resolved_name*. *resolved_name* is the resolved absolute name if the pathname is absolute or if the pathname is a relative one whose resolved name cannot be expressed relatively (for example, `../../reldir`). *resolved_name* is the resolved relative name for other kinds of relative pathnames.

Normal Completion: Value Returned

If `realpath` succeeds, it returns a pointer to *resolved_name*.

Error Condition: Value Returned

If `realpath` fails, it returns a `NULL` pointer, puts the name of the offending file in *resolved_name*, and sets `errno` to indicate the error condition. If an error occurs, `realpath` may not return to the current directory.

See Also

`getcwd` (C)

remove (C) FILES remove (C)

Name

`remove`—remove a file

Synopsis

```
#include <stdio.h>

int remove (const char *path);
```

Description

`remove` deletes a file, as `unlink` (Peterson 1991b) does, or deletes a directory, as `rmdir` (Peterson 1991b) does.

After `remove` is executed, any subsequent attempt to open the file specified by *path* will fail unless the file is created again.

Arguments

path points to the string that names the file or empty directory that `remove` is to delete.

Normal Completion: Value Returned

If `remove` succeeds, it returns 0.

Error Condition: Value Returned

If `remove` succeeds, it returns −1 and sets `errno` to indicate the error condition. See `rmdir` and `unlink` for an explanation of the error conditions that can cause `remove` to fail.

See Also

`rmdir` (Peterson 1991b), `unlink` (Peterson 1991b)

scanf (S) Formatted I/O scanf (S)

Name

`scanf`, `fscanf`, `sscanf`—convert formatted input

Synopsis

```
#include <stdio.h>

int fscanf (FILE *strm, const char *format, ...);

int scanf (const char *format, ...);

int sscanf (const char *s, const char *format, ...);
```

Description

`fscanf` reads formatted input from *`strm`*, the specified input stream.
`scanf` reads input from `stdin`, the standard input stream, converts the input according to the specified *`format`*, and stores it in the specified arguments. The conversion terminates at the end of file, at the end of the *`format`* control string, or when `scanf` encounters an input character that conflicts with the *`format`* control string.
`sscanf` reads input from *`s`*, the specified character string, formats it, and stores it in the specified arguments.
Each function reads characters, interprets the characters according to a spec-

ified *format* string, and stores its results in the locations to which its *arg* arguments point.

Each function can detect language-dependent decimal-point characters in its input string. The program's locale category LC_NUMERIC defines the decimal-point character recognized by the program. In the "C" locale, or in any locale where the decimal-point character is undefined, the default decimal-point is a period (.).

Arguments

fscanf expects three kinds of arguments: *format*; *arg*, ... , and *strm*. See a description of these arguments below.

scanf expects two kinds of arguments: *format* and *arg*, ...

sscanf expects three kinds of arguments: *arg*, ... ; *format*; and *s*.

arg, ... is a set of pointer arguments that point to locations where results are to be stored. If there are insufficient arguments to exhaust the *format* (see below), the behavior of these input functions is undefined. If *format* is exhausted while *arg*(s) still remain, these functions ignore the excess arguments.

format is a control string used by each input function. The control string usually contains conversion specifications that direct the interpretation of input sequences. *format* may contain conversion specifications, ordinary characters, and white-space characters.

conversion_specification(s) described below consist of either % or the character sequence %*digits*$; an optional assignment suppression character *; an optional decimal digit string; an optional letter l, L, or h; and a conversion code. *conversion_specification* directs the conversion of the next input field [a string of nonspace characters that extends to the next inappropriate character or until the maximum field width (if one is specified) is exhausted]. The result of the conversion is stored in the variable to which the corresponding *arg* points unless * (see below) specifies that the assignment must be suppressed.

Conversion terminates if the input function encounters an end of file during input. If the input function encounters an end of file before it has read any characters (other than white space, where allowed) that match the current specification, execution of the current specification ends with an input failure. Otherwise, execution of the following specifier (if any) ends with an input failure unless execution of the current specifier is terminated by a matching failure. The input function leaves the offending input character unread in the input stream if conversion terminates on a conflicting input character. The input functions leave any trailing white space in input items unread unless it is matched by a conversion specification.

Permissible values of *conversion_specification* are as follows:

% is used as an alternative to *%digits$* below. A control string can use % or *%digits$* but not both.

%digits$ permits the current conversion specifier to be applied to the *n*th *arg* in the argument list instead of to the next unused *arg*. *digits* is a decimal integer -*n* that gives the position of *arg* in the argument list. The first such argument is %1$; it immediately follows *format*.

* is optional. It suppresses assignment. * specifies that an input field is to be skipped.

decimal_digit_string is optional. It specifies the numerical maximum field width.

h, l, or L is optional. It indicates the size of the object that receives the results of the conversion. One or another of the h, l, or L characters can precede a d, e, f, g, i, n, o, u, or x conversion code (see below) and is ignored if it precedes any other conversion code.

h should precede d, i, or n if the corresponding *arg* points to a short int variable instead of to an int. h should precede o, u, or x if the corresponding *arg* points to an unsigned short int variable instead of to an unsigned int.

l should precede d, i, or n if the corresponding *arg* points to a long int variable instead of to an int. l should precede o, u, or x if the corresponding *arg* points to an unsigned long int variable instead of to an unsigned int. l should precede e, f, or g if the corresponding *arg* points to a double variable instead of to a float.

L should precede e, f, or g if the corresponding *arg* points to a long double variable instead of to a float.

conversion_code specifies the interpretation of the next input field. The *arg* pointer argument that corresponds to the input field ordinarily must be of a restricted type. No *arg* is given for a suppressed input field. White space that leads an input field is ignored by all of the following conversion codes except [and c.

% means that a single % is expected in the input here; no assignment is done. If an invalid conversion character follows %, the result of the operation is undefined.

c matches a character sequence whose length is specified by the field width (see *decimal_digit_string* above). The length is 1 if no field width is specified. The corresponding *arg* should point to an array that is large enough to accept the sequence. No terminating null character is added to the sequence. The usual skip over white space is suppressed.

d matches an optionally signed decimal integer. Its format is the same as the format expected for the subject sequence of strtol (C) with *base* equal to 10. The corresponding *arg* should point to an integer.

`e`, `f`, `g` matches an optionally signed floating-point number. Its format is the same as the format expected for the subject string of `strtod` (C). The corresponding *arg* should point to a floating point object.

`E` and `G` are valid under the `-Xa` and `-Xc` compilation modes of `cc` (Peterson 1991a), where they have the the same effect as `e` and `g`, respectively. They are also valid under the `-Xt` compilation modes of `cc`, where they have the the same effect as `le` and `lg`, respectively.

`i` matches an optionally signed integer. Its format is the same as the format expected for the subject sequence of `strtol` (C) with *base* equal to 0. The corresponding *arg* should point to an integer.

`n` consumes no input. The corresponding *arg* should point to an integer to which is written a count of the number of characters read from the input stream so far by the input function. If `%n` is executed, it does not increase the assignment count returned when the input function finishes execution. The success or failure of suppressed assignments and literal matches is not directly ascertainable without using the `%n` directive.

`o` matches an optionally signed octal integer. Its format is the same as the format expected for the subject sequence of `strtoul` (C) with *base* equal to 8. The corresponding *arg* should point to an unsigned integer.

`p` matches an implementation-defined set of sequences that should be identical to the set of sequences that can be created by the `%p` conversion of `printf` (S). The *arg* corresponding to `p` should be a pointer to `void`. Interpretation of an input item under the `%p` conversion depends on the implementation. Thus, if the input field is a value converted earlier during program execution, the pointer that results from the current conversion shall compare equal to the value that results from the earlier conversion; otherwise, the behavior of the `%p` conversion is not defined.

`s` matches a character string. The corresponding *arg* should be a character pointer that points to a character array large enough to accept the string and its terminating null character `0`, which is automatically added. Any white-space character terminates the input field.

`u` matches an optionally signed decimal integer. Its format is the same as the format expected for the subject sequence of `strtoul` (C) with *base* equal to 10. The corresponding *arg* should point to an unsigned integer.

`x` matches an optionally signed hexadecimal integer. Its format is the same as the format expected for the subject sequence of `strtoul` (C) with *base* equal to 16. The corresponding *arg* should point to an unsigned integer.

`X` is valid under the `-Xa` and `-Xc` compilation modes of `cc`, where it has the same effect as `x`. It is also valid under the `-Xt` compilation modes of `cc`, where it has the same effect as `lx`.

`[` matches a nonempty set of characters from the scanset, an expected set of characters. The corresponding *arg* should point to the first

character of an array that is large enough to accept the scanset and a terminating null character that is added automatically. The conversion specifier includes all subsequent characters in the `format` string, including the right bracket (]) that matches the left bracket ([). The right bracket character can be included in the scanset without being interpreted as a closing bracket if it is the first character of the scanlist (with or without a preceding ^). The scanlist, the set of characters enclosed by [and], comprises the scanset unless the character immediately following ;[is a circumflex (^), in which case the scanset is all of the characters that do not appear in the scanlist between ^ and]. If the conversion specifier starts with either [] or [^], then] is part of the scanlist; the next] matches the starting [and terminates the scanlist. Otherwise, the first] ends the specifier.
The scanset can represent a range of characters by using the construction `first-last`. For example, [012345] can be represented by [0–5]. The dash character (–) stands for itself if it is the first or last character in the scanlist or if `first` is lexically greater than `last`. At least one character must match in order for this conversion to succeed.

`ordinary_character`(s) is a character other than % that must match the next character of the input stream.

`s` specifies the character string from which `sscanf` is to read input.

`strm` specifies the input stream from which `white_space_character`(s) are blanks, tabs, newlines, or formfeeds that, with two exceptions discussed above, cause the input function to read input up to the next non-white-space character.

`fscanf` is to read input.

Normal Completion: Value Returned

`fscanf`, `scanf`, and `sscanf` return the number of successfully matched and assigned input items.

Error Condition: Value Returned

`fscanf`, `scanf`, and `sscanf` return 0 if a matching failure between an input character and the control string occurs early. They return EOF if input ends before the first conversion or matching failure.

See Also

`printf` (C), `strtod` (C), `strtol` (C), `strtoul` (C), `cc` (Peterson 1991a)

Name

`setbuf`, `setvbuf`—assign a buffer to a stream

Synopsis

```
#include <stdio.h>

void setbuf (FILE *stream, char *buf);

void setvbuf (FILE *stream, char *buf, int type,
size_t size);
```

Description

`setbuf` can assign a buffer to a stream [see `intro`] after it has been opened but before it has been read or written.

`setvbuf` can assign a buffer to a stream after it has been opened but before it has been read or written.

See `stdio` (S) for additional details about buffering.

Arguments

`setbuf`

`buf` points to the character array which will be used as a buffer for the stream instead of an automatically allocated buffer. The constant `BUFSIZ` defined in the `<stdio.h>` header file can specify a convenient buffer size, as in

```
char buf[BUFSIZ]
```

I/O will be completely unbuffered if *`buf`* is `NULL`.

`stream` specifies the stream to which *`buf`* is to be assigned.

`setvbuf`

`buf` specifies the array to be used in buffering the I/O of the specified stream unless *`buf`* is `NULL`, in which case an automatically allocated buffer will be used. *`buf`* is ignored if I/O is unbuffered.

`size` specifies the size of the I/O buffer, *`buf`*. *`size`* is ignored if I/O is unbuffered. *`buf`* will contain less than *`size`* bytes when it is full because parts

of *buf* will be used for the internal bookkeeping of the *stream*. For this reason, use an automatically allocated buffer when using setvbuf.

stream specifies the stream to which *buf* is to be assigned.

type specifies how *stream* will be buffered. *type* can have one of the following values defined in <stdio.h>:

_IOFBF specifies that I/O is fully buffered.

_IOLBF specifies that I/O is line buffered. Each time a newline is written, the buffer is full, or a newline is written, *buf* will be flushed.

_IONBF specifies that I/O is completely unbuffered.

Normal Completion: Value Returned

If setvbuf succeeds, it returns 0.

Error Condition: Value Returned

If setvbuf fails because an illegal value of *type* is provided, it returns a nonzero value.

Allocating buffer space as an automatic variable in a code block and forgetting to close the stream in the same code block is a frequent source of error.

See Also

fopen (C), getc (C), malloc (C), putc (C), stdio (C)

setjmp (C) GOTO setjmp (C)

Name

setjmp, longjmp—nonlocal goto

Synopsis

```
#include <setjmp.h>

int longjmp (jmp_buf env, int val);

int setjmp (jmp_buf env);
```

Description

setjmp saves its stack environment in *env* for later use by longjmp. longjmp restores the stack environment that was saved in *env* when `setjmp` was called with the corresponding *env* argument. When `longjmp` finishes execution, program execution resumes as if `setjmp` had just returned *val*, provided that the caller of `setjmp` has not meanwhile returned (see "Error Condition: Value Returned" below).

Arguments

env is a variable of type `jmp_buf` fined in <`setjmp.h`>] where `setjmp` stores the current state of the process.

val defines the value returned by `setjmp` when `longjmp` is called (see "Normal Completion: Value Returned" below).

Normal Completion: Value Returned

If `setjmp` succeeds, it returns 0. `longjmp` cannot make `setjmp` return 0. If `longjmp` is called with *val* equal to 0, `setjmp` returns 1.

When `setjmp` returns for the second time, all external and static variables have the same values as they did when `longjmp` was called, but the values of all register and automatic variables are undefined unless they were declared `volatile`.

`longjmp` never returns. Instead, it passes control to the return address stored in *env* by `setjmp`, after which `setjmp` returns *val*.

Error Condition: Value Returned

If `longjmp` is called without `setjmp` having first primed `env`, or if `longjmp` is called and the last call to `setjmp` was in a function that has since returned, it will cause chaos.

See Also

`sigsetjmp` (C), `signal` (Peterson 1991b)

setlocale (C) LOCALE setlocale (C)

Name

`setlocale`—alter and query a program's locale

Synopsis

```
#include <locale.h>

char *setlocale(int category, const char *locale);
```

Description

`setlocale` selects the piece of the program's locale specified by its *category* and *locale* arguments and ascertains or modifies its value.

The equivalent of

```
setlocale(LC_ALL, "C");
```

is executed at program startup; this initializes each category to the locale described by the C environment (see LC_ALL below).

Arguments

category can be one the following seven names defined in the <locale.h> header file:

LC_ALL refers to the entire locale of the program.

LC_COLLATE affects the behavior of `strcoll` (C) and `strxfrm` (C).

LC_MESSAGE affects the behavior of `catclose` (C), `catgets` (C), `catopen` (C), and `gettxt` (C) [see `catopen` (C) and `catgets` (C)].

LC_MONETARY affects the formatted monetary information that `localeconv` returns.

LC_NUMERIC affects the decimal-point character used by the formatted I/O functions and the string conversion functions, as well as the nonmonetary formatting information that `localeconv` (C) returns.

LC_TIME affects the behavior of `asctime` (C), `cftime` (C), `getdate` (C), and `strftime` (C).

LC_TYPE affects the behavior of the multibyte character functions [for example, `mbtowc` (C) and `wctomb` (C)] and the character-handling functions [for example, `isdigit` (C) and `toupper` (C)].

Each value of *category* corresponds to a set of databases containing relevant information for each locale defined. The following path points at the database: `/usr/lib/locale/`*`locale`*`/`*`category`*, where *locale* specifies the locale and *category* specifies the category. For example, the database for the LC_COLLATE type for the "`german`" locale is in `/usr/lib/locale/german/LC_COLLATE`.

locale can specify a simple locale, consisting of one locale, or a composite locale, consisting of a string that begins with a slash (`/`) followed by the locale of each category, with each category separated by a `/`. If *locale* equals `"C"`, `setlocale` gets the locale from the default environment. If *locale* equals the empty string `""`, `setlocale` gets the locale from the environment variables. The order in which setlocale checks the environment variables if *locale* equals "" depends on the value of *category* as follows:

LC_COLLATE causes setlocale to check first and LANG second.

LC_CTYPE causes setlocale to check LC_CTYPE first and LANG second.

LC_MESSAGES causes setlocale to check LC_MESSAGES first and LANG second.

LC_TIME causes setlocale to check LC_TIME first and LANG second.

LC_MONETARY causes setlocale to check LC_MONETARY first and LANG second.

LC_NUMERIC causes setlocale to check LC_NUMERIC first and LANG second.

Normal Completion: Value Returned

If *locale* is a NULL pointer, setlocale returns the current locale that is associated with *category* and leaves the program's locale unchanged.

If *locale* is a pointer to a string and *category* is not equal to LC_ALL, setlocale tries to set the locale for the specified *category* to *locale*. If setlocale succeeds, it returns *locale*.

If *locale* is a pointer to a string and *category* equals LC_ALL, setlocale tries to set the locale for all categories to *locale*. If setlocale succeeds, it returns *locale*.

Error Condition: Value Returned

If *category* does not equal LC_ALL and setlocale fails, it returns a NULL pointer and does not change the program's locale.

If *category* equals LC_ALL and setlocale fails to set the locale for any category, it returns a NULL pointer and does not change the program's locale for any category.

Files

/usr/lib/locale/C/LC_COLLATE is the LC_COLLATE database for the C locale.

/usr/lib/locale/C/LC_CTYPE is the LC_CTYPE database for the C locale.

/usr/lib/locale/C/LC_MESSAGES is the LC_MESSAGES database for the C locale.

`/usr/lib/locale/C/LC_NUMERIC` is the `LC_NUMERIC` database for the C locale.

`/usr/lib/locale/C/LC_TIME` is the `LC_TIME` database for the C locale.

`/usr/lib/locale/`*`locale`*`/`*`category`* holds files that contain locale-specific information for each locale and category.

See Also

`ctime` (C), `ctype` (C), `getdate` (C), `gettxt` (C), `localeconv` (C), `mbtowc` (C), `printf` (C), `strcoll` (C), `strftime` (C), `strtod` (C), `strxfrm` (C), `wctomb` (C), `environ` (AT&T 1990m)

sigsetjmp (C) GOTO sigsetjmp (C)

Name

`sigsetjmp`, `siglongjmp`—set up or perform a nonlocal goto with signals

Synopsis

```
#include <setjmp.h>

int sigsetjmp (sigjmp_buf env, int savemask);

void siglongjmp (sigjmp_buf env, int val);
```

Description

`sigsetjmp` saves the registers and the stack environment [see `sigalstack` (Peterson 1991b)] of the calling process in *`env`* for later use by `siglongjmp`.

`siglongjmp` restores the environment that was saved in *`env`* when `sigsetjmp` was called with the corresponding *`env`* argument. When `siglongjmp` finishes execution, program execution resumes as if `sigsetjmp` had just returned *`val`*, provided that the caller of `sigsetjmp` has not meanwhile returned (see "Error Condition: Value Returned" below).

If a signal-catching function interrupts `sleep` and calls `siglongjmp` to restore an environment that was saved before `sleep` was called, both the action associated with SIGALRM and the time SIGALRM is scheduled to be generated are undetermined (see *savemask* below).

Arguments

env is a variable of type `sigjmp_buf` [defined in `<setjmp.h>`] where `sigsetjmp` stores the registers and stack environment of the process.

savemask causes the signal mask [see `sigprocmask` (Peterson 1991b)] and the scheduling parameters [see `priocntl` (Peterson 1991b)] of the calling process to be saved if *savemask* is nonzero. `siglongjmp` restores the saved signal mask if and only if `sigsetjmp` has initialized *env* with a nonzero *savemask* argument. Unless the signal mask of a process is restored as part of the environment, it is unspecified whether or not the SIGALARM signal is blocked if a signal-catching function interrupts `sleep` and calls `siglongjmp` to restore an environment that was saved before `sleep` was called.

val defines the value returned by `sigsetjmp` when `siglongjmp` is called (see "Normal Completion: Value Returned" below).

Normal Completion: Value Returned

If `sigsetjmp` succeeds, it returns 0. `siglongjmp` cannot make `sigsetjmp` return 0. If `siglongjmp` is called with *val* equal to 0, `sigsetjmp` returns 1.

When `sigsetjmp` returns for the second time, all external and static variables have the same values as they did when `siglongjmp` was called, but the values of all register and automatic variables are undefined unless they were declared as volatile.

`siglongjmp` never returns. Instead, it passes control to the return address stored in *env* by `sigsetjmp`, after which `sigsetjmp` returns *val*.

Error Condition: Value Returned

If `siglongjmp` is called without `sigsetjmp` having first primed `env`, or if `siglongjmp` is called and the last call to `sigsetjmp` was in a function that has since returned, it will cause chaos.

See Also

`setjmp` (C), `getcontext` (Peterson 1991b), `priocntl` (Peterson 1991b), `sigaction` (Peterson 1991b), `sigalstack` (Peterson 1991b), `sigprocmask` (Peterson 1991b)

Name

sigemptyset, sigaddset, sigdelset, sigfillset, sigismember—manage sets of signals

Synopsis

```
#include <signal.h>

int sigaddset (sigset_t *set, int signo);

int sigdelset (sigset_t *set, int signo);

int sigemptyset (sigset_t *set);

int sigfillset (sigset_t *set);

int sigismember (sigset_t *set, int signo);
```

Description

The `sigaddset`, `sigdelset`, and `sigismember` functions manipulate the `sigset_t` data types that represent the set of signals supported by the implementation of System V. Any object whose type is `sigset_t` must be initialized by `sigemptyset` or `sigfillset` before any other function manipulates the object.

`sigaddset` adds the individual signal specified by *`signo`* to the set to which *`set`* points.

`sigdelset` deletes the individual signal specified by *`signo`* from the set to which *`set`* points.

`sigemptyset` initializes the signal set to which *`set`* points to exclude all signals that are defined by the system.

`sigfillset` initializes the signal set to which *`set`* points to include all signals that are defined by the system.

`sigismember` tests whether the individual signal specified by *`signo`* is a member of the set to which *`set`* points.

Arguments

`set` points to a set of signals, among which is the signal specified by *`signo`* if the function is `sigaddset`, `sigdelset`, or `sigismember`.

Normal Completion: Value Returned

If `sigaddset` or `sigdelset` succeeds, it returns 0.
If `sigismember` succeeds, it returns 1 if the specified signal is a member of the specified set or 0 if it is not.

Error Condition: Value Returned

If `sigaddset`, `sigdelset`, or `sigismember` fails, it returns −1 and sets `errno` to indicate one of the following error conditions:

14 EFAULT
`set` specifies an invalid address.

22 EINVAL
`sig` contains an invalid signal number.

See Also

`sigaction` (Peterson 1991b), `signal` (AT&T 1990m), `sigpending` (Peterson 1991b), `sigprocmask` (Peterson 1991b), `sigsuspend` (Peterson 1991b)

sleep (C) PROCESS CONTROL sleep (C)

Name

`sleep`—suspend execution for a defined interval

Synopsis

```
#include <unistd.h>

unsigned sleep (unsigned seconds);
```

Description

`sleep` suspends a process for an amount of time specified by *`seconds`*. `sleep` is implemented by setting an alarm signal and pausing until the signal (or another signal) occurs. The previous state of the alarm signal is saved and restored.

The alarm catch routine of the calling process is executed just before `sleep` returns (see "Normal Completion: Value Returned" below).

Arguments

`seconds` specifies the number of seconds that the current process is to be suspended. The actual amount of time that the process is suspended may be less than *`seconds`* because any caught signal terminates `sleep` after the signal's catching routine is executed. Also, the actual time that the process is suspended may be more than *`seconds`* because other activity in the system is scheduled. If the calling program has set up an alarm signal before calling `sleep` and *`seconds`* exceeds the time until such an alarm signal, the process sleeps only until the alarm signal would have occurred. If *`seconds`* is less than the time until such an alarm, the earlier alarm is reset to go off at the same time as it would have gone off without the intervening `sleep`.

Normal Completion: Value Returned

If the caller had an alarm set to go off before the end of the requested sleep time or another caught signal has prematurely awakened the process, `sleep` returns the amount of sleep time requested minus the time the calling process actually sleeps.

See Also

`alarm` (Peterson 1991b), `pause` (Peterson 1991b), `signal` (Peterson 1991b), `wait` (Peterson 1991b)

ssignal (C) SIGNALS ssignal (C)

Name

`ssignal`, `gsignal`—execute a software signal

Synopsis

```
#include <signal.h>

int gsignal (int sig);

int (*ssignal (int sig, int (*action) (int))) (int);
```

Description

gsignal and ssignal implement a software signal facility which behaves similarly to signal (Peterson 1991b).

gsignal raises the software signal that is specified by *sig*. When the software signal is raised, it causes the procedure, *action*, established for that signal to be executed.

ssignal associates a procedure, *action*, with the software signal *sig*.

Arguments

ssignal

action specifies a procedure which ssignal is to associate with the software signal *sig*. *action* is either the name of a user-defined function or one of the following manifest constants:

SIG_DFL (default)
SIG_IGN (ignore)

sig specifies the value of *sig* which is to be associated with *action*. *sig* can be an integer in the range from 1 through 17 inclusive.

gsignal

sig specifies the software signal which gsignal is to raise.

Normal Completion: Value Returned

If ssignal succeeds, it returns the *action* previously established for the specified *sig*.

gsignal returns 1 and takes no other action if *sig* equals SIG_IGN.

If an action function has been established for *sig*, the action is set to SIG_DFL and the action function is called with a *sig* argument, and gsignal returns the value that is returned to it by the action function.

Error Condition: Value Returned

ssignal returns SIG_DFL if no action has been established or *sig* is illegal.

gsignal returns 0 if *sig* has an illegal value or if no action was ever specified for *sig*.

gsignal returns 0 and takes no other action if *sig* equals SIG_DFL.

See Also

raise (C), signal (Peterson 1991b), sigset (Peterson 1991b)

stdio (S) USER-LEVEL BUFFERED I/O stdio (S)

Name

stdio—standard package for buffered I/O

Synopsis

```
#include <stdio.h>

FILE *stdin, *stdout, *stderr;
```

Description

The routines discussed below provide a complete means of accomplishing user-level buffered I/O.

User-level buffered I/O functions, macros, and some constants are declared in <stdio> and need no further declaration. Constants used are as follows:

BUFSIZ is an integer constant that specifies the size of buffers used by a particular UNIX System V implementation.

EOF (−1) is an integer constant that is returned by most integer functions that deal with streams if they encounter an error or an end of file.

FILENAME_MAX is an integer constant that specifies the size required for a character array large enough to contain the longest filename string that the implementation guarantees can be opened.

FOPEN_MAX is an integer constant that specifies the minimum number of files that the UNIX System V implementation guarantees can be open simultaneously. Not more than 255 files may be opened by fopen. File descriptors 0 through 255 are the only valid file descriptors.

Input Routines

getc and getchar are input macros. getc handles input characters quickly. fgetc, fgets, fread, fscanf, gets, getw, and scanf are higer-level input functions that use or behave as if they use getc, as does the getchar macro. These routines can be freely used with each other (as well as with the output routines discussed below).

Output Routines

putc and putchar are output macros. putc handles output characters quickly. fprintf, fputc, fputs, fwrite, printf, puts, and putw are higher-level output functions that use or behave as if they use putc, as does the putchar macro.

Other Routines

Other routines used with these I/O routines are the clearerr, feof, ferror, and fileno macros; the function versions of these macros; and fopen, freopen, setbuf, and setvbuf. setbuf and setvbuf [see setbuf (S)] can change a stream's buffering strategy.

Arguments

file_descriptor(s) associated with the C language standard open files stderr, stdin, and stdout are defined in <unistd.h> as follows:

STDERR_FILENO is associated with stderr (see *stream* below). Its value is 2.

STDIN_FILENO is associated with stdin (see *stream* below). Its value is 0.

STDOUT_FILENO is associated with stdout (see *stream* below). Its value is 1.

stream specifies a file that has buffering associated with it [see intro]. It is declared to be a pointer to FILE, a defined type. The fopen function creates descriptive information about the stream and returns a pointer that other I/O functions use to designate the stream. Three standard open streams have constant pointers that are defined in <stdio.h> as follows:

stderr is the standard error file. stderr, unlike other output streams, is unbuffered by default, but freopen [see fopen (S)] can be used to make it buffered or line buffered.

stdin is the standard input file.

stdout is the standard output file.

Except for stderr, output streams are line buffered if the output refers to a terminal. Otherwise, they are by default buffered if the output refers to a file.

If an output stream is unbuffered, data are queued for writing on the destination file or terminal as soon as they are written.

If an output stream is buffered, several characters are saved and written to the terminal or destination file as a block.

If an output stream is line buffered, each line of output is queued up to be written on the terminal as soon as a newline character is written or as soon as terminal input is requested (i.e., as soon as the line is finished).

stream_pointers point to streams. If a stream pointer is invalid, it can cause disorder serious enough to terminate the program (see individual functions for descriptions of error conditions). A constant NULL specifies a null pointer.

Normal Completion: Value Returned

See the entry for each function for a description of the value that it returns.

Error Condition: Value Returned

Most integer functions that handle streams return an integer constant EOF (−1) on end of file or when an error occurs (see descriptions of individual functions for details).

See Also

`ctermid` (S), `cuserid` (S), `fclose` (S), `ferror` (S), `fopen` (S), `fread` (S), `fseek` (S), `getc` (S), `gets` (S), `popen` (S), `printf` (S), `putc` (S), `puts` (S), `scanf` (S), `setbuf` (S), `system` (S), `tmpfile` (S), `tmpnam` (S), `ungetc` (S), `close` (Peterson 1991b), `lseek` (Peterson 1991b), `open` (Peterson 1991b), `pipe` (Peterson 1991b), `read` (Peterson 1991b), `write` (Peterson 1991b)

stdipc (C) INTERPROCESS COMMUNICATIONS stdipc (C)

Name

`stdipc: ftok`—supply a key for interprocess communication

Synopsis

```
#include <sys/types.h>
#include <sys/ipc.h>

key_t ftok (const char *path, int id);
```

Description

`ftok` provides one of several ways to form a key that `msgget` (Peterson 1991b), `semget` (Peterson 1991b), and `shmget` (Peterson 1991b) must have in order to obtain interprocess identifiers. All interprocess communication facilities require the user to supply such keys.

Any method used in forming the key should put the project ID in the most significant byte of the key and use the remaining portion of the key as a sequence number. The most significant byte of a key should refer to a project so that keys for different projects do not conflict across a system.

Unrelated processes can unintentionally interfere with each other if a system does not have a standard for the formation of keys.

Arguments

`id` is a character that uniquely identifies a project.
`path` must be the name of an existing file that the process can access.

Normal Completion: Value Returned

If `ftok` succeeds, it returns a key based on *id* and *path* that subsequent `msgget`, `semget`, and `shmget` calls can use. `ftok` will return the same key for linked files when it is called with the same value of *id*. It will return different keys when it is called with the same filename but with different values of *id*. If a file is removed after a call to `ftok` and the file is later re-created, subsequent calls to `ftok` are likely to return a different key than the key returned by the first call to `ftok`.

Error Condition: Value Returned

If *path* does not exist or is not accessible to the process, `ftok` returns `(key_t) - 1`. If a key still refers to the file specified by *path* after *path* has been passed to `ftok` and the file has been removed, subsequent calls to `ftok` with the same values of *id* and *path* will return an error.

See Also

`intro` (Peterson 1991b), `msgget` (Peterson 1991b), `semget` (Peterson 1991b), `shmget` (Peterson 1991b)

strcoll (C) STRING SORTING strocoll (C)

Name

`strcoll`—perform locale-specific string sorting

Synopsis

```
#include <string.h>

int strcoll (const char *s1, const char *s2);
```

Description

`strcoll` sorts strings. Its comparison of strings is appropriate to the program's locale for category LC_COLLATE [see `setlocale` (C)]. `strcoll` is intended for applications in which the number of comparisons per string is not large. Use `strxfrm` instead of `strcoll` if strings must be compared many times. Unlike `strcoll`, `strxfrm` performs transformation only once per string.

Arguments

`s1` specifies a string to be compared with string `s2`.
`s2` specifies a string to be compared with string `s1`.

Normal Completion: Value Returned

`strcoll` returns an integer that is greater than, equal to, or less than 0 if `s1` is respectively greater than, equal to, or less than s2.

Files

`/usr/lib/locale/LC_COLLATE` is the `LC_COLLATE` database for the *`locale`*.

See Also

`setlocale` (C), `string` (C), `strxfrm` (C), `colltbl` (AT&T 1990o), `environ` (AT&T 1990m)

strerror (C) STRINGS strerror (C)

Name

`strerror`—get an error message string

Synopsis

```
#include <string.h>

char *strerror (int errnum);
```

Description

`sterror` maps an error number that is contained in *`errnum`* to an error message string and returns a pointer to the string. `sterror` uses the same error message set as `perror` (C).

Arguments

`errnum` contains an error number to be mapped to an error message string.

Normal Completion: Value Returned

`sterror` returns a pointer to an error message string associated with an error number. Do not overwrite the returned string.

See Also

`perror` (C)

strftime (C) DATE AND TIME strftime (C)

Name

`strftime`, `asctime`, `cftime`—convert date and time to a string

Synopsis

```
#include <time.h>

int ascftime (char *s, const char *format, const
struct tm *timeptr);

int cftime (char *s, char *format, const time_t
*clock);

size_t *strftime (char *s, size_t maxsize, const
char *format, const struct tm *timeptr);
```

Description

`ascftime` has essentially the same effect as `strftime`. It is obsolete; use `strftime` instead.

`cftime` has essentially the same effect as `strftime`. It is obsolete; use `strftime` instead.

`strftime` puts characters in an array to which *`s`* points. It puts characters in the array under the control of a *`format`* string.

The output of `asctime`, `cftime`, and `strftime` is in American English by default. Use `setlocale` (C) to set the *`locale`* for *`category`* `LC_TIME` if the output of `asctime`, `cftime`, or `strftime` must be a language other than American English.

Arguments

strftime

format consists of zero or more directives and ordinary characters. Any ordinary character, including a terminating null character, is copied unchanged into the array. The default format for the program's locale is used if *format* is (char *)0. The default format is the same as that of "%c". Each directive in *format* is replaced by the appropriate characters described in the list below. The LC_TIME category of the program's locale and the time represented by *clock* values (see cftime arguments below) contained in the tm structure to which *timeptr* points (see *timeptr* below) jointly determine which characters are appropriate for replacing each directive in *format*. The characters which replace each directive are as follows:

%% has the same effect as %.

%a corresponds to the abbreviated weekday name for the locale.

%A corresponds to the full weekday name for the locale.

%b corresponds to the abbreviated month name for the locale.

%B corresponds to the full month name for the locale.

%c corresponds to the appropriate date and time representation for the locale as produced by date (AT&T 1990q).

%C corresponds to the appropriate date and time representation for the locale as produced by date (AT&T 1990q).

%d corresponds to the day of the month (01–31).

%D corresponds to the date (%m/%d/%y).

%e corresponds to the day of the month (1–31, with single digits preceded by a blank).

%h corresponds to the locale's abbreviated month name.

%H corresponds to the hour (00–23).

%I corresponds to the hour (01–12).

%j corresponds to the day number of the year (001–365).

%m corresponds to the month number (01–12).

%M corresponds to the minute (00–59).

%n corresponds to newline (\n).

%p corresponds to the equivalent of A.M. or P.M. for the locale.

%r corresponds to time as %I:%/M:%S [AM|PM].

%R corresponds to time as %H:%/M.

%S corresponds to seconds (00–61), allowing for leap seconds.

%t inserts a tab.

%T corresponds to time as %H:%/M:%S.

%U corresponds to week number (00–53), with Sunday as the first day of the first week. %U differs from %W below in using Sunday instead of Monday as the day that is counted as the first day of the week. With `%U`, week number 01 is the first week in January that starts with Sunday, and week number 00 contains those days in January before the first Sunday.

`%w` corresponds to weekday number (0–6), with Sunday = 0.

`%W` corresponds to week number (00–53), with Monday as the first day of the week. Week number 01 is the first week in January that starts with Monday. Week number 00 contains those days in January before the first Monday. See `%U` above.

`%x` corresponds to the date representation that is appropriate for the locale.

`%X` corresponds to the time representation that is appropriate for the locale.

`%y` corresponds to the year within the century (00–99).

`%Y` corresponds to the year, using the format *ccyy* (for example, 1991).

`%Z` corresponds to the time zone name or to no characters if no time zone exists. The time zone is gotten from the environment variable `TZ` [see `ctime` (C)].

maxsize specifies the maximum number of characters that can be put into the array at which *s* points.

s points to the array into which `strftime` puts characters.

timeptr points to a `tm` structure (defined in `time.h`) that contains values representing data and time.

asctime

format has the same effect as in `strftime` above, except for two differences. First, the default format is the same as `"%C"`, not `"%c"`. Second, `cftime` tries to use the value of the `CFTIME` environment variable before using the default *format*. Only if `CFTIME` is empty or undefined does `cftime` use the default *format*.

s points to the array into which `asctime` puts characters.

timeptr points to a `tm` structure that contains values representing data and time.

cftime

clock represents the current time.

format has the same effect as in `strftime` above, except for three differences. First, the default format is the same as `"%C"`, not `"%c"`. Second, `cftime` tries to use the value of the `CFTIME` environment variable before using the default *format*. Only if `CFTIME` is empty or undefined does `cftime` uses the default *format*. Third, the `LC_TIME` category of the program's locale and the time represented by *clock* (see *clock* above) values determine which characters are appropriate for replacing each directive in *format*.

s points to the array into which `cftime` puts characters.

Normal Completion: Value Returned

`asctime` and `cftime` return the number of characters that they put in the string to which *s* points. This number does not include the terminating null character.

`strftime` returns the total number of characters (not including the null-terminating character) that it puts in the string to which *s* points if the number of characters it puts into the string (including the terminating null character) is less than or equal to *maxsize*.

Error Condition: Value Returned

If the number of characters (including the terminating null character) that `strftime` puts into the string to which *s* points when it performs the conversion is greater than *maxsize*, `strftime` returns 0 and the contents of the string at which *s* points are undefined.

Files

`/usr/lib/locale/`*language*`/LC_TIME` is the file that contains date and time information. The file format is specific to the locale.

See Also

`ctime` (C), `getenv` (C), `setlocale` (C), `environ` (AT&T 1990m), `strftime` (AT&T 1990m), `timezone` (AT&T 1990m)

string (C) STRINGS string (C)

Name

`string`: `strcat`, `strchr`, `strcmp`, `strcpy`, `strcspn`, `strdup`, `strlen`, `strncat`, `strncmp`, `strncpy`, `strpbrk`, `strrchr`, `strspn`, `strstr`, `strok`—do string operations

Synopsis

```
#include <string.h>

char *strcat (char *s1, const char *s2);

char *strchr (const char *s, int c);
```

```
int strcmp (const char *s1, const char *s2);

char *strcpy (char *s1, const char *s2);

size_t strcspn (const char *s1, const char *s2);

char *strdup (const char *s1);

size_t strlen (const char *s);

char *strncat (char *s1, const char *s2, size_t n);

int strncmp (const char *s1, const char *s2, size_
t n);

char *strncpy (char *s1, const char *s2, size_t n);

char *strpbrk (const char *s1, const char *s2);

char *strrchr (const char *s, int c);

size_t strspn (const char *s1, const char *s2);

char *strstr (const char *s1, const char *s2);

char *strtok (char *s1, const char *s2);
```

Description

The functions described below assume that the default locale is "C".

Compare Two Strings

strcmp makes a lexicographical comparison of *s1* with *s2* and returns an integer that is less than, equal to, or greater than 0 if *s1* is respectively less than, equal to, or greater than s2. Characters that follow the null-terminating character are not compared.

strncmp makes a lexicographical comparison of the first n characters in s1 with s2 and returns an integer that is less than, equal to, or greater than 0 if s1 is respectively less than, equal to, or greater than s2. Characters that follow the null-terminating character are not compared.

Concatenate Two Strings

strcat appends a copy of string s2 to the end of string s1. The copy includes the terminating null character in s2. The initial character of s2 overrides the terminating null character of s1. strcat alters s1.

strncat appends a copy of at most n characters in string s2 to the end of string s1. The initial character of s2 overrides the terminating null character of s1. strncat alters s1.

Copy a String to Another String

strcpy copies string s2 to s1, including the null-terminating character of s2. Copying stops after the null-terminating character of s2 has been copied to s1.

strncpy copies n characters from string s2 to s1, adding null characters to s1 if s2 is shorter than s1 or truncating s2 if s2 is longer than s1. If the length of s2 is greater than n, the resulting string, s1, will not be null-terminated.

Duplicate a String

strdup returns a pointer to a newly created string that is a duplicate of the string to which s1 points. strdup uses malloc (C) to get space for the new string.

Find the First Occurrence in s1 of a Character String in s2

strstr finds the first occurrence in string s1 of the sequence of characters contained in string s2 (excluding the null-terminating character).

Find the First Occurrence of a Character in a String

strchr finds the first occurrence of c in the string to which s points (after first converting c to type char). strchr treats the null-terminating character as part of the string.

strpbrk finds the first occurrence in string s1 of any character contained in s2.

Find the Last Occurrence of a Character in a String

`strrchr` finds the last occurrence of *c* in the string to which *s* points (after first converting *c* to type `char`). `strrchr` treats the null-terminating character as part of the string.

Find the Length of a String

`strlen` returns the number of characters that are contained in the string to which *s* points. This count does not include the terminating null character.

Find the Length of the Initial Segment of s1 That Is/Is Not in s2

`strcspn` finds the length of the initial segment of string *s1* which is comprised entirely of characters that are not contained in string *s2*.

`strspn` finds the length of the initial segment of string *s1* which is comprised entirely of characters that are contained in string *s2*.

Find the Tokens in a String

`strtok` finds tokens in the *s1* string. More than one call to `strtok` is required in order to find all of the tokens in *s1* if *s1* contains more than one token.

`strtok` treat *s1* as a sequence of zero or more text tokens that are separated by spans of one or more characters contained in the separator string *s2*. The separator string *s2* may vary from call to call. The first call to `strtok` in which *s1* is specified returns a pointer to the first character of the first token and writes a null character in *s1* immediately after the returned token. `strtok` records its position in the *s1* string so that subsequent calls to `strtok` will process the remainder of the *s1* string. Subsequent calls to `strtok` have NULL as the first argument. In this way, subsequent calls to `strtok` process *s1* until no unprocessed tokens remain.

Arguments

c specifies a character.

n specifies the number of characters that are to be processed by a function.

In order to ensure that the correct collating sequence is used, some locales require that `strxfrm` (C) be applied to the argument strings described below.

s points to a null-terminated character string.

s1 points to a null-terminated character string. None of the functions described here checks for overflow of the array to which *s1* points.

s2 points to a null-terminated character string.

Normal Completion: Value Returned

`strcat` returns the number to the null-terminated string that results from its concatenation operation.

`strchr` returns a pointer to the first occurrence of *c* (after first converting *c* to type `char`) in the string to which *s* points.

`strcmp` returns an integer that is less than, equal to, or greater than 0 if *s1* is respectively less than, equal to, or greater than *s2*.

`strcpy` returns *s1*.

`strcspn` returns the length of the initial *s1* segment which consists entirely of characters that are not contained in *s2*.

`strdup` returns a pointer to a newly created string that is a duplicate of the string to which *s1* points.

`strlen` returns the number of characters in *s* other than the null-terminating character.

`strncat` returns the number to the null-terminated string that results from its concatenation operation.

`strncmp` returns an integer that is less than, equal to, or greater than 0 if *s1* is respectively less than, equal to, or greater than *s2*.

`strncpy` returns *s1*.

`strpbrk` returns a pointer to the first occurrence in string *s1* of any character that is contained in *s2*.

`strrchr` returns a pointer to the last occurrence of *c* (after first converting *c* to type `char`) in the string to which *s* points.

`strspn` returns the length of the initial *s1* segment which consists entirely of characters that are contained in *s2*.

`strstr` returns a pointer to the first occurrence of *s1* in *s2*. If *s2* points to the string "", `strstr` returns *s1*.

`strtok` returns a pointer to the first character of the first token if the current call to `srtok` is the first call to `strtok`.

Error Condition: Value Returned

`strchr` returns a NULL pointer if *c* is not in the string to which *s* points.
`strdup` returns a NULL pointer if it cannot create the new string.
`strstr` returns a NULL pointer if it does not find *s1* in *s2*.

See Also

`malloc` (C), `setlocale` (C), `strxfrm` (C)

Name

`strtod`, `atof`—convert a string to a double-precision number

Synopsis

```
#include &lt;stdlib.h&gt;

double atof (const char *nptr);

double strtod (const char *nptr, char **endptr);
```

Description

`strtod` scans a string that represents a number, converts it to a double-precision floating-point number, and returns a pointer to the double-precision floating-point number.

`strtod` continues its scan until it encounters an unrecognized character. During its scan, `strtod` recognizes an optional string of white-space characters [see `isspace` (C)], followed by an optional sign, followed by a string of digits that optionally contains a decimal character, followed by an optional exponent part that contains an `e` or E followed by an optional sign, followed by an integer.

`atof(`*`nptr`*`)` has the same effect as

`strtod(`*`nptr`*`, (char **)NULL)`

Arguments

`endptr` causes `strtod` to return a pointer (in the location to which *`endptr`* points) to the character that terminates `strtod`'s scan of the string to which *`nptr`* points (if *`endptr`* is unequal to `(char **)NULL`).

`nptr` points to a character string which `atof` or `strtod` converts to a floating-point number.

Normal Completion: Value Returned

`atof` or `strtod` returns a pointer to a floating-point number if it can form a number.

Error Condition: Value Returned

If `strtod` cannot form a number, it returns 0 and sets **endptr* equal to *nptr*. See the *endptr* argument above.

If the floating-point value produced by `atof` or `strtod` causes overflow, the function returns +HUGE or −HUGE (depending on the sign of the value) and sets `errno` to indicate the error condition discussed below. If the `-Xc` or `-Xa` compilation option was used, however, the function returns HUGE_VAL, not HUGE.

34 ERANGE

The value returned by `atof` or `strtod` cannot be represented within the precision permitted by the machine.

If the floating-point value produced by `atof` or `strtod` causes underflow, the function returns 0 and sets `errno` to indicate the following error condition:

34 ERANGE

The value returned by `atof` or `strtod` cannot be represented within the precision permitted by the machine.

See Also

`ctype` (C), `scanf` (S), `strtol` (C)

strtol (C) STRINGS strtol (C)

Name

`strtol`, `atoi`, `atol`, `strtoul`—convert a string to an integer

Synopsis

```
#include <stdlib.h>

int atoi (const char *str);

long atol (const char *str);

long strtol (const char *str, char **ptr, int base);

unsigned long strtoul (const char *str, char **ptr,
int base);
```

Description

The functions discussed below convert a string to a signed long integer or to an unsigned long integer. The long integer result can be truncated to an integer by an explicit cast or by assignment.

Conversion of Strings to Signed Long Integers

`atol(str)` has the same effect as `strtol(str, (char **)NULL, 10)` except for its behavior when an error occurs.

`strtol` converts the character string to which *`str`* points to a signed long integer value. `strtol` scans its input string, *`str`*, until it encounters the first character (if any) that is inconsistent with the base. `strtol` ignores leading white-space characters [see `isspace` (C)] during its scan.

Conversion of Strings to Unsigned Long Integers

`atoi(str)` has the same effect as `strtoul(str, (char **)NULL, 10)` except for its behavior when an error occurs.

`strtoul` has the same effect as `strtol` except that `strtoul` returns an unsigned long integer instead of a signed long integer and `strtoul` accepts larger input values than `strtol` (see *`str`* above).

Arguments

`base` is a positive number no larger than 36 used for the base of the conversion from character string to long integer. Any leading zeros after an optional leading sign are ignored. A leading "`0x`" or "`0X`" is ignored if *`base`* equals 16. If *`base`* equals 0, a leading 0 after an optional leading sign specifies octal conversion, and a leading "`0x`" or "`0X`" after an optional leading sign specifies hexadecimal conversion; otherwise, a decimal conversion base is used.

`ptr` causes `strtol` or `strtoul` to return a pointer to the location of a character that terminates the scan of the *`str`* string in the location to which *`ptr`* points (if *`ptr`* is unequal to `(char **)NULL`.

`str` specifies the character string which is to be converted to an integer. `strtol` no longer accepts input values that are greater than LONG_MAX; use `strtoul` instead if a value of *`str`* larger than LONG_MAX must be converted.

Normal Completion: Value Returned

`atoi` returns a pointer to an unsigned long integer containing the value represented by the character string *`str`*.

`atol` returns a pointer to a signed long integer containing the value represented by the character string *`str`*.

`strtol` returns a pointer to a signed long integer containing the value represented by the character string *`str`*.

`strtoul` returns a pointer to an unsigned long integer containing the value represented by the character string *`str`*.

Error Condition: Value Returned

`strtol` returns 0 and sets `errno` to indicate the following error condition if *`base`* is greater than 36:
122 EINVAL
`strtol` was supplied with an invalid argument.
`strtol` returns LONG_MAX or LONG_MIN (depending on the sign of *`str`*) and sets `errno` to indicate the following error if the value of *`str`* will cause overflow:
34 ERANGE
The value returned by `strtol` cannot be represented within the precision permitted by the machine.
`strtoul` returns ULONG_MAX and sets `errno` to indicate the following error if the value of *`str`* will cause overflow.
34 ERANGE
The value returned by `strtoul` cannot be represented within the precision permitted by the machine.

See Also

`ctype` (C), `scanf` (S), `strtod` (C)

strxfrm (C)	**STRINGS**	**strxfrm (C)**

Name

`strxfrm`—transform a string

Synopsis

```
#include <string.h>

size_t strxfrm (char *s1, const char *s2, size_t
n);
```

Description

`strxfrm` transforms the string to which *`s2`* points and puts the resulting string in the array to which *`s1`* points. If the objects to which *`s1`* and *`s2`* point overlap, the result is undefined.
The collating sequence used in the transformation is specified by the program's locale for category LC_COLLATE [see `setlocale` (C)].

If `strcmp` is applied to two transformed strings, it will return the same result as if `strcoll` were applied to the two original strings before they were transformed.

Arguments

n specifies the number of characters (including the null-terminating character) which `strxfrm` will put in the array to which *s1* points. *s1* can be a null pointer if *n* equals 0.

s1 specifies the array that is to receive the transformed *s2* string.

s2 specifies the string that is to be transformed.

Normal Completion: Value Returned

If `strxfrm` succeeds, it returns the length of the transformed string (excluding the null-terminating character). The contents of array *s1* are unpredictable if the value that `strxfrm` returns is greater than *n*.

Error Condition: Value Returned

If `strxfrm` fails, it returns `(size_t) - 1`.

Files

`/usr/lib/locale/`*`locale`*`/LC_COLLATE` contains the `LC_COLLATE` database that specifies the collating sequence used by the *locale*.

See Also

`setlocale` (C), `strcoll` (C), `string` (C), `colltbl` (AT&T 1990o), `environ` (AT&T 1990m)

swab (C) STRINGS swab (C)

Name

`swab`—swap bytes

Synopsis

```
#include <stdlib.h>

void swab (const char *from, char *to, int nbytes);
```

Description

`swab` is used to swap adjacent bytes in an array. It copies *`nbytes`* from the array to which *`from`* points to the array to which *`to`* points, swapping adjacent odd and even bytes.

Arguments

`from` specifies the array whose adjacent bytes are to be swapped.

`nbytes` specifies the number of bytes which `swab` is to process. *`nbytes`* should be even and should have a nonnegative value. If *`nbytes`* is odd and positive, `swab` uses *`nbytes`* − 1 instead of *`nbytes`*. `swab` does not swap bytes if *`nbytes`* is negative.

`to` specifies the array that receives the swapped bytes.

sysconf (S) CONFIGURABLE SYSTEM VARIABLES sysconf (S)

Name

`sysconf`—get values of configurable system variables

Synopsis

```
#include <unistd.h>

long sysconf (int name);
```

Description

`sysconf` ascertains and returns the value of a system variable (configurable system limit or option).

Arguments

`name` specifies the system variable whose value is to be ascertained and returned by `sysconf`. *`name`* is one of the set of symbolic constants defined in `<unistd.h>`. See "Normal Completion: Values Returned" below.

Normal Completion: Value Returned

`sysconf` returns one of the system variables defined in `<limits.h>` and `<unistd.h>`. The system variable that it returns depends on the value of *`name`* as follows:

_SC_ARG_MAX causes the return of ARG_MAX.

_SC_CHILD_MAX causes the return of CHILD_MAX.

_SC_CLK_TCK causes the return of CLK_TCK, whose value equals the value of sysconf(_SC_CLK_TCK); CLK_TCK can be variable, and it may or may not be a compile-time constant.

_SC_JOB_CONTROL causes the return of _POSIX_JOB_CONTROL.

_SC_LOGNAME_MAX causes the return of LOGNAME_MAX.

_SC_NGROUPS_MAX causes the return of NGROUPS_MAX.

_SC_OPEN_MAX causes the return of OPEN_MAX. This value may be changed by a call to setrlimit [see getrlimit (C)].

_SC_PAGESIZE causes the return of PAGESIZE.

_SC_PASS_MAX causes the return of PASS_MAX.

_SC_SAVED_IDS causes the return of _POSIX_DAVED_IDS.

_SC_VERSION causes the return of _POSIX_VERSION.

_SC_XOPEN_VERSION causes the return of _XOPEN_VERSION.

Error Condition: Value Returned

If sysconf fails because *name* is not defined on the system, it returns −1 but does not change the value of errno.

If sysconf fails because *name* has an invalid value, it returns −1 and sets errno to indicate the error condition.

See Also

fpathconf (C)

system (C) PROCESS CONTROL system (C)

Name

system—issue a command string to the shell

Synopsis

```
#include <stdlib.h>

int system (const char *string);
```

Description

system gives *string* to the shell [see sh (AT&T 1990q)] as input, as if *string* were typed as a command at the terminal. system executes fork

fork (Peterson 1991b) to create a child process that, in turn, execs /sbin/sh in order to execute *string* cbsee exec (Peterson 1991b)]. The current process waits until the shell has completed execution, after which it returns the exit status of the shell in the format that waitpid (Peterson 1991b) specifies.

Arguments

string specifies a string of characters to be input to the shell as a command.

Normal Completion: Value Returned

If *string* is a NULL pointer, system ascertains whether /sbin/sh exists and is executable. If /sbin/sh is available, system returns a nonzero value. Otherwise, system returns 0.

Error Condition: Value Returned

If fork or exec fails when system invokes it, system returns −1 and sets errno to indicate the error condition. If system fails, it returns −1 and sets errno to indicate one of the following error conditions:

4 EINTR

system was interrupted by an interrupt, quit, or other asynchronous signal which the user chose to catch.

11 EAGAIN

If the new process is created, the system limit on the total number of processes will be exceeded.

12 ENOMEM

The new process has asked for more memory than the system limit, MAXMEM, allows.

See Also

waitpid (C), exec (Peterson 1991b), sh (AT&T 1990q)

tcsetpgrp (C) SET PROCESS GROUP IDs tcsetpgrp (C)

Name

tcsetpgrp—set the group ID of a terminal foreground process

Synopsis

```
#include <unistd.h>

int tcsetpgrp (int fildscr, pid_t pgid);
```

Description

`tcsetpgrp` sets the foreground process group ID of the specified controlling terminal to the value specified by *pgid*.

Arguments

fildscr specifies a terminal whose process group ID is to be set to *pgid*. The file associated with *fildscr* must be the calling process's controlling terminal. Also, the controlling terminal must be associated with the session of the calling process.

pgid specifies the value to which the process group ID of the foreground process of the controlling terminal is to be set. *pgid* must equal the process group ID of a process that is in the same session as the calling process.

Normal Completion

If `tcsetpgrp` succeeds, it returns 0.

Error Condition: Value Returned

If `tcsetpgrp` fails, it returns -1 and sets `errno` to indicate one of the following error conditions:

1 EPERM

pgid is not equal to the process group ID of any existing process in the same session as the calling process.

9 EBADF

fildscr is not a valid file descriptor.

22 EINVAL

fildscr specifies a terminal that does not support the `tcsetpgrp` function, or *pgid* is invalid.

25 ENOTTY

The calling process lacks a controlling terminal, or the controlling terminal is not associated with the session to which the calling process belongs, or the specified file is not the controlling terminal.

See Also

tcsetpgrp (C), tcsetsid (C), termio (AT&T 1990o)

tmpfile (S) FILES tmpfile (S)

Name

tmpfile—create a temporary file

Synopsis

```
#include <stdio.h>

FILE *tmpfile (void);
```

Description

tmpfile creates a temporary file by using tmpnam (S). The temporary file is automatically deleted when the file is closed or when the process which uses it terminates.

Arguments

None

Normal Completion: Value Returned

If tmpfile succeeds in creating a temporary file, it returns a corresponding FILE pointer.

Error Condition: Value Returned

If tmpfile fails to open a temporary file, it returns a NULL pointer.

See Also

fopen (S), mktemp (C), perror (C), stdio (S), tmpnam (S), creat (Peterson 1991b), open (Peterson 1991b), unlink (Peterson 1991b)

tmpnam (S) FILES tmpnam (S)

Name

tmpnam, tempnam—make a name for a temporary file

Synopsis

```
#include <stdio.h>

char *tempnam(const char *dir, const char pfx);

char *tmpnam(char *s);
```

Description

tempnam and tmpnam generate filenames for temporary files. These functions generate different filenames each time they are called, except that if tempnam or tmpnam is called more than TMP_MAX [defined in <stdio.h>] times by one process, it begins to reuse previously used filenames.

If every process that creates a temporary file uses tempnam, tmpnam, or mktmp to do so, each filename created will be unique. Otherwise, it is possible for one process to create a temporary file that has the same name as a temporary file created by another process if one process creates a file between the time the other process creates a file and the time it opens the file.

tmpnam, tempnam, fopen, and creat create files that are temporary in the sense that they are in a directory that is meant for temporary use and they have unique names. However, the user must see to it that such files are removed when their usefulness ends.

In generating a filename, tmpnam always uses the path prefix defined as P_tmpdir in <stdio.h>.

tempnam, on the other hand, lets the user control the choice of a directory by using the *dir* argument tempnam. tempnam uses malloc (X) to obtain space for the filename. The pointer which tempnam returns can be used as an argument to free.

Arguments

dir points to the directory which will contain the temporary file created by `tempnam`. If *dir* is NULL or the string to which it points does not name an appropriate directory, `tempnam` uses the path prefix `P_tmpdir` defined in <`stdio.h`>. If that directory is unavailable, `tempnam` will use `/tmp` instead. If the user's environment has the variable TMPDIR, its value overrides *dir* and specifies the directory used for temporary files.

pfx specifies a prefix for the name of the temporary file created by `tempnam`. *pfx* may be NULL or it may point to a string of as many as five characters that are to be used as the first few characters of the name of the temporary file.

s causes `tmpnam` to put its result in an internal static area and return a pointer to that area if *s* is NULL. See "Normal Completion: Value Returned" below for the result when *s* is not NULL.

Normal Completion: Value Returned

If `tempnam` succeeds, it returns a pointer to the space that contains the constructed filename.

If `tmpnam` succeeds and *s* is NULL, it returns a pointer to a static area that contains the temporary filename it created. The next `tmpnam` call will destroy the contents of the static area.

If `tmpnam` succeeds and *s* is not NULL, `tmpnam` assumes that *s* points to an array that has at least `L_tmpnam` bytes [`L_tmpnam` is a constant defined in <`stdio.h`>], puts its result in that array, and returns *s*.

Error Condition: Value Returned

If `tempnam` fails for any reason (for example, the appropriate directory could not be found, or `malloc` failed and left too little space for the filename), it returns a NULL pointer.

Files

`p_tmpdir /var/tmp`

See Also

`fopen` (S), `malloc` (C), `mktemp` (C), `tmpfile` (S), `creat` (Peterson 1991b), `unlink` (Peterson 1991b)

truncate (C) FILES truncate (C)

Name

`truncate`, `ftruncate`—set a file to a given length

Synopsis

```
#include <unistd.h>

int ftruncate (int fildscr, off_t length);

int truncate (const char *path, off_t length);
```

Description

`truncate` or `ftruncate` sets the length of the specified file to the number of bytes specified by *length*.

Arguments

fildscr specifies the file whose length `ftruncate` sets. The file must be open for writing in order for `ftruncate` to be executed. Also, the effective user ID of the calling process must have write permission on the specified file for `ftruncate` to be executed.

length specifies the length to which the specified file is to be set. If the file length was greater than *length* before `truncate` or `ftruncate` was called, the bytes past *length* will no longer be available. If the file was shorter than *length*, all bytes from the EOF before the `truncate` or `ftruncate` call to the EOF after the `truncate` or `ftruncate` call will be read as zeros.

path specifies the file whose length `truncate` sets. The effective user ID of the calling process must have write permission on the specified file for `truncate` to be executed.

Normal Completion: Value Returned

If `truncate` or `ftruncate` succeeds, it returns 0.

Error Condition: Value Returned

If `truncate` or `ftruncate` fails, it returns -1 and sets `errno` to indicate the error condition.

`truncate` fails if one or more of the following error conditions occurs:

2 `ENOENT`

path specified a nonexistent file or directory.

4 `EINTR`

An asynchronous signal (for example, an interrupt or quit), which the user has decided to catch, occurred while a `truncate` was executing. If execution resumes after the signal has been processed, it will seem as if the interrupted routine returned this `EINTR`.

5 `EIO`

A physical I/O error occurred. Sometimes this error may be announced on a call following the one to which it actually applies.

13 `EACCES`

- Search permission on some component of the path prefix is denied.
- Write permission is denied on the file to which *path* points.

14 `EFAULT`

path points outside the address space of the process.

20 `ENOTDIR`

A directory is required, but the argument supplied is not a directory.

21 `EISDR`

Writing on a directory is not allowed, but an attempt was made to do so.

22 `EINVAL`

path does not specify an ordinary file.

23 `ENFILE`

Temporarily, no more `open`s can be executed because the system table is full, that is, the maximum number of files, `SYS_OPEN`, are already open.

24 `EMFILE`

An attempt was made to open more than {`OPEN_MAX`} file descriptors at one time.

26 `ETXTBSY`

The file to which *path* points is a pure-procedure program (shared text) that is being executed, but an attempt was made to open it.

30 `EROFS`

The file to which *path* points is mounted on a read-only file system, but an attempt was made to modify the file.

67 `ENOLINK`

path points to a remote machine. This error occurs if there is no virtual circuit (link) to a remote machine. This error is specific to remote file sharing (RFS).

74 `EMULTIHOP`

Some components of *path* specify hopping to remote multiple machines. The file system type does not permit this. The error is specific to remote file sharing (RFS).

78 ENAMETOOLONG

Either the path argument length is greater than {PATH_MAX}, or _POSIX_NO_TRUNC is in effect and the length of a path component is greater than {NAME_MAX} [see `limits` (AT&T 1990m)].

90 ELOOP

The number of symbolic links encountered while the pathname was being traversed is greater than MAXSYMLINKS.

`ftruncate` fails if one or more of the following error conditions occurs:

4 EINTR

An asynchronous signal (for example, an interrupt or quit), which the user has decided to catch, occurred while `ftruncate` was executing. If execution resumes after the signal has been processed, it will seem as if the interrupted routine returned this EINTR error condition.

5 EIO

A physical I/O error occurred. Sometimes this error may be announced on a call following the one to which it actually applies.

9 EBADF

fildscr is not a file descriptor that is open for writing.

11 EAGAIN

`ftruncate` failed because the file exists, mandatory file/record locking is set, and there are record locks on the file [see `chmod` (Peterson 1991b)].

22 EINVAL

fildscr is not associated with an ordinary file.

67 ENOLINK

fildscr points to a remote machine. See "67 ENOLINK" under the `truncate` error entries above.

See Also

`fcntl` (Peterson 1991b), `open` (Peterson 1991b)

tsearch (C) FILES tsearch (C)

Name

`tsearch`, `tdelete`, `tfind`, `twalk`—manipulate binary search trees

Synopsis

```
#include <search.h>

void *tdelete (const void *key, void **rootp, int
(*compar) (const void * , const void *));

void *tfind (const void *key, void * const *rootp,
int (*compar) (const void * , const void *));
```

```
void *tsearch (const void *key, void **rootp, int
(*compar) (const void * , const void *));
```

```
void *twalk (void *root, void(*action) (void *,
VISIT, int));
```

Description

`tdelete`, `tfind`, `tsearch`, and `twalk` manage binary search trees. These routines are based on the Knuth (6.2.2) Algorithms T and D. The user must supply a comparison routine that these functions can use to compare tree elements.

The user-supplied comparison routine has two arguments. These arguments point to the elements that are being compared. The comparison routine returns an integer that is less than, equal to, or greater than 0 if the element to which the first argument points is respectively less than, equal to, or greater than the element to which the second argument points. Arbitrary data may appear in the elements being compared because the comparison function need not compare every byte.

`tsearch` is used both to build and to access the binary tree. If it finds the tree datum it seeks, it returns a pointer to the datum. Otherwise, it inserts the datum in the tree and returns a pointer to it. `tsearch` copies only pointers, not other data. The calling routine must store any data which require storage.

`tdelete` deletes a node from a binary search tree.

`tfind` searches for a datum in the tree.

`twalk` traverses a binary search tree. At each node in the traversal, it executes the *`action`* routine (see the `twalk` arguments below). *`action`* has three arguments: *`first_argument`*, *`second_argument`*, and *`third_argument`*.

`first_argument` is the address of the tree node that is being visited.

`second_argument` is the first, second, or third value from an enumeration data type *`typedef`* `enum` {*`preorder`*, *`postorder`*, *`endorder`*, *`leaf`*} `VISIT` [defined in `<search.h>`] if this is respectively the first, second, or third time that the node has been visited during a depth-first, left-to-right tree traversal. *`second_argument`* is the fourth value, *`leaf`*, of the enumeration data type if the node is a leaf. The terms "preorder," "postorder," and "endorder" refer respectively to visting a node before visiting any of its children, visiting a node after visiting its left child but before visting its right child, and visiting a node after visiting any of its children.

`third_argument` specifies the level of the node in the tree, with the root having level 0.

Arguments

`tdelete`

`tdelete` has the same arguments as `tsearch`.

rootp points to a variable that will be changed if the node that was deleted was the root of the binary search tree.

`tfind`

`tfind` has the same arguments as `tsearch`.

`tsearch`

compar is a user-supplied comparison function.

key points to a datum that is to be accessed or stored. The pointer to *key* should be of type pointer-to-element and cast to type pointer-to-character.

rootp points to another variable that points to the tree root. If the variable to which *rootp* points is NULL, the tree is empty and the variable will be set to point to the tree datum which will be located at the tree root. If the calling function alters the pointer that points to the root, the results are undefined.

`twalk`

action specifies the name of a routine which is to be executed at each node of the binary search tree.

root specifies the root of the tree which it is to traverse. Any node of a binary search tree can be used as the root for a traversal below that tree node. *root* has one less level of indirection than the *rootp* arguments of `tdelete` and `tsearch`.

Normal Completion: Value Returned

`tdelete` returns a pointer to the parent of the deleted node if it finds the node.

`tfind` returns a pointer to a tree datum that equals **key* if such a datum exists.

`tsearch` returns a pointer to a tree datum that equals **key* if such a datum exists. Otherwise, `tsearch` inserts **key* in the tree and returns a pointer to it.

Error Condition: Value Returned

`tdelete` returns a NULL pointer if it does not find the datum it seeks.
`tdelete` and `tfind` return a NULL pointer if *rootp* is NULL on entry.
`tfind` returns a NULL pointer if it does not find the datum it seeks.

`tsearch` returns a NULL pointer if there is not enough space available to create a new node.

See Also

`bsearch` (C), `hsearch` (C), `lsearch` (C)

ttyname (C) I/O DEVICES ttyname (C)

Name

`ttyname`, `isatty`—find the name of a terminal

Synopsis

```
#include <stdlib.h>

char *ttyname (int fildscr);

int isatty (int fildscr);
```

Description

`isatty` ascertains whether *`fildscr`* is associated with a terminal.
`ttynam` gets the name of the terminal that is associated with the *`fildscr`* file descriptor.

Arguments

`fildscr` specifies a file descriptor.

Normal Completion: Value Returned

If `ttyname` succeeds, it returns a pointer to a string that contains the null-terminated pathname of the terminal that is associated with the *`fildscr`* file descriptor. The pointer which `ttyname` returns points to a static data area that is overwritten by each subsequent `ttyname` call.
If *`fildscr`* is associated with a terminal, `isatty` returns 1. Otherwise, it returns 0.

Error Condition: Value Returned

If *`fildscr`* is not associated with a terminal device in the `/dev` directory, `ttyname` returns a NULL pointer.

Files

`/dev/*`

Name

`ttyslot`—get the slot in the `utmp` file of the current user

Synopsis

```
#include <stdlib.h>

int ttyslot (void);
```

Description

`ttslot` gets the index of the current user's entry in the `/var/adm/utmp` file. `ttslot` gets the index by scanning files in `/dev` for the name of the terminal that is associated with the standard input, the standard output, or the standard error output (0, 1, or 2).

Arguments

None

Normal Completion: Value Returned

If `ttslot` succeeds, it returns the index of the current user's entry in the `/var/adm/utmp` file.

Error Condition: Value Returned

If `ttslot` encounters an error while searching for the terminal name, it returns −1. It also returns −1 if no terminal is associated with the standard input, the standard output, or the standard error output.

Files

`/var/adm/utmp`

See Also

`getut` (C), `ttyname` (C)

ungetc (S) CHARACTER I/O ungetc (S)

Name

`ungetc`—push a character back onto the input stream

Synopsis

```
#include <stdio.h>

int ungetc (int c, FILE *stream);
```

Description

`ungetc` inserts a specified character *c* in the buffer that is associated with an input *stream*. The next call to `getc` (S) on the *stream* will return *c*. If `ungetc` succeeds in inserting *c*, it clears the EOF indicator associated with *stream*.

It is guaranteed that four bytes can be pushed back.

After all of the pushed-back characters in the buffer associated with *stream* are read or discarded, the value of the file position indicator for the specified stream will be the same as it was before the characters were pushed back.

`fseek`, `fsetpos` (C), and `rewind` [see `getc` (S)] erase all memory of characters inserted in the buffer for the stream on which they are applied.

Arguments

c specifies a character that is to be converted to an `unsigned char` and inserted into the buffer that is associated with the specified input *stream* (see `intro`).

stream specifies the stream whose buffer is to receive the character pushed back by `ungetc`.

Normal Completion: Value Returned

If `ungetc` succeeds in inserting *c* in the buffer, it returns *c* and does not change the file that is associated with *stream*.

Error Condition: Value Returned

If *c* equals EOF, `ungetc` inserts nothing in the buffer and returns EOF. If `ungetc` is unable to insert *c* in the buffer, it returns EOF.

See Also

fseek (S), fsetpos (C), getc (S), setbuf (S), stdio (S)

vprintf (S) FORMATTED I/O vprintf (S)

Name

vprintf, vfprintf, vsprintf—print formatted output from the argument list

Synopsis

```
#include <stdarg.h>
#include <stdio.h>
```

int vfprintf (FILE **stream*, const char **format*, va_list *ap*);

int vprintf (const char **format*, va_list *ap*);

int vsprintf (char **s*, const char **format*, va_list *ap*);

Description

vfprintf, vprintf, and vsprintf are character output functions that can have a variable number of arguments. The arguments can have variable data types.

vfprintf, vprintf, and vsprintf have the same effects as fprintf, printf, and sprintf, respectively. However, vfprintf, vprintf, and vsprintf are called with an argument list as defined by the <stdarg.h> header file (see the *ap* argument below) instead of being called with a variable argument list. This makes vfprintf, vprintf, and vsprintf portable, unlike fprintf, printf, or sprintf, because different machines have different conventions for passing arguments.

Argument

ap is of the va_list data type. It is an argument of the va_arg, va_end, and va_start macros that are used for advancing through a list of arguments whose number and data types may vary. The valist data type and the va_arg, va_end, and va_start, macros are defined in <stdarg.h>. These macros have the effects discussed below.

void va_start(va_list *ap*, *parmN*); initializes *ap* for subsequent use by va_arg and va_end. It is called before any of the unnamed arguments are accessed. Together with va_end, va_start may be used to make multiple traversals of the function argument list, each traversal bracketed by `vastart` and `va_end`.

The parameters of `va_start` are as follows:

ap is the variable initialized by `va_start`.

parmN identifies the rightmost parameter in the variable parameter list (the parameter just before the `, ...`). This parameter must not be declared with the `register` storage class, or with an array or function type, or with the data type that results from default argument promotions; otherwise, the behavior of `va_start` is undefined. *parmN* is required under strict ANSI compilation but need not be supplied under other compilation modes. Under compilation modes other than strict ANSI, the second parameter of `va_start` can be left empty [i.e., `va_start(va_list ap,)`], allowing for routines that have no parameters before the `...` in the variable argument list.

type `va_arg(va_list` *ap*, *type*`);` expands to an expression that has the same type and value as the next argument of the function call.

The parameters of `va_arg` are as follows:

ap should have been initialized by `va_start` before `va_arg` was called. Each call to `va_arg` changes *ap* so that the values of successive arguments of the `vfprintf`, `vprintf`, or `vsprintf` function are returned in turn.

type specifies the type name of the next function argument that is to be returned. The type name must be specified in such a way that the type of a pointer to an object of the specified *type* can be created by prepending * to the specified *type*. The behavior of `va_arg` is undefined if *type* is not compatible with the actual type of the next argument (as promoted according to default promotion rules) or if no actual next argument exists.

`void va_end(valist` *ap*`);` cleans up after `va_start` and `va_arg`. It makes multiple traversals of the function argument list possible.

format specifies a format string that controls the conversion of output from `vfprintf`, `vprintf`, or `vsprintf`.

s specifies the character array where `vsprintf` places its output.

stream specifies the stream where `vprintf` places its output.

Normal Completion: Value Returned

If `vfprintf` or `vprintf` succeeds, it returns the number of characters transmitted.

Error Condition: Value Returned

If `vfprintf` or `vprintf` fails, it returns −1.

See Also

`printf` (S), `stdarg` (AT&T 1990m)

Part 3

libelf ELF Access Library

Part 3 has three sections:

- An introduction to `libelf` ELF access library routines,
- A classification of routines in the `libelf library, and`
- Descriptions of `libelf` library routines in alphabetical order.

intro (E) INTRODUCTION TO `libelf` ROUTINES intro (E)

Name

`intro`—introduction to `libelf` ELF object file access routines

Synopsis

```
cc [flag ...] file ... -lelf [library ...]
#include <libelf.h>
```

Description

The purpose of functions in the ELF (Executable and Linking Format) access library is to enable a program to manipulate ELF object files, archive files, and archive members.

In order for a program to use the ELF access library, the program must be compiled using the appropriate values of *`file`*, *`flag`*, and *`library`* (see "Arguments" below).

ELF Header Files

The `<libelf.h>` header must be included. It contains type and function declarations for all ELF access library services.

Information in the ELF header files consists of a part that is common to all processors and a part that is specific to one processor. If the `<sys/elf_`*NAME*`>` header file is included (where *NAME* matches the processor symbol that appears in the ELF file header), the program can make available the information that is specific to the processor. At present, the values of *NAME* are as follows (others will be added in the future):

`M32` identifies the AT&T WE 32100 processor.
`SPARC` identifies the SPARC processor.
`386` identifies the Intel 80386 processor.
`486` identifies the Intel 80486 processor.
`860` identifies the Intel 80860 processor.
`68K` identifies the Motorola 68000 processor.
`88K` identifies the Motorola 88000 processor.

For example, the processor-specific information for the Intel 80386 processor can be gotten by including the header files `<libelf.h>` and `<sys/elf_386.h>`. Only the information common to all processors can be visible if the `<sys/elf_386.h>` header file is not included.

ELF Versions

There can be three different ELF file versions in connection with a program. First, the access library is compiled with header files that identify its version. Second, an ELF object file contains a value that identifies its version. Finally, the header files with which an application program is compiled identify its version. All three of these versions should be the same, but in fact they may differ [see `elf_version` (E)].

File Classes

The ELF access library can work with several different kinds of object files produced by a variety of computer architectures, including multiple processors. An important way in which object files differ is in their capacity or class. For example, a 32-bit class supports architectures in which a 32-bit object can represent addresses, file offsets, and so on, as follows:

- An `Elf32_Addr` file object represents an unsigned address.
- An `Elf32_Half` file object represents an unsigned medium integer.
- An `Elf32_Off` file object represents an unsigned file offset.
- An `Elf32_Sword` file object represents a signed larger integer.
- An `Elf32_Word` file object represents an unsigned large integer.
- An `unsigned char` file object represents an unsigned small integer.

If it becomes necessary, file objects of other sizes will be defined to support machines with larger or smaller basic object sizes. Some of the functions discussed in this chapter [for example, `elf32_getehdr`] deal with the objects of a particular class. Others functions are independent of class [for example, `elf_begin` (E)]. The form of the name of a function indicates whether or not it is class dependent. For example, if "`32`" follows "`elf`" in the name of a function, it deals with objects of the 32-bit class.

Data Representations

The ELF access library has translation routines for converting between file representations and memory representations. Some library routines leave translation to application programs. Others convert data automatically. Whatever the case, any program that creates object files must write file-typed objects to such files. Also, any program that reads object files must read file-typed objects from such files [see `elf_xlate` (E) and `elf_fsize` (E)].

Programs can take full control over sematics and the layouts of object files, explicitly translating data, or they can use the high-level interface that the library provides for translating data. The high-level interface hides many details of object files from programs [see `elf_begin` for details].

In cross-compilation environments, there are two parallel sets of objects. One set corresponds to the native memory image of a program that is creating some files for use on a target machine. The other set corresponds to the files that are to be used on the target machine. The two files may have different byte orders. The sizes of basic objects in the two sets of files may differ, that is, the files may belong to different file classes [see `elf_fsize` (E) for additional details].

Library Names

Names associated with the ELF access library can take the following forms:

`elf_`*`name`* is the class-dependent name for a routine that performs a service, *`name`*, for the program.

`elf32_`*`name`* is the name for a routine that performs a service, *`name`*, for the program for 32-bit class files.

`Elf_`*`Type`* is the class-dependent name for a data type, *`Type`*.

`Elf32_`*`Type`* is the name for a data type, *`Type`*, for 32-bit class files.

ELF_C_*CMD* specifies one of the values of the `Elf_Cmd` enumeration. Such values are used by several functions as commands to control their action. The values can range from 0 through `ELF_C_NUM - 1`.

ELF_F_*FLAG* is used as a flag by several functions that control library action and/or status. Flags consist of bits that can be combined.

`ELF32_FSZ_`*TYPE* gives the file size (in bytes) for ELF types for files of the 32-bit class [see `elf_size` (E)].

ELF_K_*KIND* is used by `elf_kind` (E) to identify the *KIND* of file that is associated with a descriptor. Values of *KIND* are members of the `Elf_Kind` enumeration, an enumeration that ranges from 0 through ELF_K_NUM - 1.

ELF_T_*TYPE* is used to specify types by functions such as `elf_xlate` that have to deal with multiple types. *TYPE* specifies the desired type. Values of ELF_T_*TYPE* are members of the `Elf_Type` enumeration. These values can range from 0 through ELF_T_NUM - 1.

System Services

ELF library access routines such as `elf_begin` assume that a program can hold an entire file in memory without explicitly using temporary files. Such library routines bring data into memory and thereafter perform operations on the memory copy. If a program needs to read or write large object files, it must execute on a machine that has a virtual address space large enough to handle the entire file. Also, if the operating system limits the number of files that can be open at one time, the program can use `elf_cntl` to get the data from a file, after which it can close the file descriptor and reuse it.

If the higher-level interface to files that `elf_begin` (E) (see above) and related routines provide is inappropriate for a program to use, it can call the `elf_xlate` (E) data translation routines directly. These routines leave input and output operations to the program, allowing it to control its input and output models.

Arguments

Some of the arguments discussed below (*`file`*, *`flag`*, and *`library`*) are arguments for the compiler. Others are arguments of various routines discussed later in this chapter.

`data descriptor` allows the program to manipulate pieces of information that are in a file section (see *ELF `descriptor`* and *`section descriptor`* below). Each *`data descriptor`* belongs to a single *`section descriptor`*, each *`section descriptor`* belongs to a single *ELF `descriptor`*, and each *ELF `descriptor`* belongs to a single file.

Descriptors provide private file handles that a program can use to handle a file and its pieces. Even though descriptors are private, different descriptors can give access to the same data. For example, a program can combine several input files, using input data to create or update another file. The program can get a data descriptor for an input section and a data descriptor for an output section. It can then reuse the input descriptor's data to update the output descriptor; that is, although the two descriptors are distinct, they can share data bytes. This avoids the space overhead that is required if duplicate buffers are used. It also avoids the performance overhead which would be required if data were to be copied from one buffer to another.

ELF descriptor is used by a program to communicate with higher-level routines, such as elf_end (E) or elf_cntl (E). The program can use elf_begin (E) to get a new *ELF descriptor* through which it addresses the structures and information in an ELF file. A program can use such an *ELF descriptor* both to read and to write files.

file specifies files to be linked or compiled.

flag specifies compiler options.

library specifies libraries such as an ELF access library.

section descriptor can be gotten by a program after it gets an *ELF descriptor*. After it gets a *section descriptor*, the program uses it to manipulate the sections of a file [see elf_getscn (E)]. Sections of a file hold most of the real information about a file (the data, symbol table, text, and so on). A *section descriptor* is to an *ELF descriptor* as a file section is to a file.

See Also

elf_begin (E), elf_cntl (E), elf_end (E), elf_error (E), elf_fill (E), elf_flag (E), elf_fsize (E), elf_getarhdr (E), elf_getarsym (E), elf_getbase (E), elf_getdata (E), elf_getehdr (E), elf_getident (E), elf_getphdr (E), elf_getscn (E), elf_getshdr (E), elf_hash (E), elf_kind (E), elf_next (E), elf_rand (E), elf_rawfile (E), elf_strptr (E), (E), elf_update (E), elf_version (E), elf_xlate (E), a.out (AT&T 1990m), ar (AT&T 1990m), cof2elf (Peterson 1991a), "Object Files" chapter (AT&T 1990g)

class (E) CLASSIFICATION OF libelf ROUTINES class (E)

Name

class—classification of libelf ELF access library routines

Description

This section classifies the routines in the libelf ELF object file access library and points to descriptions of these routines elsewhere in this book.

Fields and Variables

Files

File Descriptor

Headers, Tables, and Data Structures

I/O Operations

Libraries

elf_begin (E) CREATE AN ELF DESCRIPTOR elf_begin (E)

Name

elf_begin—make a file descriptor

Synopsis

cc [*flag* . . .] *file* . . . -lelf [*library* . . .]
#include <libelf.h>

Elf *elf_begin (int *fildscr*, Elf_Cmnd *cmd*, Elf **ref*);

Description

elf_begin and related routines [e.g., elf_end (E), elf_next (E), and elf_rand (E)] do I/O chores on behalf of application programs. These routines provide a higher-level interface to ELF files. The interface hides many details of object files from application programs that prefer not to translate data explicitly or to have full control over the layout of object files.

elf_begin creates an ELF file descriptor through which a program can manipulate the structures and information in a file. Programs use the ELF file descriptor to communicate with a number of higher-level routines in order to create a new file, read an existing file, or update an existing file.

elf_begin works with elf_end, elf_next, and elf_rand to process ELF files, either singly or as members of archives. These functions let a program convert between memory objects and their file equivalents when reading or writing an object file.

elf_begin can be used with all files, even if they have zero bytes, provided that it can allocate memory needed for its internal structures and read any needed information that the file contains.

elf_begin can even be used on COFF files (the file format that precedes ELF). In this case, the library translates COFF structures to their ELF equivalents. This lets programs read (but not write) COFF files as if they are ELF files. Some COFF debugging information is not translated, however. Also, only the memory image of the file is translated, not the file itself. Addresses and file offsets in the ELF header, program headers, and section headers retain the original COFF values [see elf_gethedr (E), elf_getphdr (E), and elf_getshdr (E)]. If the program calls elf_update (E), the original COFF values can be adjusted (without writing the file) so that the library will present a consistent ELF view of the file. Data that are gotten by elf_getdata (E) are translated (the COFF symbol table is presented as ELF data, and so on). Data that are gotten by `elf_rawdata` (E) are not translated; this permits the program to view bytes from the file itself. See `elf_getdata` (E) and `elf_rawdata`.

Even though the ELF library supports COFF, programs should be recompiled to get ELF object files.

Any program that calls `elf_begin` must first call `elf_version` in order to coordinate versions.

Arguments

cmnd may have one of the following values:

ELF_C_NULL causes `elf_begin` to return a null pointer without opening a new file descriptor. See `elf_next`.

ELF_C_READ is used when a program must read the contents of an existing file. This command causes archive members or entire files to be examined, depending on the value of *ref*.

- If *ref* is a null pointer, `elf_begin` allocates a new ELF file descriptor in preparation for processing an entire file. `elf_begin` also readies the new ELF file descriptor so that the initial archive member can be examined when `elf_begin` is next called. This has an effect as though the program had called `elf_next` or `elf_rand` to move to the initial archive member.
- If *ref* is a nonnull ELF file descriptor that is associated with an archive file, `elf_begin` enables a program to get a separate ELF descriptor that is associated with an individual archive member. When dealing with archive members other than the initial member (which `elf_begin` prepares), the program should call `elf_next` or `elf_rand` before it calls `elf_begin` in order to position *ref* appropriately. *fildscr* should be the same file descriptor used for the parent archive.
- If *ref* is a nonnull ELF file descriptor that is not an archive, `elf_begin` increases the count of the activations for the descriptor, returns *ref*, allocates no new descriptor, and changes no read/write permissions for the descriptor. The program must call `elf_end` once per activation if the descriptor for *ref* is to be terminated. See `elf_next` (E).

ELF_C_RDWR cannot be used with archive members. It has the same action as ELF_C_READ but in addition enables the program to update the file image [see `elf_update` (E)]. ELF_C_RDWR lets the program read and write the file, but ELF_C_READ only lets the program read the file. Any nonnull *ref* must have been created with *cmnd* equal to ELF_C_RDWR.

ELF_C_WRITE is used when the program needs to ignore the contents of a file, as when it needs to create a new file. ELF_C_WRITE causes *ref* to be ignored.

fildscr is an open file descriptor used by `elf_begin` for reading or writing. The initial file offset [see `lseek` (Peterson 1991b)] is not constrained; the file offset that results is undefined.

ref modifies the meaning of *cmnd* if *cmnd* equals ELF_C_READ or ELF_C_RDWR. Otherwise, *ref* is ignored.

Normal Completion: Value Returned

If `elf_begin` succeeds, it returns a nonnull ELF file descriptor.

Error Condition: Value Returned

If an error occurs or the file is an archive that has no more members to process, `elf_begin` returns a null pointer.

See Also

`elf` (E), `elf_cntl` (E), `elf_end` (E), `elf_getarhdr` (E), `elf_getbase` (E), `elf_getdata` (E), `elf_getehdr` (E), `elf_getphdr` (E), `elf_getscn` (E), `elf_kind` (E), `elf_next` (E), `elf_rand` (E), `elf_rawfile` (E), `elf_update` (E), `elf_version` (E), `ar` (AT&T 1990m), `cof2elf` (Peterson 1991a), `creat` (Peterson 1991b), `lseek` (Peterson 1991b), `mmap` (Peterson 1991b), `open` (Peterson 1991b), `truncate` (Peterson 1991b)

elf_cntl (E) MANIPULATE AN ELF DESCRIPTOR elf_cntl (E)

Name

`elf_cntl`—manipulate a file descriptor

Synopsis

```
cc [flag . . .] file . . . -lelf [library . . .]
#include <libelf.h>

int elf_cntl (Elf *elf, Elf_Cmnd cmd);
```

Description

`elf_cntl` lets the calling program reuse file descriptors. This lets the program process many files simultaneously even if the underlying operating system limits the number of files that can be open. If the program calls `elf_cntl` with the appropriate arguments, it can close the file descriptor without interfering with the library.

`elf_cntl` achieves its effect by modifying the behavior of the library with respect to an ELF file descriptor, *`elf`* (see below). `elf_cntl` applies to all activations of *`elf`*.

Arguments

`cmd` has one of the following two values:

`ELF_C_FDDONE` causes the library not to use the file descriptor that is associated with *`elf`*. This *`cmd`* is used to avoid the overhead of reading the rest of the file after the program has requested all of the information it needs. The memory for any completed operations remains valid; however, later operations (e.g., the initial `elf_getdata` for a section) will fail unless the data are in memory already.

`ELF_C_FDREAD` has an effect similar to that of `ELF_C_FDDONE`, except that it forces the library to read the remainder of the file. This is useful if the program must close a file descriptor but has not yet read all of the data it needs to read from the file. After `elf_cntl` executes, subsequent file operations (e.g., `elf_getdata`) will use the memory version of the file without having to use the file descriptor.

In order to use raw operations after disabling the file descriptor with `ELF_C_FDDONE` or `ELF_C_FDREAD`, the program must execute raw operations explicitly beforehand; otherwise, the raw file operations will fail see `elf_rawdata` in `elf_getdata` (E)]. `elf_rawfile` (E) makes the entire memory image available, which enables subsequent `elf_rawdata` calls to work.

`elf` is an ELF file descriptor, as returned by `elf_begin`. An ELF file descriptor can have multiple activations (see `elf_begin`). Also, multiple ELF descriptors can share one file descriptor. If the ELF descriptor is associated with an archive file, descriptors for archive members will be affected as described under `ELF_C_FDDONE` and `ELF_C_FDREAD` above. However, operations on archive members do not affect the ELF descriptor for the archive unless otherwise stated.

Normal Completion: Value Returned

If `elf_cntl` succeeds, it returns 0.

Error Condition: Value Returned

If *`elf`* is null or an error occurs, `elf_cntl` returns −1.

See Also

`elf` (E), `elf_begin` (E), `elf_getdata` (E), `elf_rawfile` (E)

elf_end (E) TERMINATE AN ELF DESCRIPTOR elf_end (E)

Name

`elf_end`—end the use of an object file

Synopsis

```
cc [flag . . .] file . . . -lelf [library . . .]
#include <libelf.h>

int elf_end (Elf *elf);
```

Description

`elf_end` terminates an ELF descriptor, *`elf`*, and deallocates all data that are associated with the descriptor. The ELF descriptor can have more than one activation. Calling `elf_end` removes only one of possibly more than one activations. All of the data that are associated with an ELF descriptor remain allocated until `elf_end` terminates the last activation of the file descriptor [i.e., until the activation count (see "Normal Completion: Value Returned") reaches 0].

Termination of the ELF descriptor releases storage, after which any attempt to access such data gives undefined behavior. For this reason, any program that deals with multiple I/O files must keep the ELF descriptors active until it finishes with the files.

Any program that needs to write to the file any data that are associated with the ELF descriptor must call `elf_update` (E) before calling `elf_end`.

Arguments

`elf` should have a value that was returned earlier by `elf_begin`. To simplify error handling, *`elf`* can be a null pointer.

Normal Completion: Value Returned

If `elf_end` succeeds in removing one activation of an ELF descriptor, it returns a count of the number of activations remaining. If the count is 0, it means that the ELF descriptor no longer is valid.

See Also

elf (E), elf_begin (E), elf_update (E)

elf_errmsg (E) ERROR HANDLING elf_errmsg (E)

Name

elf_errmsg—get the internal error number of a library

Synopsis

```
cc [flag . . .] file . . . -lelf [library . . .]
#include <libelf.h>

const char *elf_errmsg (int err);
int elf_errno (void);
```

Description

elf_errno retrieves the library's internal error number if an ELF library function fails and, as a side effect, resets the internal error number to 0.

elf_errmsg takes the an error number (possibly returned by elf_errno) and returns an error message that describes the problem corresponding to the error number.

Arguments

err specifies an error number for which elf_errmsg is to get the associated error message. If *err* is 0, elf_errmsg retrieves an error message for the most recent error. If *err* is −1, elf_errmsg returns the most recent error and guarantees a nonnull return value, even if no error has occurred.

Normal Completion: Value Returned

elf_errmsg returns a null-terminated error message. The message is not terminated by a newline. If no error has occurred, elf_errmsg returns a null pointer.

elf_errno returns an error number associated with the failure of an ELF library function.

Error Condition: Value Returned

If no message is available for a specified *err*, elf_errmsg returns a message indicating this fact.

See Also

`elf` (E), `elf_version` (E)

elf_fill (E) SET AN ELF FILE FILL BYTE elf_fill (E)

Name

`elf_fill`—set a fill byte

Synopsis

```
cc [flag . . .] file . . . -lelf [library . . .]
#include <libelf.h>

void elf_fill (int fill);
```

Description

`elf_fill` specifies a fill character which the library is to use in filling holes in ELF files [see `elf_getdata` (E) for additional information about these holes].

Alignment constraints for ELF files sometimes result in holes in the data, such as when data for one section are required to begin on an eight-byte boundary, but there are too few data in the preceding section to extend to the byte immediately before the eight-byte boundary of the present section. In this case, the library must put fill characters in the resulting gap.

The application can prevent the library from filling holes in the data by setting the ELF_F_LAYOUT bit [see `elf_flag` (E)].

Arguments

`fill` specifies the fill character to be used by the library. The default fill character that the library uses is 0 unless the application calls `elf_fill` to specify a different fill character.

See Also

`elf` (E), `elf_flag` (E), `elf_getdata` (E), `elf_update` (E)

elf_flag (E) MANIPULATE FLAGS elf_flag (E)

Name

elf_flag: elf_flagdata, elf_flagehdr, elf_flagelf_, elf_flagphdr, elf_flagscn, elf_flagshdr—manage flags

Synopsis

```
cc [flag . . .] file . . . -lelf [library . . .]
#include <libelf.h>

unsigned elf_flagdata (Elf_data *data, Elf_cmd cmd, unsigned flags);

unsigned elf_flagehdr (Elf *elf, Elf_cmd cmd, unsigned flags);

unsigned elf_flagelf (Elf *elf, Elf_cmd cmd, unsigned flags);

unsigned elf_flagphdr (Elf *elf, Elf_cmd cmd, unsigned flags);

unsigned elf_flagscn (Elf_Scn *scn, Elf_cmd cmd, unsigned flags);

unsigned elf_flagshdr (Elf_Scn *scn, Elf_cmd cmd, unsigned flags);
```

Description

These functions manage the flags that are associated with the structures of an ELF file. If given a data descriptor, *data*, an ELF descriptor, *elf*, or a section descriptor, *scn*, these functions clear or set status bits in the associated *flag* and return the updated bits.

Arguments

cmd can have one of the following two values:

ELF_C_CLR causes the function to clear the bits that are asserted in `flags`. The nonzero bits in `flag` are the only bits cleared. Zero bits in `flag` do not modify the status of the descriptor.

ELF_C_SET causes the function to set the bits that are asserted in `flags`. The nonzero bits in `flag` are the only bits set. Zero bits in `flag` do not modify the status of the descriptor.

data is a data descriptor.

elf is an ELF descriptor.

flags has one of the two following values:

ELF_F_DIRTY asserts the associated information that must be written to the ELF file when the program writes an ELF file. For example, if a program is needed to update the ELF header of an existing file, it would call `elf_flagehdr` with *cmd* equal to ELF_C_SET and with the ELF_F_DIRTY bit set in *flags*. A subsequent call to `elf_update` (E) would write the marked ELF header to the file.

ELF_F_LAYOUT has meaning only for `elf_flagelf`. It causes the program to assume responsibility for determining how an output file is to be arranged. ELF_F_LAYOUT is set for an ELF descriptor. That is, the program decides where sections are to be placed, how sections are to be aligned in the file, and so on, instead of having the library making these decisions. ELF_F_LAYOUT applies to the entire ELF file associated with a descriptor.

If a flag bit is set for an item, it also affects all subitems; for example, the entire logical file is dirty if the program calls `elf_flagelf_` to set the ELF_F_DIRTY bit.

scn is a section descriptor.

Normal Completion: Value Returned

If one of these functions succeeds, it returns the updated bits.

Error Condition: Value Returned

In order to simplify error handling, all of these functions return 0 if the descriptor is null.

See Also

`elf` (E), `elf_end` (E), `elf_getdata` (E), `elf_getehdr` (E), `elf_update` (E)

elf_fsize (E) GET OBJECT FILE TYPE SIZE elf_fsize (E)

Name

elf_fsize: elf32_fsize—get the size of an object file type

Synopsis

cc [*flag* . . .] *file* . . . -lelf [*library* . . .]
#include <libelf.h>

size_t elf32_fsize (Elf_Type *type*, size_t *count*, unsigned *ver*);

Description

elf32_fsize is used in converting between two parallel sets of objects that support cross-compilation environments. One set of objects corresponds to the contents of files. The other set corresponds to the native memory image of the program that manipulates the files.

elf32_fsize finds the size (in bytes) of the 32-bit file representation of the specified number, *count*, of data objects of the specified type, *type*.

The following constant values give the file size (in bytes) of fundamental ELF types for the 32-bit class of object files:

ELF32_FSZ_ADDR whose Elf32_*Type* is ELF_T_ADDR, gives the ELF file size of an unsigned address corresponding to memory size sizeof(Elf32_Addr).

1 whose Elf32_*Type* is ELF_T_BYTE, gives the ELF file size of an unsigned small integer corresponding to memory size sizeof (unsigned char).

ELF32_FSZ_HALF whose Elf32_*Type* is ELF_T_HALF, gives the ELF file size of an unsigned medium integer corresponding to memory size sizeof(Elf32_Half).

ELF32_FSZ_OFF whose Elf32_*Type* is ELF_T_OFF, gives the ELF file size of an unsigned file offset corresponding to memory size size of (Elf32_Off).

ELF32_FSZ_SWORD whose Elf32_*Type* is ELF_T_SWORD, gives the ELF file size of a signed large integer corresponding to memory size sizeof(Elf32_Sword).

ELF32_FSZ_WORD whose Elf32_*Type* is ELF_T_WORD, gives the ELF file size of an unsigned large integer corresponding to memory size sizeof(Elf32_Word).

Arguments

count specifies the number of data objects whose size is to be ascertained by `elf32_fsize`.

type specifies the type of the data objects whose size is to be ascertained by `elf32_fsize`.

ver specifies the version used by the library in computing the size of the specified object file type.

Normal Completion: Value Returned

If `elf32_fsize` succeeds, it returns the size (in bytes) of the 32-bit file representation of the specified object file type.

Error Condition: Value Returned

If the value of *type* or *ver* is not known, `elf32_fsize` returns 0.

See Also

`elf` (E), `elf_version` (E), `elf_xlate` (E)

elf_getarhdr (E) — GET AN ARCHIVE MEMBER HEADER — elf_getarhdr (E)

Name

`elf_getarhdr`—get an archive member header

Synopsis

```
cc [flag . . .] file . . . -lelf [library . . .]
#include <libelf.h>

Elf_Arhdr *elf_getarhdr (Elf *elf);
```

Description

`elf_getarhdr` returns a pointer to an archive member header (if it exists) corresponding to the ELF descriptor *elf*. The header includes the following members:

char *arname; /* makes available an archive member name consisting of a null-terminated string that has its ar format control characters deleted. */
time_t ar_date;
long ar_uid;
long ar_gid;
unsigned long ar_mode;
off_t ar_size;
char *ar_rawname; /* contains a null-terminated string representing the original name bytes in the file, including the terminating slash and trailing blanks specified in the archive format. */

The archive format defines special archive members in addition to the regular archive members. The names of all special archive members begin with a slash (/) in order to distinguish them from regular archive members, whose names cannot begin with a slash. Special members have the following names (ar_name):

/ designates the archive symbol table, which, if present, is the first archive member. Symbol table information can be used for random archive processing [see elf_rand (E)].

// designates the archive member, which, if present, contains the string table for long archive member names. The library retrieves long member names from the string table automatically and sets ar_name to the correct value.

Arguments

elf is the ELF descriptor of the archive member whose archive member header is to be retrieved.

Normal Completion: Value Returned

If elf_getarhdr succeeds, it returns a pointer to the archive header of the specified archive member.

Error Condition: Value Returned

If no archive member exists or *elf* is null or an error occurs, elf_getarhdr returns a null value. The archive member name may not be available if certain error conditions occur. In this case, the library sets ar_name to a null pointer, but the ar_rawname member is set as usual.

See Also

elf (E), elf_begin (E), elf_getarsym (E), elf_rand (E), ar (AT&T 1990m)

elf_getarsym (E) — GET AN ARCHIVE SYMBOL TABLE — elf_getarsym (E)

Name

`elf_getarsym`—get an archive symbol table

Synopsis

```
cc [flag . . .] file . . . -lelf [library . . .]
#include <libelf.h>

Elf_Arsym *elf_getarsym (Elf *elf, size_t *ptr);
```

Description

`elf_getarsym` returns a pointer to the archive symbol table (if it exists) associated with the ELF descriptor *`elf`*. The symbol table is an array of structures. It includes the following members:

`char *as_name;` /* contains a pointer to a null-terminated symbol name. The last entry of the symbol table has a null `as_name`. */

`size_t as_off;` /* is an offset (in bytes) from the beginning of the archive to the archive member's header. The associated symbol is defined by the archive member at the given offset. The last entry of the symbol table has a ~0 value for `as_name`. */

`unsigned long as_hash;` /* is a hash value that `elf_hash` computes for the symbol name. The last entry of the symbol table has a `~0UL` value for `as_hash`. */

Arguments

`elf` is an ELF descriptor for the archive whose symbol is to be returned by `elf_getarsym`.

`ptr` points (if it is nonnull) to the location where the library stores the number of symbol table entries.

Normal Completion: Value Returned

If `elf_getarsym` succeeds, it returns a pointer to the archive symbol table.

Error Condition: Value Returned

If the archive does not have a symbol table or *elf* is null or an error has occurred, `elf_getarsym` returns a null value. If the return value is null, the value of the location to which *ptr* points is set to 0.

See Also

`elf` (E), `elf_getarhdr` (E), `elf_hash` (E), `elf_rand` (E), `ar` (AT&T 1990m)

elf_getbase (E) — BASE OFFSET OF AN OBJECT FILE — elf_getbase (E)

Name

`elf_getbase`—get the base offset of an object file

Synopsis

```
cc [flag . . .] file . . . -lelf [library . . .]
#include <libelf.h>

off_t elf_getbase (Elf *elf);
```

Description

`elf_getbase` gets the base offset of the first byte in an archive member or file. The base offset of an archive member is not the beginning of the archive member's header; it is the beginning of the member's information.

Arguments

elf is an ELF descriptor that specifies the file or archive member whose file offset is to be obtained. *elf* can be null to simplify error handling, in which case `elf_getbase` returns −1.

Normal Completion: Value Returned

If `elf_getbase` succeeds, it returns the file offset of the first byte of the specified file or archive member.

Error Condition: Value Returned

elf_getbase returns −1 if an error occurs or if the base offset is not known or cannot be gotten.

See Also

elf (E), elf_begin (E), ar (AT&T 1990m)

elf_getdata (E) GET SECTION DATA elf_getdata (E)

Name

elf_getdata, elf_newdata, elf_rawdata—get section data

Synopsis

```
cc [flag . . .] file . . . -lelf [library . . .]
#include <libelf.h>

Elf_Data *elf_getdata (Elf_Scn *scn, Elf_Data *data);

Elf_Data *elf_newdata (Elf_Scn *scn);

Elf_Data *elf_rawdata (Elf_Scn *scn, Elf_Data *data);
```

Description

elf_getdata, elf_newdata, and elf_rawdata manage the data that are associated with the specified section descriptor, *scn*. Each section will have one data buffer associated with it when an existing file is being read. The program can create a new section from individual pieces gotten from more than one data buffer. Thus, the data of a section may be thought of as a data list consisting of buffers, with each buffer accessible through a different data descriptor.

elf_getdata enables a program to step through the data list of a section. It converts data from file representations to memory representations [see elf_xlate (E)] and presents objects with memory data types to the program, as determined by the file's class. The working library version, as obtained by elf_version (E), specifies the version of the memory structures that elf_getdata should give to the program.

elf_getdata interprets the section's data according to the section type [see the section header shown in elf_getshdr (E)].

The library represents section types with memory data types for the 32-bit class as follows:

- Section type SHT_DYNAMIC represents memory data type ELF_T_DYN for the Elf32_Dyn 32-bit type.
- Section type SHT_DYNSYM represents memory data type ELF_T_SYM for the Elf32_Sym 32-bit type.
- Section type SHT_HASH represents memory data type ELF_T_WORD for the Elf32_Word 32-bit type.
- Section type SHT_NOBITS represents memory data type ELF_T_BYTE for the unsigned char 32-bit type. A section that has the special type SHT_NOBITS occupies no space in an object file even if the section header indicates a size greater than 0. Both elf_getdata and elf_rawdata (see below) set the *data* structure (see "Arguments" below) to have a null buffer pointer and the type indicated above. The d_size value (see "Arguments" below)is set to the size given in the section header. The program should use elf_newdata (see below) to add data buffers to a section when the program is creating a new section whose type is SHT_NOBITS. These new data buffers should have their d_size members set to the desired size. Their d_buf members should be set to null.
- Section type SHT_NOTE represents memory data type ELF_T_BYTE for the unsigned char 32-bit type.
- Section type SHT_NULL represents no Elf_Type memory data type.
- Section type SHT_PROGBITS represents memory data type ELF_T_BYTE for the unsigned char 32-bit type.
- Section type SHT_REL represents memory data type ELF_T_RELA for the Elf32_Rela 32-bit type.
- Section type SHT_STRTAB represents memory data type ELF_T_BYTE for the unsigned char 32-bit type.
- Section type SHT_SYMTAB represents memory data type ELF_T_SYM for the Elf32_Sym 32-bit type.
- Section type *other* represents memory data type ELF_T_BYTE for the unsigned char 32-bit type.

The library interprets the above section types according to the version. The library does not translate section data if the section belongs to a version that is newer than the working version used by the application. Since the application cannot know the format of the data if this is the case, the library presents an untranslated buffer of type ELF_T_BYTE to the program; it does the same if it encounters an unrecognized section type.

elf_newdata creates a new data descriptor for a section and appends it to any data elements that are already associated with the section. The newly created descriptor appears empty, indicating that the element contains no data. The program must set or change descriptor members as required. The descriptor's type (see `d_type` under "Arguments" below) is set equal to `ELF_T_BYTE`. The version (see `d_version` under "Arguments" below) is set equal to the working version. `elf_newdata` implicitly sets the `ELF_F_DIRTY` bit for the section's data.

`elf_rawdata` returns only uninterpreted bytes (in contrast to `elf_getdata`, which returns interpreted bytes), no matter what the section type may be; it creates a buffer that has type `ELF_T_BYTE`. `elf_rawdata` should be used only when it is necessary to avoid the automatic data translation (see below) that would otherwise occur if `elf_getdata` were used instead of `elf_rawdata` to retrieve a section image from a file that is being read. `elf_getdata` is preferable to `elf_rawdata` if `elf_getdata` provides the correct translation.

A program may not close or disable [see `elf_cntl` (E)] the file descriptor that is associated with *`elf`* before the initial raw data operation occurs, because `elf_rawdata` may read the data from the file in order to ensure that it does not interfere with the operation of `elf_getdata`.

`elf_rawfile` (E), a function related to `elf_rawdata`, applies to the entire file.

Data Alignment

The data buffers within a section must meet alignment constraints. Consequently, adjacent buffers may not be contiguous. If so, there will be holes between the buffers.

Programs can deal with these holes in one of two ways when creating output files. First, the program can call `elf_fill` (E) in order to specify the byte that the library will use when filling the holes. Otherwise, the library will fill the holes with zeroes by default. Second, the program can create its own buffers to fill the gaps between buffers. The program can then fill the gaps with values that are appropriate for the particular section being created. The program can use different fill bytes for different sections. For example, it can fill gaps in text sections with no-operation instructions and fill gaps in data sections with zeroes. If this method is used, the library finds no holes to fill because the application fills them.

Arguments

`data` points to an `Elf_Data` structure that includes the members discussed below. The program can directly manipulate the structure members.

void *d_buf; /* *d_buf points to the data buffer. If a data element contains no data, it has a null pointer. */

Elf_Type d_type; /* d_type specifies the type of the data (section) to which d_buf points. This member determines how the section's contents are to be interpreted. */

size_t d_size; /* d_size contains the total size (in bytes) of the memory that the data occupies. This size may differ from the size represented in the file. If no data exist, the memory size is 0 (see SHT_NOBITS below). */

off_t d_off; /* d_off specifies the offset within the section. The offset is relative to the beginning of the section, not to the beginning of the memory object. */

size_t d_align; /* d_align specifies the buffer's required alignment, counting from the beginning of the section. The value of d_off is a multiple of the value of this member (e.g., if the value of d_align is 4, the beginning of the buffer will be four-byte aligned within the section). The whole section will be aligned to the maximum extent of its constituents. This ensures appropriate alignment for a buffer within the section and within the file. */

unsigned d_version; /* d_version contains the version number of the objects in the buffer. The library uses the working version to control the translation of file objects to memory objects when it reads data from the object file [see elf_version (E)]. */

scn is a section descriptor.

Normal Completion: Value Returned

If *data* is null and no error occurs, elf_getdata returns a pointer to the first buffer that is associated with the specified section. If *data* is an ELF file descriptor associated with the section descriptor, *scn*, and no error occurs, elf_getdata returns a pointer to the next data element for the section.

If elf_newdata succeeds, it returns a pointer to a data descriptor.

If elf_rawdata succeeds, it returns uninterpreted bytes.

Error Condition: Value Returned

elf_getdata returns a null pointer if an error occurs or *scn* is null.

elf_newdata returns a null pointer if an error occurs or *scn* is null.

elf_rawdata returns a null pointer if an error occurs or *scn* is null.

See Also

elf (E), elf_cntl (E), elf_fill (E), elf_flag (E), elf_getehdr (E), elf_getscn (E), elf_getshdr (E), elf_rawhide (E), elf_version (E), elf_xlate (E)

elf_getehdr (E) GET AN OBJECT FILE HEADER elf_getehdr (E)

Name

elf_getehdr: elf32_getehdr, elf32_newehdr—get a class-dependent object file header

Synopsis

```
cc [flag . . .] file . . . -lelf [library . . .]
#include <libelf.h>

Elf32_Ehdr *elf32_getehdr (Elf *elf);

Elf32_Ehdr *elf32_newehdr (Elf *elf);
```

Description

elf32_getehdr returns a pointer to an ELF header (if a header exists) for a 32-bit class file for the ELF descriptor *elf*.

elf32_newehdr has the same effect as elf32_getehdr unless no header exists for the ELF descriptor, in which case elf32_newehdr allocates a clean one. elf32_newehdr does not allocate a new header if one already exists. elf32_newehdr sets the ELF_F_DIRTY bit automatically [see elf_flag (E)].

The ELF header includes the following members:

```
unsigned char  e_ident[EINIDENT]
Elf32_Half     e_type;
Elf32_Half     e_machine;
Elf32_Word     e_version;
Elf32_Addr     e_entry;
Elf32_Off      e_phoff;
Elf32_Off      e_shoff;
Elf32_Word     e_flags;
Elf32_Half     e_ehsize;
Elf32_Half     e_phentsize;
Elf32_Half     e_phnum;
Elf32_Half     e_shentsize;
Elf32_Half     e_shnum;
Elf32_Half     e_shstrndx;
```

Arguments

elf is the ELF descriptor of 32-bit class file.

Normal Completion: Value Returned

See the description above.

Error Condition: Value Returned

If an error occurs or the file is not a 32-bit class file or *elf* is null or no header exists (`elf_getehedr`) or no header file can be created (`elf_newehdr`), both functions return a null pointer.

See Also

`elf` (E), `elf_begin` (E), `elf_flag` (E), `elf_getident` (E)

elf_getident (E) GET FILE ID DATA elf_getident (E)

Name

`elf_getident`—get file ID data

Synopsis

```
cc [flag . . .] file . . . -lelf [library . . .]
#include <libelf.h>

char *elf_getident (Elf *elf, size_t *ptr);
```

Description

Various classes of ELF files differ in the size of their basic objects. Some ELF files may have basic objects whose size is 32 bits, others may have basic objects whose size is 64 bits, and so on. The ID information that is common to all ELF files, whatever their size, is placed in the initial bytes of the ELF files so that the size of a machine with a large object size will never be forced on a machine with a smaller object size.

`elf_getident` returns a pointer to the initial bytes of an ELF file that hold ID information. If the library recognizes the class of the file, it may convert the file image to the memory image.

`elf_getident` is guaranteed not to modify the ID bytes. However, the size of the unmodified area depends on the file class.

Every ELF file has an `e_ident` variable in its header that has `EI_NIDENT` bytes whose interpretations are as follows:

- Object 0, whose `e_ident` index is `EI_MAG0` and whose value is `ELFMAG0`, is used for file ID.
- Object 1, whose `e_ident` index is `EI_MAG1` and whose value is `ELFMAG1`, is used for file ID.

- Object 2, whose `e_ident` index is `EI_MAG2` and whose value is `ELFMAG2`, is used for file ID
- Object 3, whose `e_ident` index is `EI_MAG3` and whose value is `ELFMAG3`, is used for file ID.
- Object 4, whose `e_ident` index is `EI_CLASS` and whose value is `ELFCLASSNONE`, or `ELFCLASS32`, or `ELFCLASS64`, is used to specify the ELF file class.
- Object 5, whose `e_ident` index is `EI_DATA` and whose value is `ELFDATANONE`, `ELFDATA2LSB`, or `ELFDATA2MSB`, is used for data encoding.
- Object 6, whose `e_ident` index is `EV_CURRENT`, is used for the file version.
- Objects 7 through 15 are set to 0 and are not used.

Arguments

`elf` is an ELF descriptor for a file whose initial bytes are sought by `elf_getident`.

`ptr` points to the location where the library is to store a count of the ID bytes that are contained in the initial part of an ELF file. See "Error Condition: Value Returned" below.

Normal Completion: Value Returned

`elf_getident` returns a pointer to the initial bytes of an ELF file.

Error Condition: Value Returned

If an error occurs or *`elf`* is null or there are no data, `elf_getident` returns a null pointer and optionally stores 0 in the location to which *`ptr`* points.

See Also

`elf` (E), `elf_begin` (E), `elf_getehdr` (E), `elf_kind` (E), `elf_rawfile` (E)

elf_getphdr (E) — GET A PROGRAM HEADER TABLE — elf_getphdr (E)

Name

`elf_getphdr`: `elf32_getphdr`, `elf32_newphdr`—get a class-dependent program header table

Synopsis

```
cc [flag . . .] file . . . -lelf [library . . .]
#include <libelf.h>

Elf32_Phdr *elf_getphdr (Elf *elf);

Elf32_Phdr *elf_newphdr (Elf *elf, size_t count);
```

Description

elf32_getphdr returns a pointer to the program execution header table (if one exists for *elf*) for a 32-bit class file.

elf32_newphdr allocates a new program execution header table even if such a table already exists. It sets the ELF_F_DIRTY bit for the table [see elf_flag (E)].

The program execution header table consists of an array of structures whose type is Elf32_Phdr. The e_phnum member of the ELF header tells how many entries the program execution header table contains [see elf_getehdr (E)]. elf32_newphdr automatically sets the value of e_phnum to *count*.

Each structure in the program execution header table includes the following members:

```
Elf32_Word  p_type;
Elf32_Off   p_offset;
Elf32_Addr  p_vaddr;
Elf32_Addr  p_addr;
Elf32_Word  p_filesz;
Elf32_Word  p_memsz;
Elf32_Word  p_flags;
Elf32_Word  p_align;
```

If a program builds a new file, it must create the file's ELF header before creating the program execution header table.

Arguments

count specifies the number of entries in the program header table which elf32_newphdr allocates. If *count* equals 0, the existing table is deleted. This allows the program to replace or remove the program execution header table [in contrast to the behavior of elf32_newhedr in elf_ getehdr (E)] and to change the size of the table. See "Error Condition: Value Returned" below.

elf is an ELF descriptor for a 32-bit class file.

Normal Completion: Value Returned

See the description above.

Error Condition: Value Returned

elf32_getphdr and elf32_newphdr will return a null pointer if either of them is called and an error occurs or no program execution header table exists or the file is not of the 32-bit class.

See Also

elf (E), elf_begin (E), elf_flag (E), elf_getehdr (E)

elf_getscn (E) GET SECTION INFORMATION elf_getscn (E)

Name

elf_getscn, elf_ndxscn, elf_newscn, elf_nextscn—get section information

Synopsis

```
cc [flag ...] file ... -lelf [library ...]
#include <libelf.h>

Elf_Scn *elf_getscn (Elf *elf, size_t index);

Elf_Scn *elf_newscn (Elf *elf);

Elf_Scn *elf_nextscn (Elf *elf, Elf_Scn *scn);
size_t elf_ndxscn (Elf_Scn *scn);
```

Description

The functions discussed below give indexed and sequential access to the sections associated with the ELF descriptor *elf*. Any program that builds a new ELF file must create the file's ELF header before creating any new sections [see elf_getehdr (E)].

elf_getscn returns the section descriptor specified by an *index* to the section header table of a file whose ELF descriptor is *elf*. See "Normal Completion; Value Returned" below. The program can obtain a section descriptor for the section whose *index* equals 0 (the undefined section, SHN_UNDEF), but the section contains no data and the section header is present, although it is empty.

elf_ndxscn returns the section table index of the existing section descriptor that is specified by *scn*.

elf_newscn makes a new section and appends it to the list for *elf_*. The library automatically creates the SHN_UNDEF section because it is required. Accordingly, the first call to elf_newscn that is made for an ELF descriptor that has no existing sections returns a descriptor for section 1, not section 0.

After it creates a new section descriptor, the program uses elf_getshdr (E) to get the newly created, clean section header. No data will be associated with the new section descriptor. The library updates the eshnum member of the ELF header. It also sets the ELF_F_DIRTY bit for the section [see elf flag (E) for details].

elf_nextscn returns a section descriptor for the next higher section after an existing section descriptor specified by *scn*.

Arguments

elf is an ELF descriptor.

index is an index into the section header table of a file. The index ot the first real section is 1.

scn is a section descriptor. A null section descriptor used with elf_nextscn causes it to skip the section whose index is SHN_UNDEF and get the descriptor for the section whose index is 1.

Normal Completion: Value Returned

elf_getscn returns a pointer to a section descriptor corresponding to an *index* into the section header table of a file.

elf_ndxscn returns the section table index corresponding to an existing section descriptor.

elf_newscn returns a pointer to a section descriptor.

elf_nextscn returns a section descriptor for the next higher section after an existing section.

Error Condition: Value Returned

elf_getscn returns a null pointer if an error occurs or the section specified by *index* does not exist or *elf* is null.

elf_ndxscn returns SHN_UNDEF if an error occurs or *scn* is null.

elf_newscn returns a null pointer if an error occurs or *elf* is null.

elf_nextscn returns a null pointer if an error occurs or no additional sections exist.

See Also

elf (E), elf_begin (E), elf_flag (E), elf_getdata (E), elf_getehdr (E), elf_getshdr (E)

elf_getshdr (E) GET SECTION HEADER elf_getshdr (E)

Name

elf_getshdr: elf32_getshdr—get a class-dependent section header

Synopsis

```
cc [flag . . .] file . . . -lelf [library . . .]
#include <libelf.h>

Elf_Shdr *elf32_getshdr (Elf_Scn *scn);
```

Description

elf32_getshdr returns a pointer to a section header corresponding to the section descriptor, *scn*, of a 32-bit class file.

The section header has the following members:

```
Elf32_Word  sh_name;
Elf32_Word  sh_type;
Elf32_Word  sh_flags;
Elf32_Addr  sh_addr;
Elf32_Off   sh_offset;
Elf32_Word  sh_size;
Elf32_Word  sh_link;
Elf32_Word  sh_info;
Elf32_Word  sh_addralign;
Elf32_Word  sh_entsize;
```

The program must create the ELF header of a file before it creates any sections.

Arguments

scn specifies a section descriptor of a 32-bit class file.

Normal Completion: Value Returned

See "Description" above.

Error Condition: Value Returned

`elf32_getshdr` returns null if an error occurs or *scn* is null or the file is not a 32-bit class file.

See Also

`elf` (E), `elf_flag` (E), `elf_getscn` (E), `elf_strptr` (E)

elf_hash (E) CALCULATE A HASH VALUE elf_hash (E)

Name

`elf_hash`—calculate a hash value

Synopsis

```
cc [flag ...] file ... -lelf [library ...]
#include <libelf.h>

unsigned long elf_hash (const char *name);
```

Description

`elf_hash` uses a null-terminated string, *name*, to compute and return a hash value. The returned hash value can be used as a bucket index after modulus computations to ensure appropriate bounds.

`elf_hash` is used to compute the symbol hash tables of ELF files [see `elf_getdata` (E) and `elf_xlate` (E)].

`elf_hash` uses unsigned arithmetic. Thus, hash tables that are built on one kind of machine can be used on another kind of machine because possible problems caused by differences in each machine's signed arithmetic are avoided (see *name* below).

Arguments

name is a null-terminated string. Its type is given as `char*` in the function declaration above, but `elf_hash` treats it as an `unsigned char*` variable in order to avoid differences from machine to machine caused by sign extension. Using `char*` instead of `unsigned char*` in the above declaration eliminates type conflicts that can occur when expressions such as `elf_hash("string")` are used.

Normal Completion: Value Returned

`elf_hash` returns a hash value that is guaranteed not to be the bit pattern of all 1s (~0UL).

See Also

`elf` (E), `elf_getdata` (E), `elf_xlate` (E)

elf_kind (E) DETERMINE THE FILE TYPE elf_kind (E)

Name

`elf_kind`—determine the file type

Synopsis

```
cc [flag ...] file ... -lelf [library ...]
#include <libelf.h>

Elf_Kind elf_kind (Elf *elf);
```

Description

`elf_kind` returns a value that identifies the kind of file that is associated with the specified ELF descriptor, *elf*.

Arguments

elf is an ELF descriptor that should be a value previously returned by `elf_begin`. If *elf* is a null pointer, `elf_kind` returns ELF_K_NONE; this simplifies error handling.

Normal Completion: Value Returned

elf_kind returns one of the following four values:

ELF_K_AR means that the file is an archive [see ar (AT&T 1990m)]. If *elf*_ is associated with an archive member instead of with an archive, the member's type is identified.

ELF_K_COFF means that the file is a COFF object file. See elf_begin (E) for details of the library's handling of COFF files.

ELF_K_ELF means that the file is an ELF file. The class of the ELF file can be ascertained by elf_getident (E). getehdr (E) and other functions can get other kinds of file information.

ELF_K_NONE means that the library does not recognize the file type.

Values other than these four are reserved for assignment when new kinds of files are needed.

Error Condition: Value Returned

See *elf* above.

See Also

elf (E), elf_begin (E), elf_getehdr (E), elf_getident (E), ar (AT&T 1990m)

elf_next (E) SEQUENTIAL MEMBER ACCESS elf_next (E)

Name

elf_next—sequential archive member access

Synopsis

```
cc [flag . . .] file . . . -lelf [library . . .]
#include <libelf.h>

Elf_Cmd elf_next (Elf *elf);
```

Description

elf_next, together with elf_begin and elf_rand, manages archives and simple object files.

elf_next gives sequential access to the next archive member. It positions the archive to access a member that follows the archive member that is associated with the ELF descriptor, *elf*, when the program calls `elf_begin`.

Whether or not `elf_next` succeeds in positioning an archive to access the next member, `elf_begin` can use the value that `elf_next` returns (see below) to specify an action to take.

Arguments

elf is an ELF descriptor that was returned earlier by `elf_begin`.

Normal Completion: Value Returned

If `elf_next` succeeds in positioning the archive for the next member, it returns ELF_C_READ.

Error Condition: Value Returned

If `elf_next` fails in positioning the archive for the next member or an error occurs or *elf* is null or the open file is not an archive, it returns ELF_C_NULL.

See Also

`elf` (E), `elf_begin` (E), `elf_getarsym` (E), `elf_rand` (E), `ar` (AT&T 1990m)

elf_rand (E) — RANDOM ARCHIVE MEMBER ACCESS — elf_rand (E)

Name

`elf_rand`—random archive member access

Synopsis

```
cc [flag . . .] file . . . -lelf [library . . .]
#include <libelf.h>

size_t elf_rand (Elf *elf, size_t offset);
```

Description

`elf_next`, together with `elf_begin` and `elf_rand`, manages archives and simple object files.

`elf_next` gives random access to an archive member. It prepares *elf* for random access of an archive member.

Arguments

*elf_* is an ELF descriptor that was returned earlier by `elf_begin`. It must be a descriptor for the archive, not for an archive member.

offset specifies the offset (in bytes) from the beginning of the archive to the archive header of the desired member [see `elf_getarsym` (E)]. Note that an archive starts with a magic string that has SARMAG bytes. The first archive member follows immediately.

Normal Completion: Value Returned

If `elf_rand` succeeds, it returns *offset*.

Error Condition: Value Returned

If an error occurs or *elf* is null or the file is not an archive, `elf_rand` returns −1.

See Also

`elf` (E), `elf_begin` (E), `elf_getarsym` (E), `elf_next` (E), `ar` (AT&T 1990m)

elf_rawfile (E) UNINTERPRETED FILE CONTENTS elf_rawfile (E)

Name

`elf_rawfile`—get uninterpreted file contents

Synopsis

```
cc [flag . . .] file . . . -lelf [library . . .]
#include <libelf.h>

char *elf_rawfile (Elf *elf, size_t *ptr);
```

Description

`elf_rawfile` retrieves an uninterpreted byte image of a file.

`elf_rawfile` is for use only in retrieving a file that is being read, as in retrieving the bytes for an archive member.

If a program uses `elf_rawfile` to retrieve a file and also interprets that file as an object file, the program potentially has two copies of the file bytes in memory. If the program retrieves the raw image before it requests translated information (for example, by calling `elf_getehdr` or `elf_getdata`), the library will freeze the original memory copy for the raw image. The library uses this frozen memory copy to create translated objects; it does not read the file again. Thus, from the viewpoint of the application, the raw file image that `elf_rawfile` returns is a read-only buffer, unless the program changes its own view of the data translated afterward. The program can change the translated objects without changing any bytes that are visible in the raw image, whether or not the program changes its view of the data translated afterward.

`elf_rawfile` ordinarily is more efficient when the file type is unknown than when it is known to be an object file. The library leaves unknown files unmodified but translates object files in memory. If the program requests an uninterpreted image of an object file, it may cause a duplicate copy to be created in memory.

`elf_rawdata` (E), a related function, gives access to sections within a file [see `elf_getdata` (E)].

Arguments

`elf` points to a descriptor. A program that calls `elf_rawfile` may not close or disable [see `elf_cntl` (E)] the file descriptor associated with *`elf`* before calling `elf_rawfile` for the first time, because `elf_rawfile` may need to read data from the specified file if the program does not already have the original bytes in memory.

`ptr` points to the location (if *`ptr`* is not null) where the library stores the size of the file (in bytes).

Normal Completion: Value Returned

If `elf_rawfile` succeeds, it returns a pointer to an uninterpreted byte image of the specified file. If `elf_rawfile` is called more than once with the same ELF descriptor, it returns the same value each time because the library does not create duplicate copies of the file.

Error Condition: Value Returned

`elf_rawfile` returns a null pointer if an error occurs or *`elf`* is null or no data exist. In this case, 0 can optionally be stored in the location to which *`ptr`* points.

See Also

elf (E), elf_begin (E), elf_cntl (E), elf_getdata (E), elf_getehdr (E), elf_getident (E), elf_kind (E)

elf_strptr (E) CREATE A STRING POINTER elf_strptr (E)

Name

elf_strptr—create a string pointer

Synopsis

```
cc [flag . . .] file . . . -lelf [library . . .]
#include <libelf.h>

char *elf_strptr (Elf *elf, size_t section,
size_t offset);
```

Description

elf_strptr converts the offset of a string section to a string pointer and returns a pointer to the string.

In some applications, it may be more efficient to call elf_getdata (E) to retrieve an entire string table section than to call elf_strptr.

Arguments

elf is an ELF descriptor that specifies the file which contains the string section.

offset specifies the string section offset that is to be converted to a string pointer.

section specifies the section table index for the strings.

Normal Completion: Value Returned

If elf_strptr succeeds, it returns a pointer to a string (see above).

Error Condition: Value Returned

elf_strptr returns a null pointer if one of the following conditions occurs:

- An error occurs,
- *elf* is null,
- *section* is not valid, or
- *section* is not of type SHT_STRTAB.

See Also

elf (E), elf_getdata (E), elf_getshdr (E), elf_xlate (E)

elf_update (E) UPDATE AN ELF DESCRIPTOR elf_update (E)

Name

elf_update—update an ELF descriptor

Synopsis

```
cc [flag . . .] file . . . -lelf [library . . .]
#include <libelf.h>

off_t elf_updata (Elf *elf, ELf_Cmd cmd);
```

Description

elf_update makes the library examine information associated with the ELF descriptor, *elf*, and recompute all of the structural data required to create the file's image.

When it builds the output file, elf_update obeys the alignments of each data buffer to create output sections. The most strictly aligned data buffer of a section controls the alignment of that section. The library also ensures proper alignment of each data buffer by inserting any necessary padding between buffers.

When it recomputes the structural data, elf_update sets some members itself. Other members keep the values assigned by the application. Members which keep values assigned by the application are discussed below.

ELF Header Members

The application assigns values to the following ELF header members:

e_ident[EI_DATA] is set by the application. Other values of e_ident are controlled by the library. e_ident[EI_DATA] controls the data-encoding method used in the file. If it equals ELFDATANONE, it requests the use of native data encoding for the host machine. If the native encoding is not the same as a file encoding that the library knows, an error occurs.

e_type is set by the application.

e_machine is set by the application.

e_version is set by the application. It controls the version of data structures written to the file. The library uses its own internal version if e_version is EV_NONE.

e_entry is set by the application.

e_phoff is set by the application if ELF_F_LAYOUT is asserted.

e_shoff is set by the application if ELF_F_LAYOUT is asserted.

e_flags is set by the application.

e_shstrndx is set by the application.

Program Header Members

The application assigns values to all program header members. The program header members are as follows:

p_type is set by the application.

p_offset is set by the application.

p_vaddr is set by the application.

p_paddr is set by the application.

p_filesz is set by the application.

p_memsz is set by the application.

p_flags is set by the application.

p_align is set by the application.

Section Header Members

The application assigns values to the following section header members:

sh_name is set by the application.

sh_type is set by the application.

sh_flags is set by the application.

sh_addr is set by the application.

sh_offset is set by the application if ELF_F_LAYOUT is asserted.

sh_size is set by the application if ELF_F_LAYOUT is asserted.

sh_link is set by the application.

sh_info is set by the application.

sh_addralign is set by the application if ELF_F_LAYOUT is asserted.

sh_entsize is set by the library for sections that have known types, but the library cannot always know the correct value for all sections. Thus, the library relies on the program to give it the correct values for sections that have an unknown type. Set the value of sh_entsize to 0 if the entry size is not known or is not applicable.

Data Descriptor Members

The application assigns values to the following data descriptor members:

`d_buf` is set by the application.
`d_type` is set by the application.
`d_size` is set by the application.
`d_off` is set by the application if `ELF_F_LAYOUT` is asserted.
`d_align` is set by the application.
`d_version` is set by the application.

Arguments

cmd takes one of the following two values:

`ELF_C_NULL` specifies that `elf_update` is to update only the ELF descriptor's memory structures. All modified structures are flagged with the `ELF_F_DIRTY` bit. This way, the program can update the memory structure information and examine it without altering the file associated with *elf* (see *elf* below). Since the file is not changed, the ELF descriptor may permit reading, writing, or both reading and writing (see `elf_begin` (E)].

`ELF_C_WRITE` causes the same actions as `ELF_C_NULL` actions. In addition, it causes all dirty information associated with *elf* to be written to the file. In other words, if a program calls `elf_flag` (E) or `elf_getdata` (E) to supply new information for an ELF descriptor, the data will be examined, coordinated, translated (if required), and written to the file. Translation is not always transparent to the application. The application should re-establish pointers after calling `elf_update` if it has gotten pointers to data that are associated with a file [see `elf_getehdr` (E) and `elf_getdata` (E)].

Section data are written to the file in the same order in which their section header entries appear. The section header table is written at the end of the file. When items of data are written to a file, any `EFL_F_DIRTY` bits are reset to indicate that those items need not be written to the file again [see `elf_flag` (E)].

Although a program can translate a COFF file to make an image that is consistent with ELF [see `elf_begin` (E)], the `ELF_C_WRITE` command cannot update an executable COFF file because it updates both the memory image and the file. The `ELF_C_NULL` command can translate a COFF file, however, because the `ELF_C_NULL` command updates only the memory image. The absolute executable files (`a.out`) require special alignment which cannot be preserved in translating from COOF to ELF format.

elf points to an ELF descriptor that specifies the file whose structural data are to be recomputed. The `elf_begin` (E) command must be either

ELF_C_RDWR or ELF_C_WRITE at the time the ELF descriptor is created, that is, it must allow the file to be written.

Normal Completion: Value Returned

If elf_update succeeds, it returns the total size (in bytes) of the file image, not the memory image.

Error Condition: Value Returned

If elf_update fails, it returns −1.

See Also

elf (E), elf_begin (E), elf_flag (E), elf_getdata (E), elf_getehdr (E), elf_getshdr (E), elf_size (E), elf_xlate (E)

elf_version (E) COORDINATE VERSIONS elf_version (E)

Name

elf_version—coordinate application and ELF library versions

Synopsis

```
cc [flag ...] file ... -lelf [library ...]
#include <libelf.h>

unsigned elf_version (unsigned ver);
```

Description

elf_version is meant to cope with the fact that a program, an access library, and an ELF object file can each have a different notion of what constitutes the latest version of the ELF object file.

If the program, the library, and the file have different notions about the latest version, one of the following conditions can occur:

- If the program's version (the highest version that it knows about) is newer than that of the access library, important semantic knowledge that the program uses may not be known to the access library. This can cause translation routines not to work. If this happens, install a new library.

- The file's version may be newer than the program version or the library version. If this happens, the program cannot process the file correctly if it contains extra information that cannot be ignored. If this condition occurs, install a new library that understands the file's version. See "Error Condition: Value Returned" below.
- The library version may be newer than the program's version and the file's version. This is not a problem because the library understands older versions.

To cope with differences in the versions that the program, library, and file understand, `elf_version` lets a program ascertain the library's internal version. Also, the program must call `elf_version` so that it can pass the program's own working version, *`ver`*, to the library. This establishes the working version for the process. Every program that uses the ELF library must coordinate versions in this way.

The library uses the working version to accept data from the program in the correct representations, as well as to present data to the program in the correct representations. The library uses each file's version to interpret the data when it reads object files. It also uses the program's working version for file data when it writes files or converts memory types to the equivalent file types.

Each program knows its version because each program is compiled with certain header files. The EV_CURRENT macro in the `<libelf.h>` header file supplies the version to the program. Similarly, the access library is compiled with header files that specify the version that it understands. Finally, each ELF object file contains a value that identifies its version, as determined by the ELF version that the file's creator knows.

`elf_version` will not accept a version that is unknown to the library.

Arguments

`ver` specifies a version. The working version should be the same for each operation on a given *`elf`* descriptor. If the version is changed between operations on a descriptor, unexpected results may occur. See "Normal Completion: Value Returned" and "Error Condition: Value Returned" below for additional details about *`ver`*.

Normal Completion: Value Returned

`elf_version` returns the library's internal version without changing the working version if *`ver`* equals EV_NONE. `elf_version` returns the initial or previous working version number if *`ver`* is a version number that the library knows.

Error Condition: Value Returned

If *ver* is unequal to EV_NONE and *ver* is unknown to the library, elf_version returns EV_NONE.

See Also

elf (E), elf_begin (E), elf_xlate (E)

elf_xlate (E) DATA TRANSLATION elf_xlate (E)

Name

elf_xlate: elf32_xlateof, elf32_xlatetom—do class-dependent data translation

Synopsis

cc [*flag* . . .] *file* . . . -lelf [*library* . . .]
#include <libelf.h>

```
Elf_Data *elf32_xlateof (Elf_Data *dst, const
Elf_Data *src, unsigned encode);

Elf_Data *elf32_xlatetom (Elf_Data *dst, const
Elf_Data *src, unsigned encode);
```

Description

elf32_xlatom and elf32_xlatof perform data translations that are particularly useful for cross-compilation environments.

Two parallel sets of objects support cross-compilation. One set corresponds to file contents. The other set corresponds to the native memory image of the program that manipulates the file. Native memory objects should be as big as or bigger than file objects in order to avoid loss of information through truncation.

The type definitions that the header files supply work on the native machine, but the native machine may have different data encodings than the target machine. For example, the two machines may differ in word size, byte order, and so on.

elf32_xlatom translates certain data structures from their 32-bit class file representations to their appropriate memory representations.

elf32_xlatof is the inverse of elf32_xlatom; it translates memory representations to file representations.

Arguments

dst points to a destination buffer that will contain the translated data [see elf_getdata (E)]. The destination buffer (and source buffer; see below) is associated with an Elf_Data structure (descriptor) that includes the following members:

d_buf points to the data buffer. Translation routines permit the source and destination buffers to coincide, that is, dst->d_buf can equal src->d buf. In other cases, overlap of the source and destination buffers gives undefined results. The source and the destination buffers must both have valid pointers. If a data element has no data, it has a null pointer.

d_type has a value that specifies the type of data to which d_buf points, as well as the type of data that are to be created at the destination. The program must supply a d_type value in the source. The library sets the d_type of the destination to the same value as the source type. The possible values are as follows:

ELF_T_ADDR is associated with the Elf32_Addr 32-bit memory type.

ELF_T_BYTE is associated with the unsigned char 32-bit memory type. If buffers that have type ELF_T_BYTE are translated, this does not change the byte order.

ELF_T_DYN is associated with the Elf32_Dyn 32-bit memory type.

ELF_T_EHDR is associated with the Elf32_Ehdr 32-bit memory type.

ELF_T_HALF is associated with the Elf32_Half 32-bit memory type.

ELF_T_OFF is associated with the Elf32_Off 32-bit memory type.

ELF_T_PHDR is associated with the Elf32_Phdr 32-bit memory type.

ELF_T_REL is associated with the Elf32_Rel 32-bit memory type.

ELF_T_RELA is associated with the Elf32_Rela 32-bit memory type.

ELF_T_SHDR is associated with the Elf32_Shdr 32-bit memory type.

ELF_T_SWORD is associated with the Elf32_Sword 32-bit memory type.

ELF_T_SYM is associated with the Elf32_Sym 32-bit memory type.

ELF_T_WORD is associated with the Elf32_Word 32-bit memory type.

d_size contains the total size (in bytes) of the memory that the source data occupy and the size allocated for the destination data. Translation routines do not alter the contents of the destination buffer if the buffer is not large enough to contain the source data. Translation routines reset the destination's d_size member to the exact size that will be required after the translation occurs.

d_version contains the version number of the objects in the buffer. The source and destination versions are independent of each other.

encode specifies the byte encoding to be used in representing the file objects. It must equal one of the encoding values defined for the e_ident[EI_DATA] entry in the ELF header.

src points to the source buffer that contains the original data. See *dst* above.

Normal Completion: Value Returned

If elf32_xlatof or elf32_xlatom is able to translate the data, it returns *dst*.

Error Condition: Value Returned

If elf32_xlatom or elf32_xlatof fails to translate the data, it returns a null that indicates that an error such as a destination buffer overflow or incompatible data types has occurred.

See Also

elf (E), elf_fsize (E), elf_getdata (E), elf_getident (E)

nlist (E) GET NAME LIST ENTRIES nlist (E)

Name

nlist—get name list entries

Synopsis

```
cc [flag . . .] file . . . -lelf [library . . .]
#include <nlist.h>

int nlist (const char *filename, struct nlist *nl);
```

Description

`nlist` examines the name list in the file to which *`filename`* points, selectively extracts a list of values from the file, and puts the values in an array of `nlist` structures to which *`nl`* points. `nlist` looks up each variable name in the name list of the file. If `nlist` finds a name, it inserts the type, value, storage class, and section number of the name in the other fields. If the file was not compiled with the `-g` option of `cc` (Peterson 1991a), the type field can be set to 0.

If `nlist` does not find the name in the file, it sets all fields in the structure except `n_name` to 0. If the file cannot be read or if it does not contain a valid name list, `nlist` sets all value entries in the structure to 0.

Programs can get up to date system addresses by using `nlist` to examine the system name list that is kept in the `/stand/unix` file.

Arguments

`filename` specifies the executable file that contains the name list.

`nl` points to a name list that consists of an array of structures that contain names of variables, types, and values. The name list is terminated by a null name, that is, a null string that occupies the name position of the structure.

Normal Completion: Value Returned

If `nlist` succeeds, it returns 0. `nlist` always returns the information for an external symbol of a specified name if that name exists in the file. The values that `nlist` returns will be for the last occurrence of a name in the file if an external symbol of the name does not exist and the file has more than one symbol with the specified name.

Error Condition: Value Returned

If `nlist` fails, it returns −1.

See Also

`a.out` (AT&T 1990m)

Part 4

libgen General-Purpose Library

Part 4 has two kinds of sections:

- A section that classifies routines in the libgen general-purpose library, and
- A separate section for each libgen routine. These sections are arranged in alphabetical order.

class (G) CLASSIFICATION OF LIBGEN ROUTINES class (G)

Name

class—Classification of routines in the libgen general-purpose library

Description

This section classifies the routines in the libgen general-purpose library and points to the descriptions of these routines.

basename (G) — LAST COMPONENT OF A PATHNAME — basename (G)

Name

`basename`—get the last component of a pathname

Synopsis

```
cc [flag . . .] file . . . -lgen [library . . .]
#include <libgen.h>

char *basename (char *path);
```

Description

`basename` returns a pointer to the last element in the specified *`path`* and deletes any trailing "`/`" characters. For example, if given a pointer to an input string consisting of `/usr/lib`, it returns a pointer to `usr`. If given a pointer to `/usr/`, it returns a pointer to `usr`.

Arguments

`path` points to a null-terminated character string that contains a pathname.

Normal Completion: Value Returned

If `basename` succeeds, it returns a pointer to the last element of the specified *path*.

Error Condition: Value Returned

`basename` returns a pointer to a static constant "`.`" if either *path* or **path* is 0.

See Also

`dirname` (G), `basename` (AT&T 1990q)

bgets (G) READ A STREAM bgets (G)

Name

`bgets`—read a stream until a delimiter is met

Synopsis

```
cc [flag . . .] file . . . -lgen [library . . .]
#include <libgen.h>

char *bgets (char *buffer, size_t *count, FILE
*stream, const char *breakstring);
```

Description

`bgets` reads characters into the *buffer* from the specified *stream* until it encounters one of the characters in *breakstring* or until *count* is reduced to 0. `bgets` puts a null byte (`'\0'`) at the end of the characters that it reads into the *buffer*. If `bgets` encounters a character in *breakstring*, the last character in the buffer before the terminating null byte is the character in *breakstring* that terminated `bgets`'s scan.

```
bgets(buffer, sizeof buffer, stream, "\n");
```

is identical to

```
fgets(buffer, sizeof buffer, stream);
```

except that `bgets` returns a pointer to the end of the string and `fgets` returns a pointer to the beginning.

Arguments

breakstring points to a set of characters, any of which will terminate `bgets`'s scan if `bgets` encounters it. `bgets` uses the value from a previous `bgets` call if *breakstring* is a null pointer. `bgets` will not use any characters to delimit the string if *breakstring* is null on the first call. *buffer* always has enough space reserved to store the trailing null byte.

buffer points to a buffer that receives characters read from the *stream*.

count specifies the number of characters that `bgets` is to read from *stream*, subject to the conditions described under *breakstring* above.

stream specifies the stream from which `bgets` reads input.

Normal Completion: Value Returned

If `bgets` succeeds, it returns a pointer to the trailing null that terminates the characters that were read into *buffer*.

Error Condition: Value Returned

`bgets` returns `NULL` if it encounters an end of file or if an error occurs, but reporting the condition is delayed until the next `bgets` call if any characters were read but have not yet been returned.

See Also

`gets` (C)

bufsplit (G) SPLIT A BUFFER INTO FIELDS bufsplit (G)

Name

`bufsplit`—split a buffer into fields

Synopsis

```
cc [flag . . .] file . . . -lgen [library . . .]
#include <libgen.h>

size_t bufsplit (char *buffer, size_t n, char **a);
```

Description

`bufsplit` examines the field delimiter characters in a buffer, *buffer*, and divides *buffer* into several separate fields. It does this by assigning values to the array of pointers, *a*, so that a pointer points to each of the first *n* fields in *buffer* that are delimited by either tabs or newlines. `bufsplit` changes the delimiter characters in *buffer* to null bytes. The remaining bytes in the array get the same address as the null byte at the end of the buffer.

`bufsplit` will change the characters used to separate fields if it is called with *buffer* pointing to the string of characters, and *a* and *n* are set to 0. For example, to use '|', ':', ';', and ',' as field separators along with the tab and newline, execute

```
bufsplit("|:;,\t\n", 0, (char**)0 );
```

Arguments

a is an array that contains pointers to *n* fields in *buffer*.
buffer is divided into separate fields by `bufsplit`.
n specifies the number of fields into which *buffer* is to be divided.

Normal Completion: Value Returned

If `bufsplit` succeeds, it returns the number of fields assigned in the array *a* (at least field) unless *buffer* is 0. If *buffer* is 0, `bufsplit` returns 0 and does not change the array.

copylist (G) COPY A FILE TO MEMORY copylist (G)

Name

`copylist`—copy a file to memory

Synopsis

```
cc [flag . . .] file . . . -lgen [library . . .]
#include <libgen.h>

char *copylist (const char *filename, off_t
*szptr);
```

Description

`copylist` copies a list of items delimited by newlines from a file to freshly allocated memory, replacing newlines with null characters as it goes.

Arguments

filename points to the name of the file that `copylist` is to copy.
szptr points to a location where the size of the specified file is to be stored.

Normal Completion: Value Returned

If `copylist` succeeds, it returns a pointer to the freshly allocated memory.

Error Condition: Value Returned

If `copylist` cannot find the specified file or open the file if it finds it, or if `malloc` (C), which `copylist` calls, fails, `copylist` returns `NULL`.

See Also

`malloc` (C)

dirname (G) — PARENT DIRECTORY NAME OF A FILE PATHNAME — dirname (G)

Name

`dirname`—get the parent directory name of a file pathname

Synopsis

```
cc [flag . . .] file . . . -lgen [library . . .]
#include <libgen.h>

char *dirname (char *pathname);
```

Description

`dirname` accepts a pointer to a null-terminated character string that specifies a file system pathname and returns a pointer to a static constant string that specifies the parent directory of the file.

`dirname` and `basename` yield a complete pathname when used together; that is, `dirname` (*pathname*) returns a pointer to the directory where `basename` (*pathname*) is found.

Arguments

pathname points to a null-terminated character string that contains a file system pathname. No trailing `"/"` characters that the path contains are counted as part of the path. The content of *pathname* must be disposable because `dirname` sometimes puts a null byte in the pathname following the next to last element of the pathname.

Normal Completion: Value Returned

If `dirname` succeeds, it returns a pointer to a static constant string that specifies the parent directory.

Error Condition: Value Returned

`dirname` returns a pointer to the static constant `"."` if *pathname* or `*`*pathname* is 0.

See Also

`basename` (G), `basename` (AT&T 1990q), `chdir` (Peterson 1991b)

gmatch (G) SHELL GLOBAL PATTERN MATCHING gmatch (G)

Name

`gmatch`—perform shell global pattern matching

Synopsis

```
cc [flag . . .] file . . . -lgen [library . . .]
#include <libgen.h>

int gmatch (const char *str, const char *pattern);
```

Description

`gmatch` tests whether the pattern in the string to which its first argument points matches the pattern string to which its second argument points.

`gmatch` treats a backslash (`'\'`) in a pattern string as an escape character. See `sh` (AT&T 1990q) for details of pattern matching.

Arguments

pattern points to a null-terminated pattern string.

str points to a null-terminated string which `gmatch` is to compare with the string to which *pattern* points.

Normal Completion: Value Returned

If gmatch finds the pattern it seeks, it returns a nonzero (true) value. It also returns a nonzero value for any string that has an 'a' or a '-' as its last character.

Error Condition: Value Returned

If gmatch fails to find the pattern it seeks, it returns 0.

See Also

sh (AT&T 1990q)

isencrypt (G) CHARACTER BUFFER ENCRYPTION isenrypt (G)

Name

isencrypt—test whether a character buffer is encrypted

Synopsis

cc [*flag* . . .] *file* . . . -lgen [*library* . . .]
#include <libgen.h>

int isencrypt (const char **fbuffer*, size_t *ninbuffer*);

Description

isencrypt determines whether characters in a buffer are encrypted. It assumes that the buffer is not encrypted if the characters in the buffer are ASCII characters. It assumes that the characters in the buffer are encrypted if there are non-ASCII characters in the first *ninbuffer* (see below) characters of the buffer and the LC_CTYPE category of setlocale (C) is equal to ascii or C.

Arguments

fbuffer specifies the buffer that contains characters whose encryption status is to be determined.

ninbuffer specifies the number of characters in *fbuffer*. Under some circumstances, *ninbuffer* also determines how `isencrypt` decides whether *fbuffer* is encrypted. If *ninbuffer* is greater than or equal to 64 and LC_TYPE (see above) is unequal to `ascii` or C, `isencrypt` uses a chi-square test to determine whether the bytes in *fbuffer* are uniformly distributed. If they are, `isencrypt` assumes that the bytes are encrypted. If *ninbuffer* is less than 64 and LC_CTYPE is unequal to `ascii` or C, `isencrypt` tests for the presence of null characters and a terminating newline to determine whether the buffer is encrypted.

Normal Completion: Value Returned

`isencrypt` returns 1 if the buffer is encrypted. Otherwise, it returns 0.

See Also

`setlocale` (C)

mkdirp (G) CREATE/REMOVE DIRECTORIES mkdirp (G)

Name

`mkdirp`, `rmdirp`—create or remove directories in a path

Synopsis

```
cc [flag . . .] file . . . -lgen [library . . .]
#include <libgen.h>

int mkdirp (const char *pathnane, mode_t mode);

int rmdirp (char *d, char d1);
```

Description

`mkdirp` creates the missing directories in the specified *pathname* with the specified *mode*. In doing so, it uses `malloc` (X) to allocate temporary space for the string.

`rmdirp` deletes directories in the specified path, *d*. It begins at the end of the path and moves toward the root as far as it can.

Arguments

d specifies a path from which `rmdirp` is to remove directories.

d1 specifies where the remainder of a path is to be stored if `rmdirp` encounters an error condition.

mode specifies the mode in which `mkdirp` is to create directories in the specified path. See `chmod` (Peterson 1991b) for a description of the value that *mode* may have.

pathname specifies the path in which `mkdirp` is to create directories.

Normal Completion: Value Returned

If all of the directories are created or already exist, `mkdirp` returns 0.

If `rmdirp` removes every directory in the path, it returns 0.

Error Condition: Value Returned

If `mkdirp` fails to create a directory, it returns −1 and sets `errno` to one of the `mkdir` (Peterson 1991b) error numbers.

If "`.`" or "`..`" is in the path, `rmdirp` returns −2. If an attempt is made to remove the current directory, `rmdirp` returns −3. If any other error occurs, `rmdirp` returns −1.

See Also

`mkdir` (Peterson 1991b), `rmdir` (Peterson 1991b)

p2open (G) OPEN/CLOSE A PIPE TO A COMMAND p2open (G)

Name

`p2open`, `p2close`—open or close pipes to or from a command

Synopsis

```
cc [flag . . .] file . . . -lgen [library . . .]
#include <libgen.h>

int p2close (FILE *fp[2]);

int p2open (const char *cmd, FILE *fp[2]);
```

Description

`p2open` forks and execs a shell that runs the command to which *cmd* points.

`p2close` closes the file pointers opened by `p2open`. It waits for the process to terminate and returns the process status (see "Normal Completion: Value Returned" and "Error Condition: Value Returned" below).

Some commands use buffered output when they are connected to a pipe, which can make it seem as if such a command is not working properly.

Arguments

`cmd` points to a command line.

`fp`[0] points to a `FILE` pointer to write to the command's standard input. This permits the program to control the input of the command. Buffered writes on `fp`[0] can make it seem as if the command is not listening. Use `fflush` (S) calls or unbuffer `fp`[0] if this poses a problem [see `fclose` (S)].

`fp`[1] points to a `FILE` pointer to read from the command's standard output. This permits the program to control the output of the command.

Normal Completion: Value Returned

If `p2open` succeeds, it returns 0. If `p2close` succeeds, it returns 0.

Error Condition: Value Returned

If `p2open` fails, it returns −1. If `p2close` fails, it returns −1. A common reason these functions fail is that they have too few file descriptors. If the two file pointers, `fp`[0] and `fp`[1], are not from the same `p2open`, `p2close` returns −1.

See Also

`fclose` (S), `popen` (S), `setbuf` (S)

pathfind (G) — SEARCH FOR FILES IN DIRECTORIES — pathfind (G)

Name

`pathfind`—search for files in directories

Synopsis

```
cc [flag ...] file ... -lgen [library ...]
#include <libgen.h>
```

```
char *pathfind (const char *pathname, const char
*filename, const char *mode);
```

Description

`pathfind` looks for the filename, *`filename`*, in the directories specified by *`pathname`* and returns a pointer.

Arguments

`filename` specifies the filename for which `pathfind` searches. If *`filename`* begins with a slash, `pathfind` treats it as an absolute pathname and ignores *`pathname`*.

`mode` specifies the mode that the file specified by *`filename`* must have. *`mode`* is a string of one or more option letters from the set `rwxfbcdpugks`, where the option letters have the following meanings:

`b` specifies a block special file.

`c` specifies a character special file.

`d` specifies that the file is a directory.

`f` specifies a normal file.

`g` specifies that the file has its group ID bit set.

`k` specifies that the file has its sticky bit set.

`p` specifies a FIFO (pipe).

`r` specifies a readable file. This option is checked relative to the real user ID and real group ID of the process, not the effective user ID and group ID.

`s` means that the file is of nonzero size.

`u` specifies that the file has its user ID bit set.

`w` specifies a writable file. This option is checked relative to the real user ID and real group ID of the process, not the effective user ID and group ID.

`x` specifies an executable file. This option is checked relative to the real user ID and real group ID of the process, not the effective user ID and group ID.

`pathname` gives a semicolon-separated list of directories which `pathfind` searches. If *`pathname`* is empty, `pathfind` treats it as the current directory. `pathfind` does not prepend `./` when it finds the first match. Instead, it returns the unadorned *`filename`*.

Normal Completion: Value Returned

If `pathfind` finds *`filename`* (with the mode specified by *`mode`*) in any directory specified by *`pathname`*, it returns a pointer to a string that contains the member of *`pathname`*, followed by a slash (/), followed by *filename*. The string to which the pointer points is stored in a static area. Thus, the space where the string stored is reused by any subsequent `pathfind` calls.

Error Condition: Value Returned

If `pathname` fails to find a match, it returns `((char *) 0)`, a null pointer.

See Also

`getenv` (C), `access` (Peterson 1991b), `mknod` (Peterson 1991b), `sh` (AT&T 1990q), `stat` (Peterson 1991b), `test` (AT&T 1990b)

regcmp (G) COMPILE/EXECUTE A REGULAR EXPRESSION regcmp (G)

Name

`regcmp`, `regex`—compile and execute a regular expression

Synopsis

```
cc [flag . . .] file . . . -lgen [library . . .]
#include <libgen.h>

char *regcmp (const char *string1 [, char *string2,
. . .], (char *) 0);

char *regex (const char *re, const char *subject [,
char *ret0, . . .]);

extern char *__loc1;
```

Description

`regcmp` compiles the regular expression that consists of its concatenated arguments and returns a pointer to the compiled result. It uses `malloc` (C) to create space for the compiled result. If the user program iteratively calls `regcmp` without freeing vectors that are no longer needed, the program may run out of memory. The `regcmp` (Peterson 1991a) command generally eliminates the need for using the `regcmp` function at execution time.

`regex` executes the specified compiled pattern (see *re* below) against the subject string (see *subject* below).

`regcmp` and `regex` have largely been borrowed from the editor, `ed` (Peterson 1991a), but with slightly changed semantics and syntax. The symbols used with `regcmp` and `regex` are discussed below. If any of the following symbols is to be used as itself, it must be escaped by using a backslash (\).

`[ ] * . ^` are symbols that have the same meaning as in `ed`.

`$` matches the end of a string.

`n` matches a newline.

– means "through" when it is enclosed in brackets. For example, `[1-5]` has the same meaning as `[12345]`. If – is the first or last character, it can be used by itself. For example, `[]-]` matches `]` and –.

+ means "one or more times" if it follows a regular expression. For example, `[1-5]+` means the same as `[1-5][1-5]*`.

{*m*} {*m*,} {*m*, *u*} indicate the number of times the preceding regular expression is to be applied. The value *m* indicates the minimum number of times the regular expression is to be applied. If only {*m*} is present, it indicates the exact number of times the regular expression is to be applied. *u*, a number less than 256, indicates the maximum number of times the regular expression is to be applied. {*m*, } is analogous to {*m*, *infinity*}. The + and * operators have the same effect as {1, } and {0, }, respectively.

`( . . . )$`*n* indicates that the value of the enclosed regular expression is to be returned and unconditionally assigned to the (*n* + 1)th argument after the subject argument. No more than 10 enclosed regular expressions are allowed.

`( . . . )` is used for grouping, such that an operator (e.g., +, *, {}) can operate on a single character or on a regular expression that is enclosed in parentheses [for example, `(ab+)$`].

Arguments

`__loc1` is a global character that points to the location where the match began.

re specifies the compiled pattern that `regex` is to execute against the subject string.

ret0, . . ., *retn* are arguments that `regex` passes in order to receive values back.

string1 , *string2*, . . . *stringn* specify the strings to be concatenated by `regcmp`.

subject specifies a subject string.

Normal Completion: Value Returned

If `regcmp` succeeds, it returns a pointer to the string that it compiles.
If `regex` succeeds, it returns a pointer to the next unmatched character.

Error Condition: Value Returned

If `regcmp` is given an incorrect argument, it returns `NULL`. If `regex` fails, it returns `NULL`.

See Also

`malloc` (C), `ed` (AT&T 1990q), `regcmp` (Peterson 1991a)

regexpr (G) COMPILE/MATCH REGULAR EXPRESSIONS regexpr (G)

Name

`regexpr`: `compile`, `step`, `advance`—compile and match regular expressions

Synopsis

```
cc [flag . . .] file . . . -lgen [library . . .]
#include <regexpr.h>

char *compile (const char *instring, char *expbuf,
char *endbuf);

int step (const char *string, char *expbuf);

int advance (const char *string, char *expbuf);

extern char *loc1 *loc2 *locs );

extern int nbra, regerrno, reglength;

extern char *braslist[], braelist[];
```

Description

The above routines compile regular expressions in the form used by `ed` (AT&T 1990q) and match the compiled expressions against specified lines.

`compile` compiles a regular expression and returns a pointer to the expression.

`advance` steps through the string to which its *`string`* argument points until it finds a match between that string and the regular expression to which *`expbuf`* points. `advance` always restricts matches to the beginning of the string.

`step` has the same action as `advance`, except that `step` does not restrict matches to the beginning of the string.

External Variables

It is not necessary to use the external variables `braelist`, `braslist`, `loc1`, `loc2`, `locs`, and `regerrno` if the program is only testing whether or not a string matches a regular expression. The purposes of the external variables are as follows:

`braelist` is an array of character pointers that point to the end of the `nbra` expressions in the matched string. If either `advance` or `step` is called with the string `xabcdef` and the regular expression `\(abcde\)`, `braelist[0]` will point to `f`. The `braelist` array, like the `braslist` array (see below), is used by `ed` (AT&T 1990q) and `sed` (AT&T 1990q) to hold substitute replacement patterns containing the *n* notation for subexpressions.

`braslist` is an array of character pointers that point to the start of the `nbra` expressions in the matched string. If either `advance` or `step` is called with the string `xabcdef` and the regular expression `\(abcde\)`, `braslist[0]` will point to `a`.

`loc1` is one of two external character pointers (see `loc2`) that are set as a side effect of `step` if `step` finds a match between its two arguments. `loc1` points to the first character that matches the regular expression.

`loc2` is an external character pointer that is set as a side effect of `step` if `step` finds a match between its two arguments. `loc2` points to the character that follows the last character that matches the regular expression. If the regular expression matches the whole line, `loc1` points to the first character of *`string`* and `loc2` points to the null character that terminates *`string`*. `step` should be called with *`string`* equal to `loc2` if `step` is being used to find successive matches in the same string.

`locs` is an external variable. It is NULL by default. It should be set equal to `loc2` if successive matches are being sought in the same string of characters (see `loc2` above). The commands `ed` (AT&T 1990q) and `sed` (AT&T 1990q) use `locs` to prevent global substitutions like `s/y*//g` from looping forever.

`nbra` is an external variable used to determine the number of subexpressions that a compiled regular expression contains.

`reglength` is an external variable where `compile` stores the length of the compiled regular expression.

Arguments

The arguments of the `advance`, `compile`, and `step` routines are discussed below.

`advance`

`expbuf` points to the compiled regular expression that was gotten by `compile`.

`string` points to a null-terminated string of characters that are to be checked for a match.

`compile`

`endbuf` is equal to one more than the highest address where the compiled regular expression is put. *`endbuf`* is ignored if *`expbuf`* is NULL.

`expbuf` points to the location where `compile` puts the compiled regular expression. `compile` uses `malloc` (C) to allocate space to put the compiled expression if *`expbuf`* is NULL.

`instring` is a null-terminated string that represents the regular expression that `compile` compiles.

`step`

`expbuf` points to the compiled regular expression that was gotten by `compile`. If the regular expression begins with ^, `step` attempts to match only the regular expression at the beginning of the string.

`string` points to a null-terminated string of characters that are to be checked for a match.

Normal Completion: Value Returned

The value returned by each routine if it succeeds is discussed below.

`advance`

`advance` returns nonzero if the string to which *`string`* points matches the regular expression to which *`expbuf`* points.

`compile`

If `compile` succeeds, it returns a non-NULL pointer whose value depends on the value of *`expbuf`*. `compile` returns a pointer to the byte that follows the last byte in the compiled regular expression if *expbuf* is non-NULL. Otherwise, it returns a pointer to the space that malloc (C) allocates.

step

step returns nonzero if the string to which *string* points matches the regular expression to which *expbuf* points.

Error Condition: Value Returned

The values returned by each routine when it encounters an error condition are discussed below.

advance

advance returns nonzero if the string to which *string* points does not match the regular expression to which *expbuf* points.

compile

If the compiled expression that compile produces is too large to fit in *endbuf* – *expbuf* bytes, compile returns NULL and sets regerrno to 50. If an error occurs, the space which malloc (C) allocates for the compiled expression is freed, but it is the user's responsibility to free space that is not needed after the compiled expression is no longer needed. If compile encounters an error while compiling the regular expression, it returns a null pointer and sets regerrno to a nonzero number that has one of the following meanings:

11 means that the range endpoint is too large.
16 means that a number is bad.
25 means that "*digit*" is put of range.
36 means that a delimiter is illegal or missing.
41 means that there is no remembered search string.
42 means that there is a \\(~\\) imbalance.
43 means that there are too many \\(.
44 means that more than two numbers are given in \\{~\\}.
45 means that a } is expected after a \\.
46 means that the first number exceeds the second in \\{~\\}.
49 means that there is a [ ] imbalance.
50 means that there is a regular expression overflow.

step

step returns nonzero if the string to which *string* points does not match the regular expression to which *expbuf* points.

See Also

`ed` (AT&T 1990q), `grep` (AT&T 1990q), `reexp` (AT&T 1990m), `sed` (AT&T 1990q)

str (G) MANIPULATE STRINGS str (G)

Name

`str`: `strfind`, `strrspn`, `strtrns`—manipulate strings

Synopsis

cc [*flag* . . .] *file* . . . -lgen [*library* . . .]
#include <libgen.h>

int strfind (const char **as1*, const char **as2*);

char *strrspn (const char **string*, const char **tc*);

char *strtrns (const char **str*, const char **old*, const char **new*, char **result*);

Description

`strfind` finds the offset of string *as2* in string *as1* if it is a substring of string *s1*.

`strrspn` finds the first character in the string to be trimmed. All characters from the first character of *string* to its end are in *tc*.

`strtrns` transforms string *str* and copies the transformed string to *result*. In transforming *str*, `strtrns` replaces any character that appears in *old* with the character that occupies the same position in *new*.

Arguments

`strfind`

as1 points to a string which may or may not contain the string to which *as1* points.

as2 points to a string which may or may not be a substring of the string to which *as1* points.

`strrspn`

string points to the string to be trimmed.

tc specifies junk to be trimmed from the end of *string*.

`strtrns`

new specifies new characters which are to replace characters in the corresponding position of *old*.

old specifies old characters which are to be replaced.
result receives the transformed string.
str points to the string which is to be transformed.

Normal Completion: Value Returned

`strfind` returns the offset of the second string, *as2*, from the start of the first string, *as1*.

`strrspn` returns a pointer to the first character in *string* to be trimmed.

`strtrns` returns the new result of its transformation.

Error Condition: Value Returned

`strfind` returns −1 if the second string is not a substring of the first string.

See Also

`string` (C)

strccpy (G) COMPRESS/EXPAND ESCAPE CODES strccpy (G)

Name

`strccpy`: `strcadd`, `streadd`, `strecpy`—copy strings and compress or expand escape codes

Synopsis

cc [*flag* . . .] *file* . . . -lgen [*library* . . .]
#include <libgen.h>

char *strccpy (char **output*, const char **input*);

char *streadd (char **output*, const char **input*, const char **exceptions*);

char *strecpy (char **output*, const char **input*, const char **exceptions*);

Description

`strccpy` copies an input string, *input*, to an output string, *output*, compressing C-language escape sequences (e.g., `\001`, `\n`) to the equivalent character as it goes. It stops copying when it encounters a null byte in *input*, after which it appends a null byte to *output*.

strcadd has the same effect as strccpy except that it returns a pointer to the null byte that terminates *output*.

strecpy copies an input string, *input*, to an output string, *output*, expanding nongraphic characters to their equivalent C-language escape sequences (e.g., \001, \n) as it goes.

streadd has the same effect as strecpy except that it returns a pointer to the null byte that terminates *output*.

Arguments

strccpy and strcadd

input specifies an input string that is to be copied to the output string, *output*.

output points to the location that receives the transformed string. The location must be large enough to hold the result. If the location is as large as the location to which *input* points, it is large enough.

strecpy and streadd

exceptions specifies characters that are not to be expanded. If *exceptions* is 0, all nongraphic characters are expanded.

input specifies an input string that is to be copied to the output string, *output*.

output points to the location that receives the transformed string. The location that holds the result should be at least four times as large as the location to which *input* points, because each character in the input can become a slash (\) and three digits in the output.

Normal Completion: Value Returned

strcadd returns a pointer to the null byte that terminates *output*.
strccpy returns the *output* argument.
strecpy returns the *output* argument.

See Also

str (C), string (C)

Part 5

`libm` and `libsfm` Math Libraries

Part 5 has three kinds of sections:

- An introduction to `libm` and `libsfm` math library routines,
- A section that classifies `libm` and `libsfm` routines, and
- Sections that describe `libm` or `libsfm` routines. Sections that describe routines are arranged in alphabetical order.

intro (M)	**INTRODUCTION TO `libm` AND `libsfm` ROUTINES**	**intro (M)**

Name

`intro`—introduction to `libm` and `libsfm` math library routines.

Synopsis

`cc` [*`flag`* . . .] *`file`* . . . `-lm`[*`library`* . . .]

`cc -O -Ksd`[*`flag`* . . .]*`file`* . . . `-J sfm`[*`library`* . . .]

`#include <math.h>`

Description

This chapter discusses routines that are in two math libraries, `libm` and `libsfm`.

`libm` contains all of the double-precision math routines, as well as some single-precision math routines (designated by an `f` suffix) that give more speed but less precision. Some of the routines in `libm` are hand-optimized to yield more performance. The optimized routines include `atan`, `atan2`, `cos`, `exp`, `log`, `log10`, `pow`, `sin`, `sqrt`, and `tan`.

`libsfm` contains `acosf`, `asinf`, `atanf`, `cosf`, `expf`, `logf`, `log10f`, `powf`, `sinf`, and `sqrtf`. The optimizer expands the source library routines in-line in order to increase execution speed by reducing the overhead caused by passing arguments, calling functions, returning function values, and function returns. Compared to `libm`, `libsfm` achieves increased speed at the potential cost of increased size.

The math libraries are not automatically loaded at compile time. The `-J` or `-l` options of the compiler, `cc` (Peterson 1991a), must be used in order to access the libraries as follows:

`-J sfm` causes in-line expansion of functions from `libsfm`, the fast, single-precision assembly source math library. If `-O Ksd` is specified, it causes optimization for speed.

`-lm` causes the regular math library, `libm`, to be searched.

Declarations for the functions in both math libraries are contained in the `math.h` header file. The header file also contains definitions of several mathematical constants.

Arguments

`sinf` *and* `cosf` *Arguments*

The arguments of `sinf` (x) and `cosf` (x) must have values in the range

$$-\frac{\pi}{2} \leqslant x \leqslant \frac{\pi}{2}$$

`tanf Argument`

The `tanf` argument must be in the range

$$-\frac{\pi}{2} < x < \frac{\pi}{2}$$

`sqrt` *and* `logf` *and* `log10f` *Arguments*

The arguments of `logf`, `log10f`, and `sqrt` must have values greater than 0.

Definitions

See intro (C) for definitions of C-language constructs.

Error Condition: Value Returned

Details of error handling are determined by the cc (Peterson 1991a) compilation option used.

If the cc option is -Xt, math library functions return the conventional values 0, +HUGE or -HUGE, or NaN when the function in not defined for the given argument(s) or when the value returned cannot be represented. If the cc option is -Xa or -Xc, math library functions return +HUGE_VAL or -HUGE_VAL instead of +HUGE or -HUGE, respectively.

HUGE_VAL is defined in math.h to be infinity. HUGE is defined in math.h to be the largest-magnitude single-precision number.

If an error occurs, the external variable errno is always set to the value of either EDOM or ERANGE, but the value returned depends on the compilation mode, as discussed above and in the "Default Error-Handling Procedures" section in matherr (M).

Files

LIBDIR
LIBDIR/libm.a
LIBDIR/libsfm.sa

See Also

intro (C), cc (Peterson 1991a), intro (Peterson 1991b), math (AT&T 1990m), "Floating Point Operations" chapter (AT&T 1990g)

class (M) CLASSIFICATION OF libm AND libsfm ROUTINES class (M)

Name

class—classification of routines in the libm and libsfm math libraries

Description

This section classifies the routines in the libm and libsfm math libraries and points to descriptions of the routines.

bessel (M) BESSSEL FUNCTIONS bessel (M)

Name

bessel: j0, j1, jn, y0, y1, yn —perform Bessel functions

Synopsis

cc [*flag* . . .] *file* . . . -lm [*library* . . .]

```
#include <math.h>
```

```
double j0 (double x);

double j1 (double x);

double jn (int n, double x);

double y0 (double x);

double y1 (double x);

double yn (int n, double x);
```

Description

j0 and j1 and jn

j0 returns a Bessel function of x of the first kind whose order is 0.
j1 returns a Bessel function of x of the first kind whose order is 1.
jn returns a Bessel function of x of the first kind whose order is *n*.

y0 and y1 and yn

y0 returns a Bessel function of x of the second kind whose order is 0.
y1 returns a Bessel function of x of the second kind whose order is 1.
yn returns a Bessel function of x of the second kind whose order is *n*.

Arguments

j0 and j1 and jn

x is a positive value that specifies a Bessel function of x of the first kind.

y0 and y1 and yn

x is a positive value that specifies a Bessel function of x of the second kind.

Normal Completion: Value Returned

See the descriptions above.

Error Condition: Value Returned

bessel y0, y1, or yn returns -HUGE (-HUGE_VAL if the -Xa or -Xc compiler option was used), sets errno to EDOM, and prints (not if the -Xa or -Xc compiler option was used) a message indicating a DOMAIN error if its argument is not positive.

`bessel j0`, `j1`, `y0`, `y1`, or `y1` returns 0, sets `errno` to ERANGE, and prints (not if the `-Xa` or `-Xc` compiler option was used) a message indicating a `TLOSS` error if its argument is too large.

The `matherr` (M) function can change these error handling procedures, except when the `-Xc` compiler option is used.

See Also

`matherr` (M)

erf (M) ERROR FUNCTION OF X erf (M)

Name

`erf`, `erfc`—return the error function of `x`

Synopsis

```
cc [flag . . .] file . . . -lm [library . . .]

#include <math.h>

double erf (double x);

double erfc (double x);-LS2
```

Description

`erf` returns the error function of `x`, which is defined as

$$\frac{2}{\sqrt{\pi}} \int_{0}^{x} e^{-t^2}\, dt$$

`erfc` returns 1.0 – `erf(x)`. `erfc` is provided because `erf` yields very inaccurate results if it is called for large values of `x` and the returned value is subtracted from 1.0 (for example, 12 decimal places of accuracy are lost if `x` is 5).

Arguments

`x` specifies the value for which an error function is calculated.

Normal Completion: Value Returned

See the above description.

See Also

`exp` (M)

exp (M) EXPONENTS, LOGS, POWERS, SQUARE ROOTS exp (M)

Name

`exp`, `expf`, `cbrt`, `log`, `logf`, `log10`, `log10f`, `pow`, `powf`, `sqrt`, `sqrtf`—compute exponents, logarithms, powers, and square roots

Synopsis

```
cc [flag . . .] file . . . -lm [library . . .]

cc -O -Ksd [flag . . .] file . . . -J sfm [library . . .]

#include <math.h>

double exp (double x);

float expf (float x);

double cbrt (double x);

double log (double x);

float logf (double x);

double log10 (double x);

float log10f (float x);

double pow (double x, double y);

float powf (float x, float y);
```

```
double sqrt (double x);

float sqrtf (float x);
```

Description

`cbrt` returns the cube root of it argument, `x`.
`exp` and `expf` both return `e` to the `x`th power.
`log` and `logf` both return the natural logarithm of `x`.
`log10` and `log10f` both return the base 10 natural logarithm of `x`.
`pow` and `powf` both return the value of `x` raised to the *y*th power.
`sqrt` and `sqrtf` both return the nonnegative square root of `x`.

Arguments

exp and expf
`x` may have any value.

cbrt
`x` may have any value.

log and logf
`x` must have a positive value.

pow and powf
`x` can be 0 if *y* is positive
y must be an integer if `x` is negative.

sqrt and sqrtf
`x` must not have a negative value.

Normal Completion: Value Returned

See the above descriptions. If the `-Xa` or `-Xc` compiler option is used and both `x` and *y* are 0, `pow` and `powf` both return 1 with no error.

Error Condition: Value Returned

The error-handling procedures for these functions can be changed by `matherr` (M) unless the `-Xc` compiler option is used.

If the `-Xa` or `-Xc` compiler option is used, these functions return `HUGE_`

VAL on error and print no error message. Otherwise, the message printed and the value returned are as discussed below.

exp and expf

`exp` and `expf` return HUGE (HUGE_VAL if the `-Xa` or `-Xc` compiler option was used) and set `errno` to ERANGE if the result would cause overflow.

`exp` and `expf` return 0 and set `errno` to ERANGE if the result would cause underflow.

log and logf and log10 and log10f

`log`, `log10`, `logf`, and `log10f` return -HUGE (-HUGE_VAL if the `-Xa` or `-Xc` compiler option was used), set `errno` to EDOM, and print (not if the `-Xa` or `-Xc` compiler option was used) a message indicating a DOMAIN error if the argument is less than 0.

`log`, `log10`, `logf`, and `log10f` return -HUGE (-HUGE_VAL if the `-Xa` or `-Xc` compiler option was used), set `errno` to EDOM, and print (not if the `-Xa` or `-Xc` compiler option was used) a message indicating a DOMAIN error if the argument equals 0.

If the compiler option is `-Xc`, `log` and `logf` return NaN if x is negative.

pow and powf

`pow` and `powf` return 0, set `errno` to EDOM, and print on standard error a message that indicates that a DOMAIN error has occurred if y is not positive and x is 0.

`pow` and `powf` return 0, set `errno` to EDOM, and print on standard error a message that indicates a DOMAIN error has occurred if y is not an integer and x is negative.

`pow` and `powf` set `errno` to ERANGE and return +HUGE if the value they return would cause overflow.

`pow` and `powf` set `errno` to ERANGE and return -HUGE if the value they return would cause underflow.

sqrt and sqrtf

`sqrt` and `sqrtf` return 0, set `errno` to EDOM, and print on standard error a message indicating a DOMAIN error if x is negative.

See Also

`hypot` (M), `matherr` (M), `sinh` (M)

floor (M) ABSOLUTE VALUE, CEILING, FLOOR, REMAINDER floor (M)

Name

floor, floorf, ceil, ceilf, copysign, fmod, fmodf, fabs, fabsf, rint, remainder—compute floor, ceiling, remainder, or absolute values

Synopsis

cc [*flag* . . .] *file* . . . -lm [*library* . . .]

```
#include <math.h>

double floor (double x);

float floorf (float x);

double ceil (double x);

float ceilf (float x);

double copysign (double x, double y);

double fmod (double x, double y);

float fmodf (float x, float y);

double fabs (double x);

float fabsf (float x);

double rint (double x);

double remainder (double x, double y);
```

Description

ceil and ceilf return the largest integer that is greater than or equal to *x*.

copysign returns *x* but gives *x* the same sign as *y*.

fabs and fabsf return $|x|$, the absolute value of *x*.

floor and floorf return the largest integer that is less than or equal to x.

fmod and fmodf return the floating-point remainder that results from division of x by y. That is, they return a number f such that f has the same sign as x, and x is equal to (i * y + f) for some integer i and for |f| < |y|.

remainder returns the floating-point remainder that results from division of x by y. That is, it returns the value r = (x - y * n), where n is the integer that is nearest the exact value of (x /y). n is even if 0.5 equals |n - x/y|.

rint returns the integer that is closest to its double-precision floating-point argument x. It rounds the returned value according to the current machine-rounding mode. The returned value will be rounded to the nearest even integer if the round-to-nearest mode (the default mode) is set and the difference between the x and the rounded result is exactly equal to 0.5.

Arguments

See the above descriptions.

Normal Completion: Value Returned

See the above descriptions.

Error Condition: Value Returned

fmod and fmodf return x, set errno to EDOM, and print (not if the compilation mode is -Xa or -Xc) on standard error a message indicating a DOMAIN error if y equals 0.

remainder returns NaN, sets errno to EDOM, and prints (not if the compilation mode is -Xa or -Xc) on standard error a message indicating a DOMAIN error if y equals 0.

These error-handling procedures can be changed by matherr (M).

See Also

abs (C), matherr (M)

gamma (M) LOG GAMMA FUNCTION gamma (M)

Name

gamma, lgamma—return a log gamma function

Synopsis

```
cc [flag ...] file ... -lm [library ...]

#include <math.h>

double gamma (double x);

double lgamma (double x);

extern int signgam;
```

Description

`gamma` and `lgamma` return the log of the gamma function of `x`; that is,

$$\ln(|\Gamma(x)|)$$

where $\Gamma(x)$ is defined as

$$\int_0^\infty e^{-t} t^{x-1}\, dt$$

The sign of (x) is returned in the external integer variable `signgam`. The value of the gamma function can be computed by using the following C-code fragment:

```
if ((y = gamma(x)) > LN_MAXDOUBLE)
error (); /* error handling here */
y = signgam * exp(y);
```

Arguments

`x` must be a positive integer.

Normal Completion: Value Returned

See the above description.

Error Condition: Value Returned

`gamma` and `lgamma` return HUGE (HUGE_VAL instead of HUGE if the compiler option is `-Xa` or `-Xc`), set `errno` to EDOM, and print on standard error output a message indicating a `SING` error (no message if the compiler option is `-Xa` or `-Xc`) if `x` is not a positive integer.

gamma and lgamma return HUGE and set errno to ERANGE if the result would overflow.

The error-handling procedures for these functions can be changed by matherr (M) unless the compiler option is -Xc.

See Also

exp (M), matherr (M), values (AT&T 1990m)

hypot (M) EUCLIDEAN DISTANCE FUNCTION hypot (M)

Name

hypot—compute the Euclidean distance function

Synopsis

cc [*flag* . . .] *file* . . . -lm [*library* . . .]

```
#include <math.h>
```

double hypot (double *x*, double *y*);

Description

hypot returns the value of

sqrt(*x* * *x* + *y* * *y*)

It takes precautions against overflow.

Error Condition: Value Returned

hypot returns HUGE (HUGE_VAL if the -Xa or -Xc compiler option was used) and sets errno to ERANGE if the correct result would overflow.

The error-handling procedure for this function can be changed by matherr (M) unless the compiler option is -Xc.

See Also

matherr (M)

matherr (M) MANAGE MATH ERROR MESSAGES matherr (M)

Name

matherr—manage errors

Synopsis

cc [*flag* . . .] *file* . . . -lm [*library* . . .]

```
#include <math.h>

int matherr (struct exception *x);
```

Description

When a function in the math library encounters an error, it calls matherr unless the -Xc compiler option was used in compiling the program.

A user-defined error-handling procedure can be substituted for the default matherr procedure by including a function named matherr in the program. When an error occurs, the user-supplied matherr function will be passed a pointer to the exception structure x defined in the <math.h> header file. The structure is defined as follows:

```
struct exception {
    int type;
    char *name
    double arg1, arg2, retval
};
```

type is an integer constant that tells what error has occurred. It may be one of the following constants:

DOMAIN indicates that an argument domain error has occurred.
OVERFLOW indicates that an overflow range error has occurred.
PLOSS indicates that a partial loss of significance has occurred.
SING indicates that an argument singularity error has occurred.
TLOSS indicates that a total loss of significance has occurred.
UNDERFLOW indicates that an underflow range error has occurred.

name points to a string that contains the name of the function that encountered the error.

arg1 is an argument with which the function was called.

arg2 is an argument with which the function was called.

`retval` is set to the default value that will be returned by the function if the user's `matherr` function does not set it to another value.

Default Error-Handling Procedures

The values returned by default error handling procedures are as follows:

- `bessel y0`, `y1`, or `yn` returns `-HUGE` (`-HUGE_VAL` if the `-Xa` or `-Xc` compiler option was used), sets `errno` to EDOM, and prints (not if the `-Xa` or `-Xc` compiler option was used) a message indicating a `DOMAIN` error if its argument is not positive.
- `bessel j0`, `j1`, `y0`, `y1`, or `y1` returns 0, sets `errno` to `ERANGE`, and prints (not if the `-Xa` or `-Xc` compiler option was used) a message indicating a `TLOSS` error if its argument is too large.
- `exp` and `expf` return HUGE (`HUGE_VAL` if the `-Xa` or `-Xc` compiler option was used) and set `errno` to ERANGE if the result would cause overflow.
- `exp` and `expf` return 0 and set `errno` to ERANGE if the result would cause underflow.
- `log`, `log10`, `logf`, and `log10f` return `-HUGE` (`-HUGE_VAL` if the `-Xa` or `-Xc` compiler option was used), set `errno` to EDOM, and print (not if the `-Xa` or `-Xc` compiler option was used) a message indicating a `DOMAIN` error if the argument is less than 0.
- `log`, `log10`, `logf`, and `log10f` return `-HUGE` (`-HUGE_VAL` if the `-Xa` or `-Xc` compiler option was used), set `errno` to EDOM, and print (not if the `-Xa` or `-Xc` compiler option was used) a message indicating a `DOMAIN` error if the argument equals 0.
- `pow` and `powf` return 0, set `errno` to EDOM, and print on standard error output a message indicating that a `DOMAIN` error has occurred if *y* is not positive and *x* is 0.
- `pow` and `powf` return 0, set `errno` to EDOM, and print on standard error output a message indicating that a `DOMAIN` error has occurred if *y* is not an integer and *x* is negative.
- `pow` and `powf` set `errno` to ERANGE and return `+HUGE` if the value they return would cause overflow.
- `pow` and `powf` set `errno` to ERANGE and return `-HUGE` if the value they return would cause underflow.
- `sqrt` and `sqrtf` return 0, set `errno` to EDOM, and print on standard error output a message indicating a `DOMAIN` error if *x* is negative.
- `fmod` and `fmodf` return *x*, set `errno` to EDOM, and print (not if the compilation mode is `-Xa` or `-Xc`) on standard error output a message indicating a `DOMAIN` error if *y* equals 0.
- `remainder` returns `NaN`, sets `errno` to EDOM, and prints (not if the

compilation mode is -Xa or -Xc) on standard error output a message indicating a DOMAIN error if *y* equals 0.

- gamma and lgamma return HUGE (HUGE_VAL instead of HUGE if the compiler option is -Xa or -Xc), set errno to EDOM, and print on standard error output a message indicating a SING error (no message if the compiler option is -Xa or -Xc) if *x* is not a positive integer.
- gamma and lgamma return HUGE andd set errno to ERANGE if the result would overflow.
- hypot returns HUGE (HUGE_VAL if the -Xa or -Xc compiler option was used) and sets errno to ERANGE if the correct result would overflow.
- acosh returns NaN (HUGE_VAL if the -Xa or -Xc compiler option was used), sets errno to EDOM, and prints (not if the -Xa or -Xc compiler option was used) on standard error output a message indicating that a DOMAIN error has occurred if *x* is less than 1.
- atanh returns NaN (HUGE_VAL if the -Xa or -Xc compiler option was used), sets errno to EDOM, and prints (not if the -Xa or -Xc compiler option was used) a message indicating that a DOMAIN error has occurred if the absolute value of *x*, $|x|$, is greater than 1.
- atanh returns NaN (HUGE_VAL if the -Xa or -Xc compiler option was used), sets errno to EDOM, and prints (not if the -Xa or -Xc compiler option was used) a message indicating that a SING error has occurred if $|x|$ equals 1.
- sinh, sinhf, cosh, and coshf return HUGE (HUGE_VAL if the -Xa or -Xc compiler option was used) and set errno to ERANGE if their result is one that would overflow.
- sinh and sinhf return -HUGE (HUGE_VAL if the -Xa or -Xc compiler option was used) and set errno to ERANGE if *x* is negative.
- asin, asinf, acos, and acosf return 0, set errno to EDOM, and print (not if the -Xa or -Xc compiler option was used) on standard error output a message indicating that a DOMAIN error has occurred if the magnitude of *x* is greater than 1.
- atan2 and atan2f return 0, set errno to EDOM, and print (not if the -Xa or -Xc compiler option was used) on standard error output a message indicating that a DOMAIN error has occurred if both argument are 0.

Arguments

x points to the exception structure described above.

Normal Completion: Value Returned

If the user's matherr function returns nonzero, errno will not be set and no error message will be printed.

Error Condition: Value Returned

If no `matherr` function is supplied by the user, a math function that encounters an error will call the default `matherr` function and set `errno` to either EDOM or ERANGE, after which program execution will resume.

sinh (M) HYPERBOLIC FUNCTIONS sinh (M)

Name

`sinh`, `sinhf`, `cosh`, `coshf`, `tanh`, `tanhf`, `asinh`, `acosh`, `atanh`—compute hyperbolic functions

SYNOPSIS

```
cc [flag . . .] file . . . -lm [library . . .]

#include <math.h>

double sinh (double x);

float sinhf (float x);

double cosh (double x);

float coshf (float x);

double tanh (double x);

float tanhf (float x);

double asinh (double x);

double acosh (double x);

double atanh (double x);
```

Description

`asinh`, `acosh`, and `atanh`, respectively, return the inverse hyperbolic sine, cosine, and tangent of their argument.

`sinh`, `cosh`, and `tanh`, respectively, return the double-precision hyperbolic sine, cosine, and tangent of their argument.

sinhf, coshf, and tanhf, respectively, return the single-precision hyperbolic sine, cosine, and tangent of their argument.

Error Condition: Value Returned

Error-handling procedures for the above functions can be changed by matherr if the program was compiled with the -Xc option.

acosh returns NaN (HUGE_VAL if the -Xa or -Xc compiler option was used), sets errno to EDOM, and prints (not if the -Xa or -Xc compiler option was used) on standard error output a message indicating that a DOMAIN error has occurred if *x* is less than 1.

atanh returns NaN (HUGE_VAL if the -Xa or -Xc compiler option was used), sets errno to EDOM, and prints (not if the -Xa or -Xc compiler option was used) a message indicating that a DOMAIN error has occurred if the absolute value of *x*, $|x|$, is greater than 1.

atanh returns NaN (HUGE_VAL if the -Xa or -Xc compiler option was used), sets errno to EDOM, and prints (not if the -Xa or -Xc compiler option was used) a message indicating that a SING error has occurred if $|x|$ equals 1.

sinh, sinhf, cosh, and coshf return HUGE (HUGE_VAL if the -Xa or -Xc compiler option was used) and set errno to ERANGE if their result is one that would overflow.

sinh and sinhf return -HUGE (HUGE_VAL if the -Xa or -Xc compiler option was used) and set errno to ERANGE if *x* is negative.

See Also

matherr (M)

trig (M) TRIGONOMETRIC FUNCTIONS trig (M)

Name

trig: sin, sinf, cos, cosf, tan, tanf, asin, asinf, acos, acosf, atan, atanf, atan2, atan2f—compute trigonometric functions

Synopsis

cc [*flag* . . .] *file* . . . -lm [*library* . . .]

cc -O -Ksd [*flag* . . .] *file* . . . -J sfm [*library* . . .]

```
#include <math.h>

double sin (double x);

float sinf (float x);

double cos (double x);

float cosf (float x);

double tan (double x);

float tanf (float x);

double asin (double x);

float asinf (float x);

double acos (double x);

float acosf (float x);

double atan (double x);

float atanf (float x);

double atan2 (double y, double x);

float atan2f (float y, float x);
```

Description

`acos` and `acosf` return the arccosine of `x`. The angle is in the range $[0, +\pi]$.

`asin` and `asinf` return the arcsine of `x`. The angle is in the range $[-\pi/2, +\pi/2]$.

`atan` and `atanf` return the arctangent of `x`. The angle is in the range $[-\pi/2, +\pi/2]$.

`atan2` and `atan2f` return the arctangent of *y*/ `x`, in the range $[-\pi, +\pi]$. The quadrant of the return value is determined by the signs of both arguments.

`sin`, `cos`, and `tan`, respectively, return the double-precision sine, cosine, and tangent of their argument, `x`, measured in radians.

sinf, cosf, and tanf, respectively, return the single-precision sine, cosine, and tangent of their argument, x, measured in radians.

Error Condition: Value Returned

Error-handling procedures for the above functions can be changed by matherr if the program was compiled with the -Xc option.

asin, asinf, acos, and acosf return 0, set errno to EDOM, and print (not if the -Xa or -Xc compiler option was used) on the standard error output a message indicating that a DOMAIN error has occurred if the magnitude of x is greater than 1.

atan2 and atan2f return 0, set errno to EDOM, and print (not if the -Xa or -Xc compiler option was used) on standard error output a message indicating that a DOMAIN error has occurred if both arguments are 0.

See Also

matherr (M)

Part 6

Specialized Libraries

Part 6 has two kinds of sections:

- A section that classifies the routines in the UNIX System V specialized libraries, and
- Sections that describe routines in the specialized libraries. These are arranged in alphabetical order.

CLASSIFICATION OF SPECIALIZED ROUTINES

class (X)

Name

`class`—classification of routines in specialized libraries

Description

This section classifies routines in the specialized libraries and points to these routines.

Diagnostics

Miscellaneous Routines

assert (X) ERROR MESSAGE MANAGEMENT assert (X)

Name

assert—verify the truth value of an expression

Synopsis

```
#include <assert.h>

void assert (int expression);
```

Description

assert is used for putting diagnostics into programs. If assert is executed, it prints

Assertion failed: *expression*, file *xyz*, line *nnn*

on the standard error output and aborts if *expression* is false (zero).

nnn is the number of the source line that contains the assert statement. The value of *nnn* is the value of the preprocessor macro, __LINE__.

xyz is the name of the source file that contains the assert statement. The value of *xyz* is the value of the preprocessor macro, __FILE__.

Assertions can be stopped from being compiled into a program if the preproccesor control statement #define NDEBUG is placed in front of the #include <assert.h> statement or if the program is compiled with the preprocessor option -DNDEBUG [see cc (Peterson 1991a)].

Arguments

expression is an expression whose truth value is tested by assert. *expression* may not contain any string literals because assert is a macro.

See Also

abort (C), cc (Peterson 1991a)

crypt (X) PASSWORD AND FILE ENCRYPTION crypt (X)

Name

crypt—manage password and file encryption functions

Synopsis

cc [*flag* . . .] *file* . . . -lcrypt [*library* . . .]

```
#include <crypt.h>

char *crypt (const char *key, const char *salt);

void setkey (const char *key);

void encrypt (char *block, int flag);

char *des_crypt (const char *key, const char *salt);

void des_setkey (const char *key);

void des_encrypt (char *block, int flag);

int run_setkey (int *p, const char *key);

int run_crypt (long offset, char *buffer, unsigned
int count, int *p);

int crypt_close (int *p);
```

Description

crypt_close terminates the connection with the crypt utility when encryption is completed.

In order to use crypt routines, the program must be linked with the libcrypt.a object file access routine library.

crypt, encrypt, and setkey, are front-end routines. They call des_crypt, des_encrypt, and des_setkey, respectively.

des_crypt uses a one-way hashing encryption algorithm to encrypt passwords. The algorithm has variations that are intended to prevent hardware implementations of a key search.

des_encrypt also provides access to the actual hashing algorithm (see "Arguments" below).

des_setkey also provides access to the actual hashing algorithm (see "Arguments" below).

run_crypt provides cryptographic capabilities compatible with the crypt (AT&T 1990q) user-level utility. run_crypt uses the crypt utility to transform a cleartext block of characters into a ciphertext block of characters or to transform a ciphertext block of characters into a cleartext block.

run_setkey also provides cryptographic capabilities compatible with the crypt (AT&T 1990q) user-level utility to applications such as ed (AT&T 1990q) and vi (AT&T 1990q). run_setkey establishes a two-way pipe connection with the crypt (AT&T 1990q) utility.

Arguments

crypt

See des_crypt.

crypt_close

p specifies the pipe which is to be closed.

des_crypt

key is the password typed by the user.

salt is a two-character string that is used to perturb the hashing algorithm in one of 4096 different ways, after which the password repeatedly is used to encrypt a constant string. The two-character string is chosen from the set [a-zA-Z0-9./].

encrypt

See des_encrypt.

des_encrypt

block points to a character array whose length is 64 characters. Each character has the numerical value 0 or 1. This array is modified in place to become a similar array that represents the bits of the argument after it has been hashed using the *key* established by des_setkey.

`flag` causes `block` to be encrypted if `flag` is 0. `block` is not encrypted if `flag` is not 0 (see "Error Condition: Value Returned" below).

`des_setkey`

`key` points to a character array whose length is 64 characters. Each character has the numerical value 0 or 1. If the character string is divided into groups of eight, the low-order bit in each group is ignored. This creates a 56-bit key that is set into the machine. `key` will be used by the hashing algorithm to encrypt the string `block` with the function `des_encrypt`.

`run_crypt`

`buffer` contains the result of encryption or decryption.

`count` specifies the number of characters in `buffer`.

`offset` specifies the distance from the beginning of the file (in bytes) of the beginning of the block of text that will be encrypted or decrypted in `buffer`.

`p` specifies the source of bytes which are to be encrypted or decrypted.

`run_setkey`

`key` is the password argument (see `des_crypt`) used by `run_setkey` in establishing a two-way pipe connection with `crypt` (AT&T 1990q).

`p` specifies the pipe which is to get a two-way connection with `crypt`.

`setkey`

See `des_setkey`.

Normal Completion: Value Returned

`crypt` returns points to a static area that is overwritten by each subsequent `crypt` call.

`des_crypt` returns a pointer to the encrypted password. The first two characters of the encrypted password are the `salt` itself (see "Arguments" above).

`run_crypt` returns 0 if it can do I/O with the pipe attached to `crypt`.

`run_setkey` returns 0 if a null `key` is passed to it. It returns 1 otherwise.

Error Condition: Value Returned

Although decryption is provided with the domestic version of `crypt` (which is part of the Security Administration Set), decryption is not provided in the international version of `crypt` (which is part of the C Development Set).

If decryption is attempted with the international version of `des_encrypt` (i.e., if the flag argument of the international version of `des_encrypt` is

1), it sets `errno` to ENOSYS and prints a message to indicate that the capability to encrypt is not available.

If the flag argument of the international version of `encrypt` is 1, it sets `errno` to ENOSYS to indicate that the capability to encrypt is not available.

`run_crypt` returns −1 if it cannot do I/O operations with the pipe attached to `crypt`.

`run_setkey` returns −1 if it cannot establish a connection with the `crypt` utility, as will be the case in the international versions of UNIX in which `crypt` is not available.

See Also

`getpass` (C), `crypt` (AT&T 1990q), `login` (AT&T Peterson 1990q), `passwd` (AT&T 1990o), `passwd` (AT&T 1990q)

dlclose (X) — CLOSE A SHARED OBJECT — dlclose (X)

Name

`dlclose`—close a shared object

Synopsis

```
cc [flag . . .] file . . . -ldl [library . . .]

#include <dlfcn.h>

int dlclose (void *handle);
```

Description

`dlclose` dissociates the current process from a shared object that was previously opened by `dlopen` (X). This makes the object's symbols unavailable to (X). If such symbols are referenced thereafter, it causes undefined behavior.

`dlclose` also closes all objects that were automatically loaded as the result of calling `dlopen` on the referenced object.

If `dlclose` succeeds in closing an object, it does not guarantee that the object will be removed from the address space of the process. Objects that are loaded by one call to `dlopen` may also be loaded by another call to `dlopen` (i.e., the same object may be opened multiple times). All references to an object through an explicit call to `dlopen` must be closed, and all other objects that implicitly refer to the object must be closed, before the object is removed from the process's address space.

Arguments

handle is a value that was returned by an earlier call to `dlopen` (X).

Normal Completion: Value Returned

`dlclose` returns 0 if it succeeds in closing the specified object.

Error Condition: Value Returned

`dlclose` returns a nonzero value if it fails to close the specified object or if *handle* does not specify an open object.

The `dlerror` (X) routine gives additional diagnostic information.

See Also

`dlerror` (X), `dlopen` (X), `dlsym` (X)

dlerror (X) GET A DIAGNOSTIC STRING dlerror (X)

Name

`dlerror`—get a diagnostic information string

Synopsis

cc [*flag* . . .] *file* . . . -ldl [*library* . . .]

```
#include <dlfcn.h>

char *dlerror (void);
```

Description

`dlerror` returns a string that describes the last error that occurred during dynamic linking and returns it. The string that `dlerror` returns is stored in a static buffer that is overwritten by each subsequent call to `dlerror`. Any program that needs to save such a string must copy it to another buffer.

Arguments

None

Normal Completion: Value Returned

If a dynamic linking error has occurred since the last time `dlerror` was called, `dlerror` returns a null-terminated character string that describes the error. The string lacks a trailing newline character.

If no dynamic linking error has occurred since the last time `dlerror` was called, `dlerror` returns a NULL. Therefore, `dlerror` will return NULL if it is called a second time immediately after being called the first time.

See Also

`dlerror` (X), `dlopen` (X), `dlsym` (X)

dlopen (X) OPEN A SHARED OBJECT dlopen (X)

Name

`dlopen`—open a shared object

Synopsis

`cc` [*`flag`* . . .] *`file`* . . . `-ldl` [*`library`* . . .]

`#include <dlfcn.h>`

`void *dlopen (char *`*`pathname`*`, int `*`mode`*`);`

Description

`dlopen` opens a shared object, thereby making it available to a running program.

`dlopen` is one of several routines that give direct access to dynamic linking facilties [see the "C Compilation System" chapter (AT&T 1990g)]. The library that contains these routines is loaded if `cc` (Peterson 1990a) or `ld` (Peterson 1990a) is executed with the `-ldl` option.

Objects loaded by one call to `dlopen` cannot directly reference symbols from objects that are loaded by a different call to `dlopen`. However, such symbols can be indirectly referenced by using dlsym (X). Objects that are loaded by a single call to dlopen can import symbols from each other or from any other object that is automatically loaded during program startup.

dlopen automatically loads any other shared objects that were link-edited with *pathname* (see below) when *pathname* was built.

dlopen can repeatedly open objects that have names which resolve to the same absolute or relative pathname, but the object that is referenced will be loaded only once into the address space of the current process. If the same object is referenced by two different pathnames, it may be loaded more than once.

Arguments

mode determines the processing of references that a shared object makes to symbols whose addresses are not known until the object is loaded into the address space of a process. Such references must be relocated before the process can access the symbols. Values of *mode* determine the relocation of these symbols as follows:

RTLD_LAZY causes relocation of data symbols only. Relocation of references to a function is deferred until the function is called for the first time. RTLD_LAZY may result in better performance because a given process might not refer to all of the functions in a given shared object.

RTLD_NOW causes all necessary relocations to be done when an object is first loaded. This will cause wasted effort if symbols that are never referenced are relocated. However, if an application must know as soon as an object is loaded that all of the symbols that it references will be available, RTLDNOW must be used.

pathname is the pathname of the object opened by dlopen. The pathname can be relative to the new directory or it can be an absolute path.

If *pathname* equals 0, dlopen makes the symbols in the original a.out file and the objects that were loaded with a.out at program startup available through dlsym (X). Some of the symbols defined in a.out may not be available to the dynamic linker. The symbol table that ld (Peterson 1991a) creates for the dynamic linker to use might contain only those symbols referenced by the shared object with which the a.out file is linked.

The directory search path used in finding *pathname* and other needed objects can be specified by setting the environment variable LD_LIBRARY_PATH to a colon-separated list of directories that has the same format as the PATH variable [see sh (AT&T 1990q)]. LD_LIBRARY_PATH will be ignored if the calling process is running setgid (Peterson 1991b) or setuid (Peterson 1991b) [see exec (Peterson 1991b)] or if *pathname* contains a slash (/), that is, it is not a simple filename.

Normal Completion: Value Returned

If `dlopen` succeeds, it returns a *`handle`* to the process which the process can use in subsequent calls to `dlsym` (X) and `dlclose` (X).

Error Condition: Value Returned

`dlopen` returns NULL if *`pathname`* cannot be found or cannot be opened for reading or is not a shared object, or if an error occurs when *`pathname`* is being loaded or when its symbolic references are being relocated. The `dlerror` (X) routine gives additional diagnostic information.

See Also

`dlclose` (X), `dlerror` (X), `dlsym` (X), `cc` (Peterson 1991a), `exec` (Peterson 1991b), `ld` (Peterson 1991a), `sh` (AT&T 1990q), "C Compilation System" chapter (AT&T 1990g)

dlsym (X) — ADDRESS OF A SYMBOL IN A SHARED OBJECT — dlsym (X)

Name

`dlsym`—get the address of a symbol in a shared object

Synopsis

`cc` [*`flag`* . . .] *`file`* . . . `-ldl` [*`library`* . . .]

`#include <dlfcn.h>`

`void *dlsym(void *`*`handle`*`, char *`*`name`*`);`

Description

`dlsym` enables a process to get the address of a symbol that is defined in a shared object that was previously opened by `dlopen` (X). The shared object must not have been closed by `dlclose`.

Arguments

`handle` is a value previously returned by `dlopen`. It corresponds to a shared object. `dlsym` searches for the specified symbol (see *`name`*) in all of

the shared objects that are automatically loaded as the result of loading the shared object referenced by *handle* [see `dlopen` (X)].

name is the symbol's name, expressed as a character string.

Normal Completion: Value Returned

`dlerror` returns the address of a symbol defined in a shared object previously opened by `dlopen`.

Error Condition: Value Returned

`dlerror` returns `NULL` if the specified symbol, *name*, cannot be found in any of the objects associated with *handle* or if *handle* does not specify a valid object opened by `dlopen`.

The `dlerror` (X) routine gives additional diagnostic information.

See Also

`dlerror` (X), `dlopen` (X), `dlsym` (X)

libwindows (X) WINDOWING TERMINAL LIBRARY libwindows (X)

Name

`libwindows`—windowing terminal library

Synopsis

`cc` [*flag* . . .] *file* . . . `-lwindows` [*library* . . .]

`int openagent (void);`

`int New (int` *cntlfd*`, int` *origin_x*`, int` *origin_y*`, int` *corner_x*`, int` *corner_y*`);`

`int Newlayer (int` *cntlfd*`, int` *origin_x*`, int` *origin_y*`, int` *corner_x*`, int` *corner_y*`);`

`int openchan (int` *chan*`);`

`int Runlayer (int` *chan*`, char *`*command*`);`

```
int Current (int cntlfd, int chan);

int Delete (int cntlfd, int chan);

int Top (int cntlfd, int chan);

int Bottom (int cntlfd, int chan);

int Move (int cntlfd, int chan, int origin_x, int
origin_y);

int Reshape (int cntlfd, int chan, int origin_x, int
origin_y, int corner_x, int corner_y);

int Exit (int cntlfd);
```

Description

`Bottom` puts the layer associated with *`chan`* (see "Arguments" below) beneath all overlapping layers.

`Top` puts the layer associated with *`chan`* on top of all overlapping layers.

`Move` moves the layer associated with *`chan`* from its present location to a new screen location whose origin is at (*`origin_x`*, *`origin_y`*) and maintains its size and contents.

`Reshape` reshapes the rectangular layer associated with *`chan`*, giving it the new coordinates (*`origin_x`*, *`origin_y`*) and (*`corner_x`*, *`corner_y`*). The user can define the layer rectangle interactively if all of the coordinate arguments are 0.

`Current` attaches the layer associated with the channel argument, *`chan`*, to the keyboard, that is, makes it current.

`Delete` removes the layer that is associated with the channel argument *`chan`* and kills the host processes that are associated with the channel.

`Exit` causes `layers` to exit and kills all processes that are associated with it.

The `libwindows` library lets programs that run on UNIX host systems execute windowing terminal functions [see `layers` (AT&T 1990q)].

`New` creates a new layer with a separate shell. The new layer appears on top of any overlapping layers. The new layer is not attached to the keyboard, that is, it is not made current.

`Newlayer` has the same effect as `New`, except that it does not execute a separate shell.

`openagent` opens the control channel of the `xt(7)` channel group to which the calling process belongs. Applications should use `/dev/xt/??/[0-7]` instead of `/dev/xt??/[0-7]` when accessing the `xt` driver.

`openchan` opens the channel argument *`chan`* which is gotten from `New` or `Newlayer`.

`Runlayer` executes *`command`* (see "Arguments" below) in the layer that was previously created by `Newlayer` and associated with *`chan`*. Any processes that are attached to this layer will be killed. The new process will have the environment of the `layers` process.

Arguments

`chan` is the channel argument gotten from `New` or `Newlayer`.

`command` specifies a command to be executed in the layer associated with *`chan`*.

`cntfld` is the file descriptor that was returned by a previous call to `openagent`.

`corner_x` specifies the x-coordinate of a corner of the layer rectangle. The values of *`corner_x`* and other layer rectangular coordinates depend on the type of terminal. Some terminals expect these coordinates to be passed as character positions (bytes). Other terminals expect them to be passed as pixels (bits). This dependency affects the four routines that pass layer rectangular coordinates: `Move`, `New`, `Newlayer`, and `Reshape`. For example, `New`, `Newlayer`, and `Reshape` take minimum values of 8 (pixels) for *`origin_x`* and *`origin_y`* and 792 (pixels) for *`corner_x`* and 1016 (pixels) for *`corner_y`* when the terminal is the AT&T 5620 DMD.

`corner_y` specifies the y-coordinate of a corner of the layer rectangle.

`origin_x` specifies the x-coordinate of the origin of the layer rectangle. If *`origin_x`*, *`origin_y`*, *`corner_x`*, and *`corner_y`* are 0, the user must define the layer rectangle interactively.

`origin_y` specifies the y-coordinate of the origin of the layer rectangle.

Normal Completion: Value Returned

If `Bottom`, `Current`, `Delete`, `Exit`, `Move`, `Reshape`, or `Runlayer` succeeds, it return 0.

If `New` succeeds, it returns the `xt(7)` channel number that is associated with the new layer it creates.

If `Newlayer` succeeds, it returns the `xt(7)` channel number that is associated with the new layer it creates.

If `openagent` succeeds, it returns a file descriptor, *`cntfld`*, that can be passed to any other `libwindow` function except `openchan` and `Runlayer`. In addition, the file descriptor can be passed to `close` (Peterson 1991b).

If `openchan` succeeds, it returns a file descriptor that `write` (Peterson 1991b) or `close` (Peterson 1991b) can use as an argument.

Error Condition: Value Returned

If any of the above functions fails, it returns −1.

Files

ULIBDIR ordinarily is `/usr/lib`.
ULIBDIR`/libwindows.a` is the windowing terminal function library.

See Also

`close` (Peterson 1991b), `jagent` (AT&T 1990m), `layers` (AT&T 1990q), `write` (Peterson 1991b)

maillock (X) — CREATE A LOCKFILE FOR A USER'S MAILFILE — maillock (X)

Name

`maillock`—creat a lockfile for the user's mailfile

Synopsis

```
cc [flag ...] file ... -lmail [library ...]

#include <maillock.h>

int maillock (const char *user, int retrycnt);

int mailunlock (void);
```

Description

`maillock` tries to create a lockfile for the user's mailfile. It assumes that the user's mailfiles are in the standard place, as defined in `maillock.h`. It also assumes that the content of any already existing lockfile is the process ID (a null-terminated ASCII string) of the process that created the lockfile by a previous call to `maillock`.

`mailunlock` should be called to remcve any lock that is no longer needed.

`mailunlock` removes the lockfile created by the most recent call to `maillock`. If `maillock` is called for different users without any intervening calls to `mailunlock` being made, the lockfiles initially created will remain, possibly blocking subsequent message delivery until the process terminates.

Arguments

`retrycnt` specifies the number of times that `maillock` will try to create a lockfile before it indicates an error if the process that created the lockfile is still alive. If the process that created the lockfile is still alive, `maillock` sleeps for 5 seconds times the `maillock` attempt number. The first sleep will be for 5 seconds, the next will be for 10 seconds, and so on until the number of attempts reaches *`retrycnt`*.

`user` specifies the login name of the user for whose mailbox the lockfile is being created.

Normal Completion: Value Returned

If `maillock` succeeds in creating a lockfile or `mailunlock` succeeds in removing it, the function returns the following constant defined in `maillock.h`:

L_SUCCESS equals 0; it means that the lockfile was created or removed.

Error Condition: Value Returned

If `maillock` fails, it returns one of the following constants defined in `maillock.h`:

L_ERROR equals 5; it means that `errno` must be checked to determine the reason for failure.

L_NAMELEN equals 1; it means that the recipient's name exceeds 13 characters.

L_TMPLOCK equals 2; it means that the `tmp` file cannot be created.

L_TMPWRITE equals 3; it means that the *`pid`* cannot be written into the lockfile.

L_MAXTRYS equals 4; it means that `maillock` failed.

Files

LIBDIR/llib-mail.ln
LIBDIR/mail.a
/var/mail/*
/var/mail/*.lock

malloc (X) MEMORY ALLOCATION malloc (X)

Name

malloc, free, realloc, calloc, mallopt, mallinfo—memory allocation

Synopsis

```
cc [flag . . .] file . . . -lmalloc [library . . .]

#include <stdlib.h>

void *malloc (size_t size);

void free (void *ptr);

void *realloc (void *ptr, size_t size);

void *calloc (sizet nelem, size_t elsize);

include <malloc.h>

int mallopt (int cmd, int value);

struct mallinfo mallinfo (void);
```

Description

`calloc` allocates space for an array of elements and initializes it to zeroes.

`free` frees previously allocated memory.

`mallinfo` returns a structure (see "Normal Completion: Value Returned" below) that describes space usage.

`malloc` and `free` jointly provide general-purpose memory allocation capability.

`malloc` allocates memory.

`mallopt` controls the space allocation algorithm. It may be called repeatedly, but not after the first small space is allocated.

`realloc` changes the size of the block pointed to by *ptr* to the size specified by *size* and returns a pointer to the block. It may move the block, but the contents up to the lesser of the new and old sizes are unchanged.

The function prototypes for `calloc`, `free`, `malloc`, and `realloc` are also defined in <`malloc.h`> in order to have compatibility with old applications. New applications which need to access the prototypes for these functions should include <`stdio.h`>.

Arguments

`malloc`

`size` specifies a block of at least *`size`* bytes that `malloc` is to allocate. If the space that *`size`* specifies is overrun, undefined results occur.

`free`

`ptr` points to a block, previously allocated by `malloc`, which `free` is to free. If *`ptr`* is not a null pointer, `free` destroys the contents of this block [but see `mallopt` (X)] and makes the block available for further allocation. If *`ptr`* is a null pointer, `free` takes no action. If *`ptr`* is some random number, undefined results occur.

`realloc`

`ptr` points to a block, previously allocated by `malloc`, whose size `realloc` is to change. `realloc` acts like the `malloc` function for the specified size if *`ptr`* is a null pointer. If *`ptr`* is not a null pointer and *`size`* (see below) is 0, the block to which *`ptr`* points is freed.

`size` specifies the size, in bytes, of the block to which *`ptr`* points.

`calloc`

`elsize` specifies the size of elements in an array for which `calloc`20is to allocate space.

`nelem` specifies the number of elements in an array for which `calloc`20is to allocate space.

`mallopt`

`cmd` is one of several constants defined in `malloc.h` whose effects are as follows:

MGRAIN sets *`grain`* to *`value`*, which must be larger than 0. The size of any block that is smaller than *`maxfast`* is rounded up to the nearest multiple of *`grain`*. The default value of *`grain`* is the smallest number of bytes that permit the alignment of a data type. When *`grain`* is set, the value will be rounded up to a multiple of the default.

M_KEEP causes data in a freed block to be preserved until the next time `calloc`, `malloc`, or `realloc` is called. Unlike `malloc` (C), these functions do not preserve the contents of a block when it is freed unless this option is used. This option is provided to ensure compatibility with the old `malloc` version. Otherwise, do not use it.

MMXFAST sets *maxfast* to *value* (see *value* below). The algorithm allocates all blocks that are smaller than *maxfast* in large groups of blocks and gives the blocks out quickly. The default for *maxfast* is 24.

MNLBLKS sets *numblks* to *value*. *numblks* specifies the number of blocks in each large group of blocks which is to be allocated. *numblks* must be greater than 0. Its default is 100.

value specifies a value to which a variable is to be set. The specific variable that is set to *value* depends on the value of *cmd* above.

Normal Completion: Value Returned

Each of the memory allocation routines returns a pointer to space that is suitably aligned (possibly after pointer coercion) for storage of any type of object.

`realloc` returns a pointer to the block whose size it changes.

`mallinfo` returns a structure which is defined in `malloc.h`. Its members are as follows:

```
struct mallinfo {/*
    int arena; /* total arena space */
    int ordblks; /* number of ordinary blocks */
    int smblks; /* number of small blocks */
    int hblkhd; /* space in holding block headers */
    int hblks; /* number of holding blocks */
    int usmblks; /* space in use in small blocks */
    int fsmblks; /* space in free small blocks */
    int uordblks; /* space in use in ordinary blocks */
    int fordblks; /* space in free ordinary blocks */
    int keepcost; /* space penalty if cmd is M_KEEP */
}
```

`malloc` returns a pointer to a block of at least *size* bytes suitably aligned for any use.

Error Condition: Value Returned

`calloc`, `malloc`, and `realloc` return a NULL pointer if not enough memory is available to satisfy an allocation request. The block to which *ptr* points is left intact if `realloc` returns NULL.

`mallopt` returns 0 if *cmd* or *value* is invalid or if `mallopt` is called after an allocation.

See Also

malloc (C), brk (Peterson 1991b)

sputl (X) ACCESS LONG INTEGERS sputl (X)

Name

sputl, sgetl—machine-independent access to long integers

Synopsis

cc [*flag* . . .] *file* . . . -lld [*library* . . .]

```
#include <ldfcn.h>

void sputl (long value, char *buffer);

void sgetl (const char *buffer);
```

Description

sgetl gets four bytes from *buffer* and returns the bytes in the same order that the host machine uses.

sputl puts the four bytes of the long integer in *value* into memory, starting at the location to which *buffer* points. The byte order is the same for every machine.

Arguments

buffer points to the location in which sputl puts bytes or from which sgetl gets bytes.

value specifies the long integer whose bytes sputl puts into the location to which *buffer* points.

Normal Completion: Value Returned

sgetl returns the four bytes of the long integer value stored at *buffer*.

Bibliography

AT&T. 1984. *AT&T Bell Labotatories Technical Journal 63*. No. 8, Part 2. October.

AT&T. 1985. *UNIX System V Interface Definition, Issue 1*. Short Hills, New Jersey.

AT&T. 1988a. *UNIX System V/386 Programmer's Guide*. Englewood Cliffs, New Jersey: Prentice-Hall.

______. 1988b. *UNIX System V/386 User's Guide*. Second Edition. Englewood Cliffs, New Jersey: Prentice-Hall.

______. 1988c. *UNIX System V/386 User's Reference Manual*. Englewood Cliffs, New Jersey: Prentice-Hall.

______. 1989a. *UNIX System V/386 Programmer's Reference Manual*. Englewood Cliffs, New Jersey: Prentice-Hall.

______. 1989b. *UNIX System V/386 System Administrator's Reference Manual*. Englewood Cliffs, New Jersey: Prentice-Hall.

______. 1990a *UNIX System V Release 4 ANSI C Transition Guide*. Englewood Cliffs, New Jersey: Prentice-Hall.

______. 1990b *UNIX System V Release 4 BSD/XENIX Compatibility Guide*. Englewood Cliffs, New Jersey: Prentice-Hall.

______. 1990c *UNIX System V Release 4 Device Driver Interface/Driver-Kernal Interface (DDI/DKI) Reference Manual*. Englewood Cliffs, New Jersey: Prentice-Hall.

______. 1990d *UNIX System V Release 4 Migration Guide*. Englewood Cliffs, New Jersey: Prentice-Hall.

______. 1990e *UNIX System V Release 4 Network User's and Administrator's Guide*. Englewood Cliffs, New Jersey: Prentice-Hall.

______. 1990f *UNIX System V Release 4 Product Overview and Master Index*. Englewood Cliffs, New Jersey: Prentice-Hall.

______. 1990g *UNIX System V Release 4 Programmer's Guide: ANSI C and Programming Support Tools*. Englewood Cliffs, New Jersey: Prentice-Hall.

———. 1990h *UNIX System V Release 4 Programmer's Guide: Character User Interface (FMLI and ETI)*. Englewood Cliffs, New Jersey: Prentice-Hall.

———. 1990i *UNIX System V Release 4 Programmer's Guide: Networking Interfaces*. Englewood Cliffs, New Jersey: Prentice-Hall.

———. 1990j *UNIX System V Release 4 Programmer's Guide: POSIX Conformance*. Englewood Cliffs, New Jersey: Prentice-Hall.

———. 1990k *UNIX System V Release 4 Programmer's Guide: STREAMS*. Englewood Cliffs, New Jersey: Prentice-Hall.

———. 1990l *UNIX System V Release 4 Programmer's Guide: System Services and Application Packaging Tools*. Englewood Cliffs, New Jersey: Prentice-Hall.

———. 1990m *UNIX System V Release 4 Programmer's Reference Manual*. Englewood Cliffs, New Jersey: Prentice-Hall.

———. 1990n *UNIX System V Release 4 System Administrator's Guide*. Englewood Cliffs, New Jersey: Prentice-Hall.

———. 1990o *UNIX System V Release 4 System Administrator's Reference Manual*. Englewood Cliffs, New Jersey: Prentice-Hall.

———. 1990p *UNIX System V Release 4 User's Guide*. Englewood Cliffs, New Jersey: Prentice-Hall.

———. 1990q *UNIX System V Release 4 User's Reference Manual*. Englewood Cliffs, New Jersey: Prentice-Hall.

Banahan, Mark, and Andy Rutter. 1983. *The UNIX Book*. New York: John Wiley.

Bell Laboratories. 1978. "UNIX Time-Sharing System." *The Bell System Technical Journal 57*. No. 6, Part 2, July-August.

Bourne, S.R. 1982. *The Unix System*. Reading, Massachusetts: Addison-Wesley.

Christian, Kaare. 1983. *UNIX Command Reference Guide*. New York: John Wiley & Sons.

———. 1988. *The UNIX Operating System*. New York: John Wiley and Sons.

Clukey, Lee Paul. 1985. *UNIX and XENIX Demystified*. Blue Ridge, Pennsylvania: Tab Books, Inc.

Gauthier, Richard. 1981. *Using the UNIX System*. Englewood Cliffs, New Jersey: Reston.

Harbison, Samuel P., and Guy L. Steele, Jr. 1987. *C: A Reference Manual*. 2nd Edition. Englewood Cliffs, New Jersey: Prentice-Hall.

Kernighan, Brian W., and Rob Pike. 1984. *The UNIX Programming Environment*. Englewood Cliffs, New Jersey: Prentice-Hall.

Lomuto, Ann, and Nico Lomuto. 1983. *A UNIX Primer*. Englewood Cliffs, New Jersey: Prentice-Hall.

Morgan, Rachel, and Henry McGilton. 1987. *Introducing UNIX System V*. New York: McGraw-Hill.

O'Reilly & Associates, Inc. 1986, 1987. *UNIX in a Nutshell*. Newton, Massachusetts: O'Reilly & Associates, Inc.

Peterson, Baird. 1991a. *UNIX System V Commands: Programmer's Rapid Reference*. New York: Van Nostrand Reinhold.

———. 1991b. *UNIX System V System Calls: Programmer's Rapid Reference*. New York: Van Nostrand Reinhold.

Rochkind, Marc J. 1957. "The Source Code Control System." *IEEE Transactions on Software Engineering*. December.

SCO. 1989a. *SCO UNIX System V/386 Development System: Programmer's Guide*. Santa Cruz, California: The Santa Cruz Operation, Inc.

______. 1989b. *SCO UNIX System V/386 Development System: Programmer's Reference*. Santa Cruz, California: The Santa Cruz Operation, Inc.

______. 1989c. *SCO UNIX System V/386 Development System: Library Guide*. Santa Cruz, California: The Santa Cruz Operation, Inc.

______. 1989d. *SCO UNIX System V/386 Development System: The STREAMS Network Programmer's Guide*. Santa Cruz, California: The Santa Cruz Operation, Inc.

______. 1989e. *SCO UNIX System V/386 Development System: The STREAMS PRIMER*. Santa Cruz, California: The Santa Cruz Operation, Inc.

______. 1989f. *SCO UNIX System V/386 Development System: The STREAMS Programmer's Guide*. Santa Cruz, California: The Santa Cruz Operation, Inc.

______. 1989g. *SCO UNIX System V/386 Operating System: User's Reference*. Santa Cruz, California: The Santa Cruz Operation, Inc.

______. 1989h. *SCO UNIX System V Development System: Programmer's Reference*. Santa Cruz, California: The Santa Cruz Operation, Inc.

______. 1990. *SCO UNIX System V/386 Operating System: Administrator's Reference*. Santa Cruz, California: The Santa Cruz Operation, Inc.

Shaw, Myril Clement, and Susan Soltis Shaw. 1986. *UNIX And XENIX System V Programmer's Guide*. Blue Ridge Summit, Pennsylvania: Tab Books, Inc.

Thomas, Rebecca, Lawrence R. Rogers, and Jean L. Yates. 1986. *Advanced Programmer's Guide to UNIX System V*. Berkeley, California: Osborne McGraw-Hill.

Thomas, Rebecca, and Jean L. Yates. 1982. *A User Guide to the UNIX System*. Berkeley, California: Osborne McGraw-Hill.

Western Electric Co. 1985. *UNIX System V Documents*. Greensboro, North Carolina; Western Electric Co.

INDEX

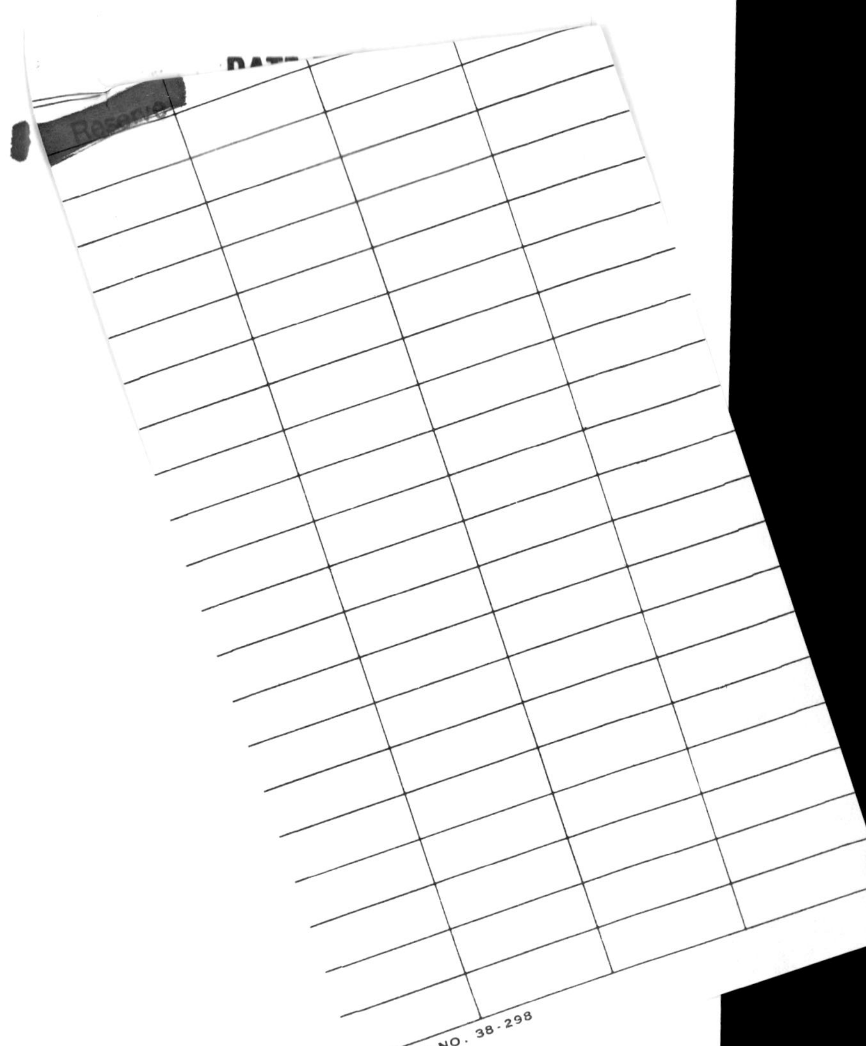
DATE
Reserve
DEMCO NO. 38-298